GPS Backup
with a Mark 3 Sextant

All Instructions and Tables Included;
For Any Ocean, Any Day;
No Background in Celestial Navigation Required.

by

David Burch

★ ★ ★
★   ★
STARPATH.

ISBN 978-0-914025-60-3

Published by
Starpath Publications
3050 NW 63rd Street, Seattle, WA 98107
Manufactured in the United States of America
starpathpublications.com
10 9 8 7

1. OVERVIEW

This booklet is intended to teach the necessary steps to finding your position at sea with sextant sights of the sun and *Polaris,* using the simplest possible procedures and tables. This booklet should be stored with a Davis Mark 3 plastic sextant, along with a few other items. All will fit into a Davis plastic sextant case, that in turn should be stored in a waterproof bag. If you are not wearing a watch at all times, with known UTC, then an inexpensive one should be stored in the box as well. Without accurate time we can find Latitude, but not Longitude. If you are not familiar with timekeeping in navigation, see Section 8.1.

In principle, a navigator with no knowledge of celestial navigation should be able to learn how to use the Mark 3 sextant and related tables in this booklet to find their position at sea to within about 5 to 10 nautical miles, on any date, on any ocean. It is an easy process with no math beyond addition and subtraction. A review of latitude, longitude, nautical miles, and dead reckoning (DR) is given in Section 8.2.

The Mark 3 is small, lightweight, and inexpensive, which makes it an ideal choice for a backup sextant. For successful and long-term use, however, we must treat it as we would an expensive instrument, and to that end we recommend using a bold, black marker to write "**$900**" right on outside of the sextant case in large letters, to remind us to treat this instrument as if it had cost that much. Complaints about the instrument, that we periodically read in blogs, can usually be traced to violation of this principle—or simply not knowing how to use the sextant. When we read a complaint that the mirror settings changed after being left on deck in the bright sun for several hours, we ask if they would have left a $900 sextant on the deck that way? Those experienced with a high-end metal sextant, who try the Mark 3 for the first time and disparage its accuracy and usability, have likely not taken the time to learn how to use it, nor recognize its value for its intended purpose.

2. SEXTANT SIGHTS WITH THE MARK 3 SEXTANT

The Mark 3 design is based on the lifeboat sextant used by the US Navy in WWII. It is not as accurate as a full-size metal sextant, but it is more than adequate for backup navigation. It comes with a *Mark 3 User's Guide,* also available online. This booklet expands and improves on that guide, based on our experience teaching celestial navigation for over thirty years, to thousands of students, using both metal and plastic sextants. We also add easier, more accurate solutions to the sights, using expanded almanac data.

Taking a celestial navigation sight means measuring the angular height of the sun or a star above the visible horizon using a sextant, as shown schematically in Figure 2-1. This angle is called

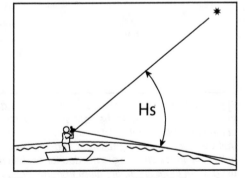

Figure 2-1. *Sextant height (Hs) is the angle of a celestial body above the visible horizon. Later we apply a couple corrections to this measurement.*

the *sextant height* (Hs). Figure 2-2 shows how the sextant works. A light ray from the sun or a star reflects from the *index mirror* to the *horizon mirror* and back to the eye, while simultaneously a light ray coming from the horizon passes by the horizon mirror directly to the eye. Because of the double reflection, the angle between these two rays is twice the Hs we want, but that is accounted for automatically on the sextant scales. Thus we read Hs directly from the sextant. The double reflection design is an ingenious way to measure this angle accurately while still moving around in a seaway.

Reading the Sextant Scales

The sextant angle (Hs) will be in the form 23° 45' (degrees and minutes), with 1° = 60'. Read the degrees part of Hs from the scale on the sextant arc. Choose the degrees value that is just to the right of the 0' line on the vernier scale below it. Read the minutes part of Hs directly from the vernier scale on the sliding index arm. Choose the

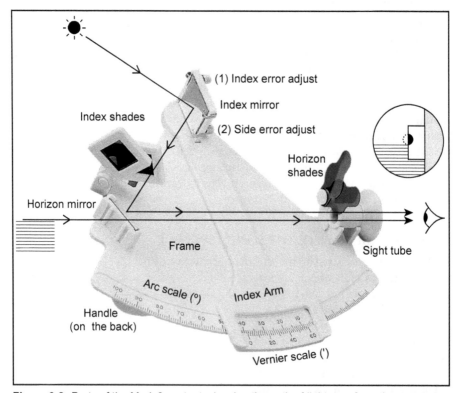

Figure 2-2. *Parts of the Mark 3 sextant, showing the path of light rays from the sun and the horizon. The inset on the right shows how the sun should be aligned on the horizon at the time of the sight—sliding the arm along the arc moves the sun up and down in that view, corresponding to larger and smaller angles. The angle read from the sextant is called Hs. Index shades are needed for essentially all sun sights. The horizon shades are used when there is a bright glare from the horizon itself, although they may be combined with index shades for a very bright sun. The goal in shade selection is to have the sun disc prominent, without a perception of brightness. The two adjustments screws are used to align the mirrors with the sextant set to 0° 0'—usually in an iterative process of one and then the other, then repeat, with smaller adjustments.*

minutes reading that most closely aligns with an index mark on the degrees scale above it. Reading the dials is greatly assisted by a small magnifying glass, which are just a few dollars at the local drug store—a valuable addition to a GPS backup kit. See Figure 2-3 for practice reading the scales.

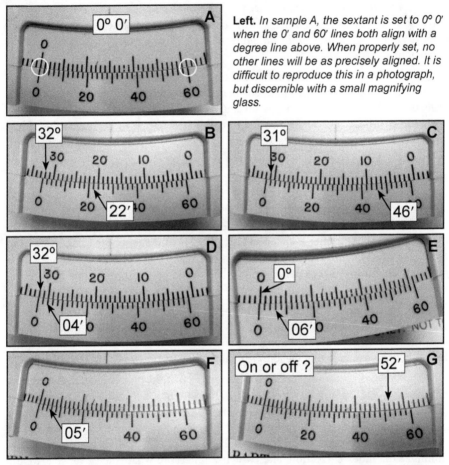

Left. *In sample A, the sextant is set to 0° 0' when the 0' and 60' lines both align with a degree line above. When properly set, no other lines will be as precisely aligned. It is difficult to reproduce this in a photograph, but discernible with a small magnifying glass.*

Figure 2-3. *Sample sextant readings. Reading the scales is a crucial step in using the Mark 3. A small magnifying glass is very helpful. In B, the 0' line is just left of the 32° line, which tells you the degrees part. Then the 22' line is best lined up with a degree line above it. In C, the 0' line is just slightly to the right of the 32° line, so the degrees part would be 31°, and we look for minutes alignment at the high end of the vernier scale.* **Tip:** *If the 0' line on the vernier is almost exactly aligned with a whole degree on the arc, then check the vernier carefully to decide if it is just above the degree line by noting that a low minute lines up (as in D). If it is just below it, a high minute will line up (as in G). In these cases, don't look at the 60' line, as it will share the same ambiguity as the 0' line. E, F, and G are index correction measurements. In F we see that 4' and 6' are equally unaligned in opposite directions, but both are closer than any others, so we choose the midpoint of 5' "on the scale." In G we can only tell that this is off the scale because a high minute (52') lines up, which means the index correction is 8' "off the scale."*

Adjusting the Index Mirror

Preliminary Note: *We go over this process systematically, in detail, because we assume you will be doing this for the first time, on your own, with only these instructions to go by. It may seem a long process at first reading, but after doing it once or twice, it will be easy and intuitive, and you will not need to go through all of the steps. The discussion is also longer because there are different ways to do it depending on what you have to look at for reference. Read through the full process before starting with your sextant so all the optional methods are understood.*

The principle of the double-reflection sextant measurement relies on the two mirrors (index and horizon) being perfectly parallel when the sextant reads 0° 0'. It is unlikely this will be the case with a new sextant, so our first step will be to adjust the index mirror to get these as close as possible to parallel, and then to measure the residual offset, called the *index correction (IC)*, which we will then apply to subsequent sights.

When taking sextant sights, this offset is treated like a speedometer that reads 2 mph when you are parked. Then, when you start moving and the speedometer reads 30 mph, you know you are only going 28 mph. Likewise, if the speedometer was reading 2 mph below 0 when parked, and you read 30 mph on the dial when moving, you would know you are now going 32 mph. The former correction is called "on the scale" (above the zero reading); the latter is called "off the scale" (below the zero reading), so we can make a simple rule for applying the correction: When it is on, take it off; when it is off, put it on. This is a far better approach than thinking of plus or minus corrections, which are prone to errors.

It is not practical to attempt to adjust out all of the offset (i.e., IC = 0), nor is it required. We set it as close as we can with reasonable effort, then spend our time measuring what is left as carefully as we can. In other words, it is not important that the index correction be zero, only that we know its value, whatever it is, as best we can.

On the Mark 3, the horizon mirror is fixed in position, perpendicular to the frame of the sextant and cannot be adjusted, so all adjustments are on the index mirror. We make the mirrors parallel in two steps. Referring to Figure 2-4, we first make the index mirror perpendicular to the frame, called removing the *side error*, and then we tilt the index mirror to make the mirrors parallel on both axes. This last adjustment is to minimize the index correction, after which we measure what is left over that we did not get out.

There are several approaches to this adjustment, depending on what you have to look at for reference. If we assume you will be at sea when this is first needed, then the best time to do the adjustments is during twilight when you can see both a star (or planet) and the sea horizon, but any time during the day will work. Section 8.3 shows ways to do this on land. With a sharp sea horizon in view, we do the adjustment in two steps.

Index Mirror Adjustment Using Only a Sea Horizon

Step 1. Set the sextant to 0° 0' as shown in Figure 2-3 (sample A). Then, holding the sextant in your right hand, look through the sighting tube toward the horizon. You will likely see something similar to that shown in the left part of Figure 2-5. The direct

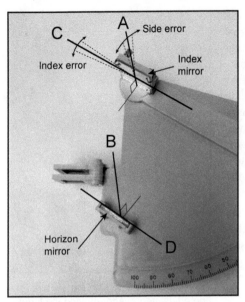

Figure 2-4. *Geometry of the mirrors. Line B along the face of the horizon mirror is perpendicular to the frame. Line D along the face of the index mirror is parallel to the frame. When the sextant is set to 0° 0', we strive to have line A along the face of the index mirror parallel to line B, which makes both mirrors perpendicular to the frame, and we strive to have line C along the face of the index mirror be parallel to line D. When A is not parallel to B, we have side error, and when C is not parallel to D we have index error. A small amount of side error does not affect the accuracy of the sights, but we must know the size of the index error so we can account for it (the index correction) in each sight we take.*

view and the reflected view of the horizon will not line up. This implies there is indeed an index error and most likely a side error as well, but we can't know the latter from this view alone.

Step 2. While keeping your eye on this view, move the index arm back and forth along the arc just a small amount to see the reflected view of the horizon rise above and below the direct view. This gives you a feeling for the sensitivity of the adjustment. Moving the reflected horizon from the middle of the horizon mirror to the top or bottom of the mirror is only a movement of ± 2.5° along the degrees scale on the arc, so we are talking about very small movements here. **Tip:** Figure 2-5a shows one way for controlled small motions of the index arm. The final adjustment is more of a squeeze and release of the thumb against the index arm, rather than what might be considered a push.

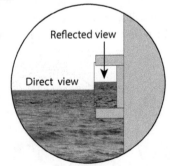
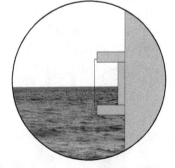

Figure 2-5. *Left. View of the index mirror through the sight tube with the sextant set to 0° 0', but reflected view of horizon does not line up with direct view. This means there is an index correction to adjust out or measure. Right. View of the index mirror after we have moved the index arm to align the horizon views. We are not adjusting nor measuring the index error at this point in Step 3, we are just setting it this way temporarily so we can remove the side error most effectively.*

Step 3. Adjust the index arm till the horizons align as shown in the right side of Figure 2-5. At this point, the sextant reading will no longer be 0° 0' but line C will be parallel to line D in Figure 2-4. With this first-step alignment done, we can check for side error by rocking the sextant. This means—using vessel motion terminology—slowly rolling the sextant about the eyepiece-to-index-mirror axis, without any yaw or pitch. When side error is present, you will see the horizon split as shown in Figure 2-6.

To correct the side error with only a sea horizon to work with, rock it to the side that shows the largest split—they won't necessarily be the same—and reach over the top of the index mirror to adjust the screw nearest the frame (#2 in Figure 2-2). As you turn this and watch the split horizon, one direction will increase the split and one will decrease it. If possible, turn it until the horizon is a flat line, checking the roll to the other direction periodically. The roll should not be more than 45° to either side. If you can remove all of it with just a turn or two, then

Figure 2-5a. *How to hold the sextant for fine adjustments. After moving the index arm to the approximately right position, make final adjustments with four fingers firmly pressing on the frame to steady it against the right hand holding the handle. Use a squeezing motion of the thumb for fine adjustments to either align the horizons or take sun sights.*

the view will look like that of Figure 2-7, but don't worry if all of the side error cannot be removed at this step. This is an iterative process and we will come back to this as needed.

Tip: After making an adjustment, check the horizon, and then tap the plastic mount of the index mirror gently a couple times and check the horizon again to see if that makes a difference on the alignment. Don't tap it any harder than you would tap your nose! Even with a gentle tap or gentle push you will see the horizon move notably during the process, but it will spring back, which reflects both the sensitivity of the measurement and the limitations of a plastic device.

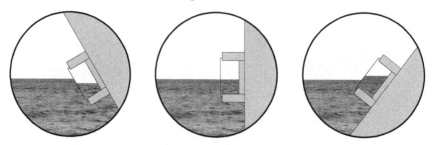

Figure 2-6. *The effect of side error when the sextant is rocked to the left and right. This means that line A is not parallel to line B in Figure 4. The split can be different in the two directions.*

Figure 2-7. *This is the way the horizon view should behave when there is no side error. This view also implies you have either moved the index arm to compensate for any index error as in Step 3, or you have adjusted out the index error as in Step 4.*

Step 4. At this point we have most or all of the side error removed, but we have not addressed the index error. We now effectively start again with Step 1. Set the sextant to 0° 0' as before, look to the horizon, and again see what we saw in the left side of Figure 2-5. But this time we will use the top screw (#1 in Figure 2-2) to bring the reflected horizon in line with the direct view as best we can. Again, try a gentle tap after each adjustment. Once this has been set at close as possible visually, then read the dial of the sextant to see what is left, and that is your index correction (IC). Review notes in Figure 2-3 on reading this IC. Determine if the reading is "on the scale" (low minutes line up) or "off the scale" (larger minutes line up).

Record the IC value, using an "on" or "off" label, then move the arm away from horizon alignment, and then bring it back into alignment and read the value again and re-record IC. Do this several times to determine an average value. This will also give you a feeling for the uncertainty in the subsequent sights. The accuracy of the sights is affected by your accuracy in reading the dials, and your concept of horizon alignment.

Index Mirror Adjustment with a Star

With a star or planet in view, we can do both adjustments another way, and then compare what we find from horizon alone. It is a quicker process, but ultimately the horizon is what we use for a reference in the sights, so that is the true measure of the effective index correction. When doing any celestial sight, we must see the horizon, so we will use that to check the IC before every sight session. In the description below, we are either starting from scratch, or using the view of a star to check what we did with the horizon alone.

Step 1. Set the sextant to 0° 0' and point the sextant toward a star and view it through the sight tube, and you will see something like what is shown in Figure 2-8. You will have to move the view around a bit to position the reflected star view right on the edge of the mirror, near the center as shown. With both side error and index error, you will see two views of the star, offset from each other. The left-right offset is the side error, the up-down offset is the index error.

Step 2. With this graphic display of the effect of both errors in view, we can adjust them both as we watch the results. Turn adjustment screw #1 to bring them together vertically (removing the index error) and then turn screw #2 to remove the horizontal separation. This last side error adjustment is not crucial to the final results as long as it is small. In fact a small offset using stars can help tune out the index correction. Again, this is an iterative process, so alternating between the two adjustments is often a successful approach. Again, slight taps on the back of the index mirror housing can sometimes help to settle in the adjustments.

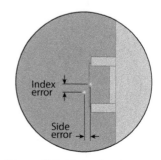

Figure 2-8. *View of a star through the sight tube with the sextant set to 0° 0'. We see the effects of both side error and index error. This view can be used to adjust out both errors.*

Step 3. Once you have the star looking like Figure 2-9, you are done and can then read the IC from the sextant scales. Record what you have for IC, marked "on" or "off", and then repeat a few times—or if the horizon is in view, then switch to the horizon for the checks of the IC.

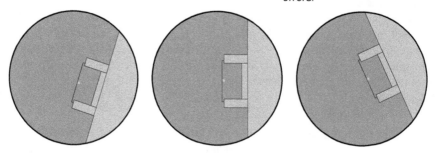

Figure 2-9. Below. *View of a star when rocking the sextant and there is no side error or index error.*

Index Mirror Adjustment with Cloud Edges

This method is frequently available as a quick way to see the effects of the mirror offsets. Like the use of stars, it offers a way to get most of the corrections removed before we switch to the horizon for the final IC measurement. An example is in Figure 2-10. Follow the procedures listed with the star example using the top and side edges of the clouds for index error and side error adjustments. Then turn to the horizon for fine tuning.

Figure 2-10. *Using cloud edges as a quick way to adjust the index mirror, before turning to the horizon for final adjustments. Left is before adjustments; right is after removing side and index errors.*

3. TAKING SUN SIGHTS

You might find that you can adjust the index mirror for index and side errors once, and then on subsequent sights just measure the IC and use that value without actually adjusting the mirror again. Determine that by checking the IC and side error at each sight session. If either has changed much since the last session, readjust it and get a new IC value for the present sight session. With a metal sextant these adjustments rarely change, but with a plastic sextant they can change, depending on how the instrument has been stored and handled.

TIP: After moving the arm to line up the horizons to measure the IC, try yawing the view to the left and right slightly to see if you can detect any small bump moving right and left where the horizons meet. If the views are not exactly aligned you can sometimes see this indication better than just visually aligning the two views of the horizon.

For the simplified methods we use here, the sun sights are taken during the middle part of the day, centered halfway between sunrise and sunset. At this time the sun will be approaching its peak height for the day, at which time it will bear either due south or due north. It will "hang" at its peak height for a short time and then begin to descend as it moves to the west. The time of the peak height is called your *local apparent noon* (LAN). We find our Latitude (Lat) from the peak height at LAN, and we find our longitude (Lon) from the time of LAN.

We need to know the UTC (GMT) of this event, which we determine from our watch time (WT), watch error (WE), and the zone description (ZD) our watch is set to:

$$UTC = WT \pm WE \pm ZD,$$

where WE can be positive (slow watch) or negative (fast watch), and ZD is positive for Lon-west and negative for Lon-east. Time keeping is reviewed in Section 8.1. We need to know the WT of each sight we take. To accomplish this in practice, it is easiest to have an assistant who records the time when you announce that you have the sun aligned with the horizon in the sextant, as discussed below. You say "mark" and they read the time on their watch (seconds first, then minutes, then hours) and record it. Remind them that you will actually need to read what they wrote, which I emphasize with seasoned reason!

Doing the sights and recording them by yourself takes a bit more practice. After aligning the sun on the horizon, you turn away from the sextant, still holding it in one hand and being careful not to bump the dials, and read your watch, seconds first, then minutes, then hours. Then you must write down this time, which takes some choreography on a moving vessel. Some navigators attach a small notepad to an arm and keep a pencil on a lanyard, others manage by switching hands on the sextant, and using a notepad and pencil from their pocket or tucked under a line running tight across the cabin top. In either event, the main challenge is not bumping the dials or bumping the hand holding the sextant in the process. This is more of a challenge with a Mark 3 than it is with a metal sextant that is less susceptible to angle changes.

Figure 3-1 shows a sample set of "noon sights." That means a set of Hs and WT that spans the peak height. We have a table, as might be recorded in a notepad, along with a plot of Hs vs. WT on graph paper (a notepad option), which can be useful for finding the peak and central time when the measurements are sparse.

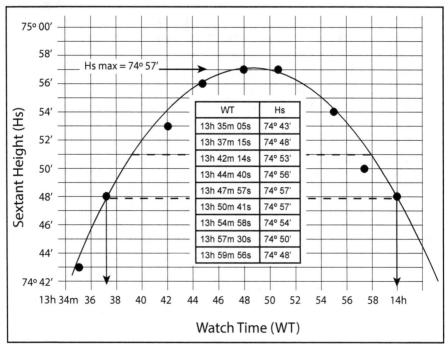

WT	Hs
13h 35m 05s	74° 43'
13h 37m 15s	74° 48'
13h 42m 14s	74° 53'
13h 44m 40s	74° 56'
13h 47m 57s	74° 57'
13h 50m 41s	74° 57'
13h 54m 58s	74° 54'
13h 57m 30s	74° 50'
13h 59m 56s	74° 48'

Figure 3-1. *Sextant sights spanning LAN, July 14, WE = 3 sec fast, ZD = +7 hr, HE = 8 ft, IC = 4' off the scale. The DR position is 36° 40' N, 133° 20'W. Based on the approximate times of the Hs = 74° 48' sights, the WT of LAN was (1360+1337)/2 = 13h 48m 30s. We can get a more accurate value averaging actual WT correcting for WE.*

Aligning the Sun on the Horizon

Start your sights 10 or 20 min before LAN. You may know this time from the previous day's work, or you can judge the approach to noon from the true bearing to the sun. Section 8.4 shows a way to calculate the time of LAN based on your DR-Lon using the Sun Almanac and Increments Table.

After measuring and recording the IC, put one index shade in place, and estimate the height of the sun visually; halfway up the sky is Hs = 45°. Set the sextant to that estimated height and look toward the horizon directly below the sun—we always look toward the horizon, not up at the sun. Any shadows on the boat, show precisely the direction to look. Then, move the arm along the arc to find the sun in the reflected view. The reflected view gets much brighter as it approaches the sun, at which point the second index shade should be added. With the sun in view, you might need to add one of the horizon shades as well, or, on a hazy day, it could be that one index shade and one of the horizon shades will be best. The goal is to get a sharp image of the sun disk without glare or perception of undo brightness.

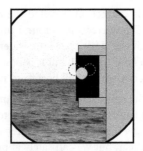

Figure 3-2. *Sun aligned with the horizon for a sun sight. Dashed lines show how it moves when rocking the sextant. The bottom of the sun should just touch the horizon when the sextant is vertical. The rocking tilt (roll) is very small in both directions, but you have to make slight yaw and pitch adjustments to the keep the sun in view. The color of the sun depends on the combination of shades in place, but the background will be opaque with most choices.*

Once the sun is in view on the horizon mirror, bring it into alignment with the horizon as shown in the center of Figure 3-2. As described in the IC measurement, the sextant should be slightly rocked to ensure that it just touches the horizon at its lowest point. With a slight roll counterclockwise, the sun rises slightly on the right, but rolling clockwise the sun would go off the mirror, so we need to make a very slight turn to the left to keep it in view. With just little practice, the motion and alignment becomes more intuitive, which is testimony to the double-reflection design of sextants.

Once it is aligned as shown, record the time and Hs as described above.

4. A COOKBOOK APPROACH TO FINDING POSITION

The primary intention of this booklet is teach you to find your position at sea when your GPS has failed, and to do so as directly as possible. As such, we first present the process as a cookbook recipe with a list of ingredients and how to use them to find your latitude (Lat) and longitude (Lon). For those who wish to understand the principles of how this works, please refer to Section 8.5. A review of Lat, Lon, nautical miles (nmi), and DR is given in Section 8.2.

Correcting the Sextant Height to get the Observed Height

For all celestial sights we need to know the true angular height of the center of the celestial body sighted, above the true horizon, independent of our height above the water, and corrected for refraction as the light enters the atmosphere from the vacuum of space. These corrections are in addition to the sextant's index correction, discussed previously. Thus the first step in any celestial sight is to convert sextant height (Hs) to *observed height* (Ho) by applying these corrections.

Index correction (IC). This is the sextant's zero angle offset that we must measure at the start of each sight session. It can be a + or − correction that we determine by measurement. If "on the scale," we take it off (a − correction); if "off the scale," we put it on (a + correction).

Height of eye (HE). As we stand with our sextant some height (HE) above the surface, we are seeing over the true flat horizon at our location, so the angles we measure will always be slightly too big. This correction is called the *dip of the horizon* (Dip) and it is always negative (–). The Dip correction is found in the Dip Correction Table. It depends only on your height of eye (HE) above the water level at the location you are taking the sights. This HE can be estimated, but it is best to measure it once and then record it. For most vessels this correction will be a fixed number, used for all sights.

Semi-diameter (SD). This is the angular width of the sun from its top or bottom edge to the center. We measure Hs from the visible horizon to the bottom edge (called its *lower limb*), but we need to know the height of its center so we must add SD to Hs. SD varies slightly throughout the year, but we can safely approximate it as a constant: SD = +16'.

Refraction (Ref). When a light ray from the sun or a star enters the atmosphere from the vacuum of space, it bends down toward the earth slightly due to refraction. We view and measure this bent light ray, and thus perceive the height of the body to be slightly higher than it really is. Thus we have a minus (–) Ref correction for all sights, which we determine from the Refraction Correction Table. This correction is largest for low sights and near zero for high sights. The Ref correction will be more important for *Polaris* sights than for sun sights, but it is easy to add in either case, so there is no need to ignore it.

In summary:

$$Ho = Hs \pm IC - Dip + SD - Ref.$$

Finding Latitude and Longitude From the Sun

Again, an illustrated background of the principles behind what we are doing is given in Section 8.5. For now we just note that the sun rises in the east and climbs in the sky as it moves westward around the horizon. Its peak height above the horizon occurs when it crosses your longitude line (called *meridian passage*). We determine our Lat from the value of this peak height, and we determine our Lon from the time this peak height occurs.

The Recipe

(1) Measure the IC, and take a series of sun sights throughout the middle of the day to determine the maximum Hs and the WT of that peak height (LAN). Record your DR-Lat and DR-Lon for the approximate time of the sights.

(2) Convert Hs to Ho, and convert WT to UTC.

(3) Find the *zenith distance* (z): $z = 90° - Ho$

(4) Look up the *declination* (Dec) of the sun from the Sun Almanac at the UTC of LAN (time of the peak Hs). For this step the UTC can be rounded to the nearest hour.

(5) Your Lat is the sum of, or difference between, zenith distance (z) and declination (Dec). Compare the two choices with your DR-Lat to decide which is correct—more on this choice later.

(6) Your Lon is the *Greenwich hour angle* (GHA) of the sun at the UTC of LAN, which we find in the Sun Almanac. There are two steps: find the GHA for the hours part of the UTC in the Sun Almanac, then find the minutes and seconds part in the Increments Tables. Add these two parts for the full GHA. This will be your Lon when in western

longitudes. If the GHA you find turns out to be more than 180°, then your eastern longitude will be 360° - GHA.

Finding the Peak Height of the Sun

This is usually an easy process if you started 5 or 10 min before the peak (Section 10 tells how to predict this time). You will see the height rise, level out, and then descend, and you can typically determine this from just the tabulated list of your sights. With scarce sights, or values that bounce around near the peak, it is best to plot a curve of Hs vs. WT on graph paper using any convenient scale and draw a smooth symmetric curve through the data by eye, trying to go through as many points as possible, leaving as many above the curve as below it—and disregarding any that are notably off of the curve.

Graph paper notebooks, even waterproof versions, are easy to find. A grid of 0.25" or 5 mm squares is common. A plot using 1 min of WT per grid line on the horizontal scale and a 1' of Hs per grid line on the vertical scale, would be a typical starting point to vary as needed.

Finding the Time of LAN

Longitude is very easy to solve once we are confident we know the time of local apparent noon (LAN), which is the time the midday sun reaches its peak height in the sky, bearing either due south or due north. The problem is the path of the sun across the sky is fairly flat at midday, so finding the precise peak based on Hs measurements takes some care. This flat curve at midday makes finding Lat easy and not sensitive to the actual time of the sight, but it also makes finding a precise time of the actual peak height more difficult.

There are two approaches to finding this peak. The easiest, though not necessarily the shortest, is to just start the sights 10 or 15 minutes before the peak, and measure enough values of Hs and WT on either side of the peak that we can then plot the curve of Hs vs. WT on graph-paper and find the symmetric center of the curve as shown in Figure 3-1.

Alternatively, we can take two or three sights in the morning, well before the sun reaches its peak, as shown in Figure 4-1, then put the sextant away until midday when we take another few sights to determine the peak height for Lat.

Then note the time interval between the last morning sight (Hs3) and a rough estimate of the time of LAN from the Lat sights, and go back on deck in time to catch the sun as it descends to the Hs3 height. If Hs3 was, say, 22 minutes before your estimated LAN, then be ready to go at about 20 min after LAN. Set the sextant to precisely the Hs3 value, and without further adjustment of the arm, watch

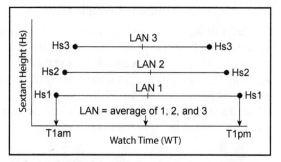

Figure 4-1. *Ways to find the midpoint of LAN sights. The average could be found from the numbers without plotting.*

the sun in the mirror with a rocking motion, and when you see it descend to just touch the horizon, read your watch and record the time. Then set the sextant to Hs2, and repeat the process to get its corresponding afternoon time, and so on. We now have two or three measurements of the midpoint, i.e., LAN 1 = (T1pm – T1am)/2. The average of these should be a good measure of the time of LAN.

In principle this could be done with just one such measurement, but the average of several will be much better. We need to know this time as accurately as we can. Recall that a 1-min error in this time will be a 15' error in Lon. With care we can find this to within ± 0.5 min (30 sec), meaning our Lon uncertainty will be ± 8' or so. This does not mean it will be wrong by that much, just that it will be uncertain by that much.

Note that this method of finding Lon is not standard procedure in celestial navigation. With full training in the subject there are better ways that are faster and more systematic, but it takes extra tables and procedures beyond the goal of this booklet. We use here a backup method that should easily meet our needs when we lose the convenience of GPS.

Sailing Under the Sun

No matter what methods are used, nor what type of sextant, a noon sight for Lat becomes more difficult when the sun is higher than about 85°. It is doable, but more difficult because it is difficult to know which way to point the sextant as you rock it for the best alignment. Thus extra uncertainty arises when the sights are very high, which occurs when your Lat approaches the declination (Dec) of the sun. Check the Sun Almanac for values on specific dates. On Jun 21, for example, the Dec is about N 23°, so sailing between Lat 26 N and 20 N, we must count on more difficult LAN Lat sights when we rely on this technique alone.

On the other hand, the Lon determination is not much affected. It is even assisted to some extent as the sun gets higher, because the curve is less flat at the top and the midpoint easier to determine. Even when the sun is too high for good Lat sights, we can take the three AM and PM reference sights of Figure 4-1 well before the sun is too high, so Lon determination is not affected.

5. WORKED LAN EXAMPLES

Latitude Example 1

Refer to the data from Figure 3-1, which is repeated in Table 5-1. See from the graph or table that the peak height Hs was 74° 57'. The measured IC was 4' Off the scale; the HE was 8 ft. The date was July 14 with sights taken from a DR position of 36° 40' N, 130° 10' W. The watch was set to ZD = +7, with a WE = 3 sec fast = –3 sec. This data can be put into a simple forms as in Table 5-2 to solve for Lat.

Apply the corrections to convert Hs to Ho:

$$Ho = Hs \pm IC - Dip + SD - Ref.$$

Table 5-1. LAN Data from Figure 11	
WT	Hs
13h 35m 05s	74° 43'
13h 37m 15s	74° 48'
13h 42m 14s	74° 53'
13h 44m 40s	74° 56'
13h 47m 57s	74° 57'
13h 50m 41s	74° 57'
13h 54m 58s	74° 54'
13h 57m 30s	74° 50'
13h 59m 56s	74° 48'

Table 5-2. Find Lat		
DR -Lat =	36° 40'	N
DR-Lon =	130° 10'	W
UTC LAN =	20h 49m	
Hs Max =	74°	57'
±IC =		+4'
–Dip =		-2.7'
+SD =		+16'
–Ref =		-0.3'
Sum above		
Ho =	74°	74.0'
Ho =	75°	14.0'
90° =	89°	60.0'
–Ho =	75°	14.0'
z =	14°	46.0'
Dec =	N 21°	34.6'
Lat = z + Dec =	35°	80.6'
Lat =	36°	20.6'

Here the IC is 'off the scale' so we put it on, a + correction. The HE of 8 ft implies a Dip correction (see Dip Table) of –2.7'. The SD is a constant correction of +16', and the refraction correction (Ref) at Hs of about 75° is –0.3' (halfway between the 70° and 80° values).

Then find zenith distance (z):

$$z = 90° - Ho.$$

Now we need the declination of the sun (Dec) at the UTC of LAN.

$$UTC = WT \pm WE \pm ZD$$

For Lat, we only need the time accurate to the hour (we can skip the WE), which we can read from Table 5-1 as WT 13h 49m, which we round to WT 1400, and with a ZD = +7, we get UTC = 21h. From the Sun Almanac for July 14 at 21h we find Dec = N 21° 34.6' (Figure 5-1).

Refraction Correction	
Hs	Ref Cor
4°	–11.7'
6°	–8.5'
8°	–6.6'
10°	–5.3'
12°	–4.5'
14°	–3.8'
18°	–3.0'
20°	–2.6'
26°	–2.0'
32°	–1.5'
42°	–1.1'
50°	–0.8'
60°	–0.6'
70°	–0.4'
80°	–0.2'

Dip Correction		
HE(ft)	HE(m)	Dip Cor
4	1.2	–1.9'
6	1.8	–2.4'
8	2.4	–2.7'
10	3.0	–3.1'
12	3.7	–3.4'
15	4.6	–3.8'
20	6.1	–4.3'
25	6.7	–4.9'
30	9.1	–5.3'
35	9.8	–5.5'
40	12.2	–6.1'

Note: These are truncated tables. See Section 12 for full versions.

July 14				
Hr	GHA		Dec	
00	178°	32.3'	N021°	42.6'
01	193°	32.2'	N021°	42.2'
02	208°	32.1'	N021°	41.8'
03	223°	32.1'	N021°	41.5'
04	238°	32.0'	N021°	41.1'
05	253°	31.9'	N021°	40.7'
06	268°	31.9'	N021°	40.3'
07	283°	31.8'	N021°	39.9'
08	298°	31.7'	N021°	39.6'
09	313°	31.7'	N021°	39.2'
10	328°	31.6'	N021°	38.8'
11	343°	31.5'	N021°	38.4'
12	358°	31.5'	N021°	38.0'
13	013°	31.4'	N021°	37.7'
14	028°	31.3'	N021°	37.3'
15	043°	31.3'	N021°	36.9'
16	058°	31.2'	N021°	36.5'
17	073°	31.1'	N021°	36.1'
18	088°	31.1'	N021°	35.7'
19	103°	31.0'	N021°	35.3'
20	118°	30.9'	N021°	35.0'
21	133°	30.9'	N021°	34.6'
22	148°	30.8'	N021°	34.2'
23	163°	30.7'	N021°	33.8'

Figure 5-1. Sun Almanac

With Lat and Dec in hand, we can apply the *Easy LAN Rule*, to find our Lat as the sum of the two, or Lat = 36° 20.6' N, which shows that our DR-Lat was off by about 20 nmi. (If we had subtracted the two, we would have got a Lat of 6° 48.6', which is clearly wrong.)

Easy LAN Rule

Your Lat will always be the sum of, or difference between, zenith distance (z) and declination (Dec). When subtracting, take the smaller from the larger. The Easy LAN Rule on whether to add or subtract that works in most cases is:

"Add them, and if that is nonsense, subtract them."

Compare with your DR-Lat to decide. Adding versus subtracting will usually make a big difference.

The only times this Easy LAN Rule does not work is when *twice* either term (z or Dec) is small comparable to our DR uncertainty. Declination is small (< 2°) for about a week on either side of the equinoxes (Mar 21 and Sep 23), and the zenith distance (90° – Ho) is small whenever Ho is higher than 88° or so. This in turn happens at LAN whenever your Lat is within 2° of the sun's declination, which can be found for any date in the Sun Almanac. In practice we can't do LAN sights very well in these conditions (sailing under the sun) in any event, so the Easy LAN Rule works most of the time. When sailing near the equinoxes, use the Universal Rule for LAN given in Section 8.7.

Longitude Example 1

To find our Lon we just need to determine the UTC of LAN more carefully. More analysis of the curve in Figure 3-1 can be done as explained earlier, but for now we just compare the times of the two sights, either side of LAN, with Hs = 74° 48'. These data are entered into Table 5-3 to find the midpoint at WT = 13h 48m 36s. Now we apply the watch error (WE) and zone description (ZD) in Table 5-4 to get the UTC of LAN = 20h 48m 33s. Use that time to enter the Sun Almanac (sample in Figure 5-1) to get the GHA for the 20 hr (118° 30.9') and then turn to the Increments Tables to find the increment in GHA for the 48m 33s (12° 8.0') as shown in top of Figure 5-2. These values are shown in Table 5-5 to find Lon = 130° 39' W.

We used decimals in these computations even though the sights are precise only to ± 2' or so; but other data used are more accurate, and we do not want to throw away precision when we don't have to. In the end, the Lat we find will be ± 3' *at best* and the Lon ± 8' *at best*—not necessarily wrong that much, but uncertain that much.

Table 5-3. Find WT of LAN			
Times	hr	min	sec
T1am	13	37	15
T1pm	13	59	56
sum	26	96	71
LAN	13	48	36

Table 5-4. Find UTC			
times	hr	min	sec
WT	13	48	36
WE			-3
ZD	+7		
UTC	20	48	33

Table 5-5. Find Lon		
Hs Max UTC	20h 48m 33s	
GHA 20h	118°	30.9'
GHA 48m 33s	12°	8.0'
GHA	130°	38.9'
Lon = GHA =	130°	38.9'

48 Min		
Sec	0	'
0	12	0
4	12	1
8	12	2
12	12	3
16	12	4
20	12	5
24	12	6
28	12	7
32	12	8
36	12	9
40	12	10
44	12	11
48	12	12
52	12	13
56	12	14
60	12	15

Figure 5-2.
Increments Table segments.

43 Min		
Sec	0	'
0	10	45
4	10	46
8	10	47
12	10	48
16	10	49
20	10	50
24	10	51
28	10	52
32	10	53
36	10	54
40	10	55
44	10	56
48	10	57
52	10	58
56	10	59
60	11	0

Latitude Example 2

Next consider the June 2 example from the *Mark 3 User's Guide*. The height of eye (HE) was 10 ft, the index correction (IC) was 5' on the scale. This IC value means that when the two horizons were aligned, the dials looked like those of Figure 2-3 (sample F). Since this is "on the scale," the IC is a negative correction. Hs max was measured to be 84° 56' at 21h 43m 30s UTC, which can be rounded to 22h for the Lat solution. These data are summarized in Table 5-2a to find Lat = 27° 12.4' N. Our value is ± 3', which we can improve for specific years with the Declination Correction Table (Page 93). Note: the *Mark 3 User's Guide* is not as accurate.

Longitude Example 2

The UTC of LAN was given as 21h 43m 30s, which is used in Table 5-5a to find a Lon of 146° 21.4' W. This differs from the value in the guide by 4.1', primarily due to Almanac data.

Table 5-5a. Find Lon		
Hs Max UTC =	21h 43m 30s	
GHA 21h	135°	28.9'
GHA 43m 30s	10°	52.5'
GHA =	145°	81.4'
Lon = GHA =	146°	21.4'

June 2				
Hr	GHA		Dec	
00	180°	31.0'	N022°	09.4'
01	195°	30.9'	N022°	09.7'
02	210°	30.8'	N022°	10.0'
03	225°	30.7'	N022°	10.4'
04	240°	30.6'	N022°	10.7'
05	255°	30.5'	N022°	11.0'
06	270°	30.4'	N022°	11.3'
07	285°	30.3'	N022°	11.6'
08	300°	30.2'	N022°	12.0'
09	315°	30.1'	N022°	12.3'
10	330°	30.0'	N022°	12.6'
11	345°	29.9'	N022°	12.9'
12	000°	29.8'	N022°	13.2'
13	015°	29.7'	N022°	13.6'
14	030°	29.6'	N022°	13.9'
15	045°	29.5'	N022°	14.2'
16	060°	29.4'	N022°	14.5'
17	075°	29.3'	N022°	14.8'
18	090°	29.2'	N022°	15.2'
19	105°	29.1'	N022°	15.5'
20	120°	29.0'	N022°	15.8'
21	135°	28.9'	N022°	16.1'
22	150°	28.8'	N022°	16.4'
23	165°	28.7'	N022°	16.7'

Figure 5-3. *Sun Almanac.*

Table 5-2a. Find Lat		
DR -Lat =	28°	N
DR-Lon =	146°	W
Hs Max =	84°	56'
±IC =		-5'
-Dip =		-3.1'
+SD =		+16'
-Ref =		-0.1
Sum above	———	
Ho =	84°	64.0'
Ho =	85°	04.0'
90° =	89°	60.0'
-Ho =	85°	04.0'
z =	4°	56.0'
Dec =	N 22°	16.4'
Lat = z + Dec =	26°	72.4'
Lat =	27°	12.4'

6. LATITUDE BY POLARIS

At any Lat above about 5° N, we can measure the Hs of *Polaris* (the North Star), and from it quickly determine our latitude. *Polaris* is not visible from southern latitudes, and at low northern latitudes it is difficult to see because it is not a bright star. The procedures for taking the sights are the same as described for doing sun sights, we just put *Polaris* on the horizon rather than the sun. The sights have to be taken during twilight, morning or evening, when we can see both the star and the horizon. There is a 20 to 30-min time slot available for this, depending on Lat.

Polaris has a declination (Dec) of near N 90°, which puts it overhead when standing at the North Pole. As we go south from there, the star will move off of overhead, descending in the sky in sync with the angular distance we move away from the pole. Thus the observed height of *Polaris* (Ho) will always be equal to our latitude. See Section 8.5 for background on this.

But we can't just measure the Hs of *Polaris* to get Lat. First we have to convert Hs to Ho in the usual manner: Ho = Hs ± IC – Dip – Ref. There is no SD for stars. Then, we have to correct for the fact that the Dec of *Polaris* is not exactly 90°; it is 89° 20', which puts the star 40' off of the true pole. This means that *Polaris*, like all other stars, circles the true pole once a day. To find Lat by *Polaris*, we have to correct for that offset. We determine the observed height of *Polaris* (Ho), and then figure how high above or below the pole is it at that time, called the Polaris correction (Q). Then we find Lat as:

$$Lat = Ho ± Q.$$

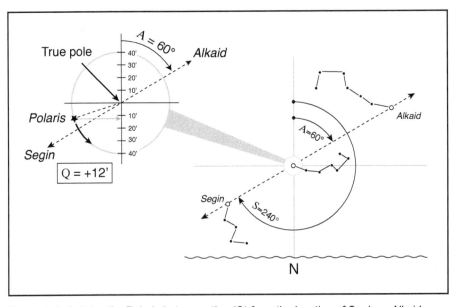

Figure 6-1. *Judging the Polaris Lat correction (Q) from the location of Segin or Alkaid relative to Polaris. Polaris is on the Segin side (Cassiopeia side) of the true pole. The left side shows a zoomed in view of Polaris circling the pole. Polaris is about 15° behind the Alkaid-Segin line as it rotates counterclockwise around the true pole once a day. The Polaris correction tables specifies the orientation of Alkaid-Segin line relative to a true compass rose centered on Polaris, with the N-S line perpendicular to the horizon.*

Polaris Correction			Polaris Correction		
S	A	Q	S	A	Q
180	000	+39'	000	180	-39'
195	015	+35'	015	195	-35'
210	030	+28'	030	210	-28'
225	045	+20'	045	225	-20'
240	060	+12'	060	240	-10'
255	075	00'	075	255	00'
270	090	-10'	090	270	+10'
285	105	-20'	105	285	+20'
300	120	-28'	120	300	+28'
315	135	-35'	135	315	+35'
330	150	-39'	150	330	+39'
345	165	-40'	165	345	+40'
000	180	-39'	180	360	+39'

Note: *These are truncated tables. See Section 12 for full versions.*

The correction varies as *Polaris* circles the pole at a radius of 40'. (Figure 6-1). When *Polaris* is directly below the pole, we add 40' to Ho to get the true height of the pole, which is our Lat. When Polaris is directly above the pole, we subtract 40'. There is no correction when *Polaris* is just to the right or left of the Pole, at an equal height above the horizon.

The *Polaris* correction (Q) can be estimated from the location of the trailing star *Segin* in Cassiopeia or from the trailing star *Alkaid* in Ursa Major. *Polaris* is on the Segin side of the pole.

The task at hand is to estimate the angle made between the *Segin-Alkaid* line and the horizon, or more practically, a line parallel to the horizon that goes through *Polaris*. The correction table lists the orientation of this line using either Segin or Alkaid, because at latitudes lower than about 45 N, one of these stars could be below the horizon.

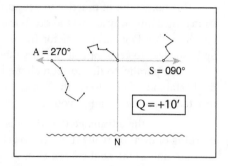

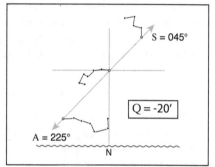

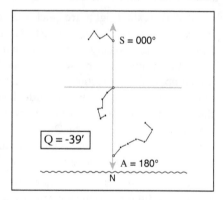

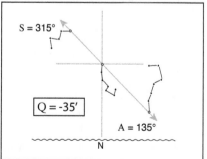

Figure 6-2. *Polaris correction examples. Either star can be used to find the orientation of the line to use in the Tables.*

This takes a bit of practice to get optimum values, as these are big constellations, stretching a long way across the sky. It is easier at lower latitudes than at higher. Looking through a Douglas protractor (or any equivalent) centered on *Polaris* with north up is one way to get a more accurate value than just estimating by eye. Or hold up two sticks, one parallel to the horizon aligned with Polaris and the other aligned with the target star and *Polaris* to set the angle, then use a protractor or plotting sheet compass rose to determine the angle you set.

We have the advantage that there is no rush on this sight; you can take the full morning or evening twilight period to get the best value. The disadvantage is the three stars are not bright, so it takes a clear night to see both *Polaris* and a target star. With practice we can get this correction to ± 5' or so, with maybe twice that in most cases by just looking at the stars, the latter giving a Lat accurate to ± 10 nmi. (Practicing ahead of time in the presence of any city light pollution, with possibly an obscured horizon, makes it seem harder than it is on a clear dark night with a good horizon.)

Latitude by *Polaris* Example

We measure Hs *Polaris* of 38° 12' with *Segin* above *Polaris*, about 15° above due west on the protractor (S = 285). From the Polaris Correction Table, we see this implies a Q correction = -20'. The height of eye was 8 ft. The index correction was 2' on the scale. Note that the time and date do not matter for this sight.

Polaris sextant sights are quick and easy when the sky is clear. The main challenge is estimating the correction (Q), but there is plenty of time for that. In full celestial navigation training, with use a full *Nautical Almanac*, we can compute this correction very accurately from the time of the sight. Unfortunately, to include the needed information would double the size of the backup almanac we use here, not to mention that the Q correction depends on the date. The method used here is an approximation that does not depend on special almanac data nor the date.

Table 6-1. Latitude by Polaris		
Hs =	38°	12.0'
IC =		-2.0
Dip =		-2.7'
Ref =		-1.3'
Ho =	38°	6.0'
Q =		-20.0'
Lat =	37°	46.0'

Figure 6-3 shows several other ways to find due north, which is useful for steering without a compass.

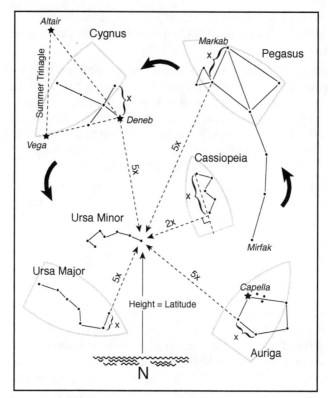

Figure 6-3. *Ways to find the North Star, Polaris*

7. PLOTTING POSITIONS AND DR TRACKS

Finding your Lat and Lon from the sextant is just the first step in ocean navigation. We must plot this on a chart of some form, and layout our DR track to navigate with until our next sextant sights. Section 8.2 is a review of Lat, Lon, nmi, and DR as needed.

If you do not have a chart of the ocean at your location, you can make one with a universal plotting sheet (UPS), several of which can be included in a GPS back-up kit. A UPS is a way to make a small nautical chart for any region on earth. The chart covers a rectangular area of roughly 120 nautical miles in all directions around the mid-latitude and mid-longitude that you choose for the sheet.

Setting Up a Universal Plotting Sheet

(1) Choose and label the mid-latitude on the center horizontal line, as shown in Figure 7-1. This would be the nearest whole degrees of Lat to your DR-Lat. The horizontal lines are latitude lines; the vertical lines are longitude lines. Then label the latitudes above and below your mid-latitude. In northern latitudes, latitude increases to the north, that is, to the top of the page. South of the equator, the latitude lines increase to the south.

(2) Next, draw a horizontal line on the longitude diagram in the bottom right-hand corner at the position of your mid-latitude. This line is then the longitude scale you will use for reading and plotting the longitudes of points on the chart.

(3) Label the central vertical line with your mid-longitude (the nearest to your DR-Lon). And now draw in the other longitude lines, which is the main job in setting up these sheets.

(4) On the *outside scale* on the central compass rose, to the right of the mid-longitude line, go up from the mid-latitude line (0 on the curved scale) to your mid-latitude along the curved scale. If your mid-latitude is 40° N, go up 40°. Mark a point at this spot. Then go down from the center latitude line and mark another point in the same way. Draw a line between the two points to get the longitude line. You can do the same thing to the left of the center line to get another longitude line, but in this case the outer scale is not labeled, so you must just count off the degrees.

(5) Label the new longitude lines, remembering that west of Greenwich longitude increases to the west, or left. The chart is now set up and ready to go.

Using the Plotting Sheet

(1) The latitude of any point is read from the vertical center line. Each tick mark is equal to 1′ of latitude. Each latitude line is separated by 60 marks, since 60′ = 1°.

(2) The longitude of any point is read from the diagram in the bottom right hand corner. For example, to set your dividers on 45' of longitude, set one side of them on the 40' mark and the other side halfway between the second and third mark to the right of 0'. Each division on the right side of the diagram is equal to 2' of longitude. This special diagram is taking into account how the longitude scale changes with latitude. The changes that apply for different latitudes on the same plotting sheet are so small you can use the same mid-latitude line for reading any longitude on the page.

(3) For measuring distances between points, always use the central, vertical latitude scale. Each 1′ of latitude equals 1 nmi. Recall that 1° of latitude always equals 60 nmi, but the number of miles per 1° of longitude changes with your latitude. At the equator 1° of longitude is 60 nmi, but as you go north, it gets smaller. Check the example page to see that at latitude 40°N the distance between each longitude line is 46 nmi. This takes into account the convergence of the longitude lines at the north pole. Since the earth is symmetric about the equator, everything is the same for southern latitudes. The only thing that changes is the labels. In the south, latitude increases toward the bottom of the page.

When you find a latitude it will be a horizontal line of position (LOP) on the UPS. Plot that Lat on the chart, and draw a horizontal line through it. You are somewhere on that line. When you find Lon, it will be a vertical LOP on the UPS. If you find them at the same time, their intersection is your plotted position fix, and you can start a new DR track from that point and time (Section 8.2).

Getting by Without Dividers

In routine navigation we measure and transfer distances on the chart and UPS with dividers, and most navigation stations will have a pair. It is not required to store another pair of these in a GPS backup kit because you either already have a pair or you can use a ruler or protractor scale to make the same measurements. Or we fall back to the standard of two tick marks on the edge of a piece of paper.

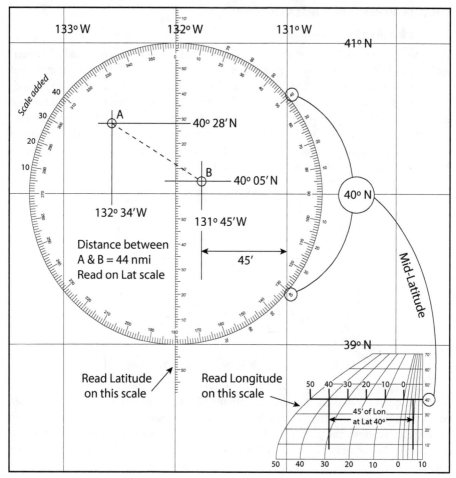

Figure 7-1. Above. *A universal plotting sheet set up with a mid-latitude of 40° N. Once the meridians are drawn in as explained in the instructions, longitude is read from the diagram in the bottom right. Latitude is read from the vertical scale in the center. For mid-latitudes that are not even tens, we must estimate where to draw in the line on the longitude scale diagram. The direction A to B (133 T) can be found from the azimuth scale on the UPS, or easier by centering the Douglas protractor on point A with North aligned and reading the true direction from the protractor.*

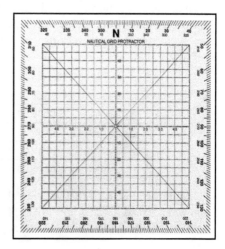

Figure 7-2. Right. *A 5"-square Douglas protractor used for measuring bearings and track lines.*

8. BACKGROUND INFORMATION

8.1 Timekeeping in Navigation

To find Lon we need to know universal coordinated time (UTC), once called Greenwich Mean Time (GMT). These are the same time systems; we still see both names used in navigation and weather. Ideally we would know the UTC accurate to the second, but for backup positions, we can get by with ± a few seconds, keeping in mind that for every 4 seconds our UTC is wrong, the Lon we determine from it will be wrong by 1'. Lon and time are related by the rate the earth rotates: 360°/24 hr = 15°/hr = 15'/min = 1'/4 sec. The relation between Lon and nmi is given in Table 8.1-1. At the equator, a 4-sec error is a 1 nmi error, and less at higher latitudes.

Table 8.1-1. Length of 1° and 1' of Lon		
Lat (N or S)	1° Lon (nmi)	1' of Lon (nmi)
0	60.0	1.0
15	58.0	1.0
30	52.0	0.9
45	42.4	0.7
60	30.0	0.5
75	15.5	0.3

Finding Your Watch Rate... Before You Depart!

All watches gain or lose time to some extent. This is called the *rate* of the watch. A typical quartz watch has a rate of less than ±10 sec/month, or 2 or 3 sec/week. This could be gaining (a positive rate) or losing (a negative rate). Since we need the time as accurate as possible, the procedure is to set the watch you will be using on some easy date to remember, and then record this set date and rate with the watch in the GPS backup kit.

Finding the watch rate is a preparatory step to take before your departure—you cannot do this at the time you might need it. Your GPS backup kit should have a warning on the label to remind you to do this. To find the rate of the watch you will be using for navigation, use your phone or computer (connected a network) to find the correct time, then over the next week or two, every other day or so, make a table like Table 8.1-2.

Table 8.1-2. Finding Watch Rate			
Date	Correct Time	Watch Time	Watch Error
July 4	12:05:00	12:05:00	0 sec (set)
July 9	13:55:30	13:54:28	2 sec slow
July 12	10:42.00	10:41:57	3 sec slow
July 14	10:15:00	10:14:56	4 sec slow

From this you learn that your watch loses 4 sec/10days, and it was set on July 4. Then when I read a *watch time* (WT) of 09:20:32 on Aug 3, 30 days later, I know my *watch error* (WE) = (30 day x 4 sec/10 day) = 12 sec slow.

Then we need to know the time zone the watch is set to. That is simply how many hours you must add to the WT to get UTC. In west Lon this is a positive number; in east Lon it is negative. Pacific Daylight time is +7 hr, for example, but it does not matter what the zones are called. At some point before stowing the watch or leaving the dock with the watch on your arm, confirm the time difference between watch and UTC. The time zone of the watch can be called ZD for *zone description*.

This leaves us with the basic time computation we must do when evaluating sextant sights:

$$UTC = WT \pm WE \pm ZD$$

Using the above example values for Aug 3,

$$UTC = 09h\ 20m\ 32s + 12s + 7h = 16h\ 20m\ 44s.$$

8.2 Lat, Lon, nmi, and DR

A nautical mile (nmi) is precisely 1852 m, which is about 6,000 ft. It is the standard unit of distance in marine navigation. A speed of 1 knot is 1 nmi/hr. It is defined to match the Lat scale on a nautical chart, where $1° = 60'$:

Latitude Distances	
Lat	Distance
1°	60 nmi
1'	1 nmi = 6,000 ft
0.1'	600 ft = 185.2m
0.01'	60 ft
0.001'	6 ft

More generally, 1° along any great circle on earth corresponds to 60 nmi.

Lat-Lon is the rectangular grid used on nautical charts. The horizontal lines are constant Lat (*parallels*); vertical lines are constant longitude (*meridians*). Figure 8.2-1 shows how these grids are defined in terms of angles.

Dead Reckoning (DR) navigation means finding your position

Figure 8.2-1. *Definitions of Lat and Lon and how they show up on charts. East Lon increases to the right; South Lat increased toward the bottom.*

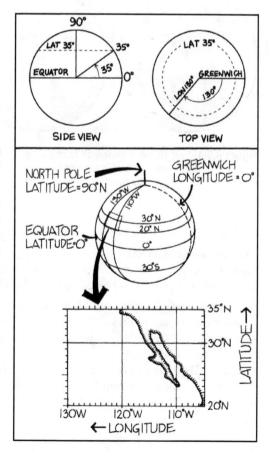

from measurements taken from the boat (compass and log), often supplemented by knowledge of measured or forecasted current patterns, and known leeway of your vessel. A *DR position* is your best estimate of your location based on all the information you have about the vessel's movement since its last position fix. Ocean navigation proceeds by a sequence of positions fixes, with DR navigation between them. Once a new fix is achieved, the next DR track emanates from that position.

8.3 Adjusting the Index Mirror on Land

On land you can still use clouds and stars, but often a distant flat rooftop or hill will serve as a horizon for the index error adjustments, and any prominent vertical structure such as pole or building edge can be used for the side error adjustments. The landmarks used, however, must be a mile or more away to be valid. Closer landmarks will appear to behave properly, but the resulting sextant adjustments will not be correct for true sights. Samples are shown in Figure 8.3-1. Refer to earlier discussion of the adjustment process for the steps involved.

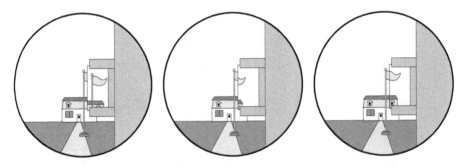

Figure 8.3-1. *Left shows a view with both side error and index error. On the left, the side error screw (#2) is too tight; in the middle, it is too loose. On the right, the side error and index error have been removed.*

8.4 Predicting the Time of LAN From Your DR-Lon

After you have observed LAN once, you will know its watch time, and on the following day the time will not be much different. But starting from scratch, or to fine tune this on any day, we can use this procedure to predict the time of LAN.

LAN occurs when the GHA of sun crosses your meridian, which puts it due south or due north of your position. We can estimate this time from your DR-Lon. The Sun Almanac lists its GHA for each hour of the day, which increases at the rate of 15° per hour. Step one is find in the Almanac, on the day of your sights, the whole hour of UTC that has a GHA just east of your DR-Lon—for west longitudes, that will be the GHA value that is just less than your DR-Lon. Now we need to figure how long it takes to get from that GHA to your actual DR-Lon, which we can get from the from the Increments Table.

July 14		
Hr	GHA	
00	178°	32.3'
01	193°	32.2'
02	208°	32.1'
03	223°	32.1'
04	238°	32.0'
05	253°	31.9'
06	268°	31.9'
07	283°	31.8'
08	298°	31.7'
09	313°	31.7'
10	328°	31.6'
11	343°	31.5'
12	358°	31.5'
13	013°	31.4'
14	028°	31.3'
15	043°	31.3'
16	058°	31.2'
17	073°	31.1'
18	088°	31.1'
19	103°	31.0'
20	118°	30.9'
21	133°	30.9'
22	148°	30.8'
23	163°	30.7'

Figure 8.4-1.

Left. *Section from the Sun Almanac for July 14. At 21 hr the sun moving west with increasing GHA is at 133° 30.9, which is past our DR, so we choose the hour prior to that (20 hr).*

Right. *Section of the Increments Table that happens to have a result of 11° 39'. We need the min and seconds that corresponds to that result, i.e., 46m 36s.*

Table 8.4-1 Find UTC Increment						
DR-Lon W	130°	10.0'		h	m	s
Previous whole-hour GHA	118°	30.9'	=	20		
Difference from DR-Lon	11°	39.1'	=		46	36
UTC			=	20	46	36
- ZD			=	-7		
WT LAN			=	13	46	

46 Min		
Sec	°	'
0	11	30
4	11	31
8	11	32
12	11	33
16	11	34
20	11	35
24	11	36
28	11	37
32	11	38
36	11	39
40	11	40
44	11	41
48	11	42
52	11	43
56	11	44
60	11	45

Consider Example 1 covered earlier. The DR-Lon was 130° 10' W on July 14. We then found from sun sights that LAN occurred at 20h 48m 33s UTC—which showed that our actual Lon was 130° 39' W. So the question is, what time would we have predicted that LAN would occur in this example based on our midday DR? From that time we can decide when to start the sights so we do not miss it.

We find the UTC of LAN assuming we were at our DR-Lon and not moving, then we convert that to WT, then we start our sights about 10 or 15 minutes earlier than that to account for the uncertainty in our DR-Lon and to give us time to measure the peak Hs.

Figure 8.4-1 shows a section of the Almanac for this date. We see that 20h with GHA = 118° 30.9' is the last whole hour with a GHA less than 130° 10', so that is the hour part of the UTC of LAN. Then we subtract that from our DR-Lon and the interval left is found in Table 8.4-1 to be 11° 39.1'. Now we go to the Increments Table to figure out how much time that is, with the sun moving west at 15° Lon/hr. We enter the Increments Table "backwards," in that we know the answer we want (11° 39.1') and are looking to see what time interval corresponds to that. The answer does not have to match precisely, as we only need to know the time to the minute to predict the time of LAN, but we get it to the second from the table.

The result is that, moving at 15°/hr, the sun takes 46m and 36s to cross over 11° 39' of Lon. We add that time interval to 20h to get the result: UTC of LAN = 20h 46m 36s if we happened to be precisely at Lon 130° 10' W at the time. In this example we added 7 hr to our WT to get UTC (i.e., ZD = +7) so to go from UTC to WT we subtract the 7 hr to get the predicted WT LAN = 1346.

Dec 25		
Hr	GHA	
00	180°	03.6'
01	195°	03.3'
02	210°	03.0'
03	225°	02.7'
04	240°	02.4'
05	255°	02.0'
06	270°	01.7'
07	285°	01.4'
08	300°	01.1'
09	315°	00.8'
10	330°	00.5'
11	345°	00.2'
12	359°	59.9'
13	014°	59.6'
14	029°	59.3'
15	044°	58.9'
16	059°	58.6'
17	074°	58.3'
18	089°	58.0'
19	104°	57.7'
20	119°	57.4'
21	134°	57.1'
22	149°	56.8'
23	164°	56.5'

Figure 8.4-2.

Left. *Section from the Sun Almanac for Dec 25. DR-Lon of 153° 40' E, corresponds to a GHA of 206° 20'. At 02 hr the sun moving west with increasing GHA is at 210° 03.0, which is past our DR-Lon (converted to GHA), so we choose the hour prior to that (01 hr).*

Right. *Section of the Increments Table that happens to have a result of 11° 16.7' (rounded to 17'). We need the min and seconds arguments that corresponds to that result, i.e., 45m 8s.*

45 Min		
Sec	°	'
0	11	15
4	11	16
8	11	17
12	11	18
16	11	19
20	11	20
24	11	21
28	11	22
32	11	23
36	11	24
40	11	25
44	11	26
48	11	27
52	11	28
56	11	29
60	11	30

Table 8.4-2 Find UTC Increment					h	m	s
DR-Lon E converted to GHA	206°	20.0'					
Previous whole-hour GHA	195°	03.3'	=	01			
Difference from DR-Lon	11°	16.7'	=			45	08
UTC				=	01	45	08
- ZD = - (-10) = +10				=	+10		
WT LAN				=	11	45	

For an east longitude example, suppose it is Dec 25 and our DR-Lon = 153° 40' E, off the coast of Australia. The ZD of our watch is -10 hr. That is, on this vessel we find UTC by reading our watch and subtracting 10 hr.

In Nautical Almanacs, the sun's GHA increases in the westerly direction from 0° at the Greenwich Meridian to 360° as it returns to Greenwich Meridian after circling the earth. Our longitude east, on the other hand, increases to the east from 0° at Greenwich to 180° E at the dateline. So a longitude of 153° 40' E will be passed by the sun when its GHA = 360° – 153° 40' = 206° 20'. An hour later the GHA will be 15° higher. So we can do the same thing now entering the almanac looking for the first whole GHA before 206° 20', which is 01h as shown in Figure 8.4-2. Once the DR-Lon E has been converted to a GHA, the process of predicting the UTC and WT of LAN is the same as in west longitudes. Another example is given in Section 10.2.

8.5 Principles of the Noon Sight for Lat and Lon

From our perspective on a rotating earth, the sun circles the earth once a day. We can track its position as it does so by thinking of the point on earth directly below the sun, which is called its geographic position (GP). As the earth rotates beneath the sun each day, the GP of the sun moves west along the surface of the earth at a near-constant latitude, at a rate of 360° of longitude in 24 hr = 15°/hr = 15'/min. The longitude of GP at any moment is called the Greenwich Hour Angle (GHA) of the sun. The latitude of the GP is called the declination (Dec) of the sun. The GHA and Dec of the sun for any time of day, on any day of the year, is listed in the *Nautical Almanac*, a shortened version of which we have in this book. On a yearly basis, as the earth circles the sun, the latitude

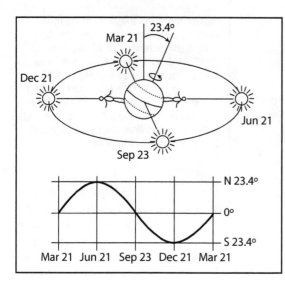

Figure 8.5-1. *The sun's declination is the Lat of the point below it, which varies from N 23.4° to S 23.4°, defining the tropics. Turning points are at the solstices, Jun 21 and Dec 21, the longest and shortest days of the year. The sun crosses the equator on the equinoxes, Mar 21 and Sep 23, at which times the lengths of day and night are the same. The declination changes most rapidly near the equinoxes (about 24' per day) and most slowly near the solstices. This seasonal oscillation of the declination occurs because the tilt of the earth's axis remains constant as it circles the sun— here shown in reverse, with the sun circling the earth.*

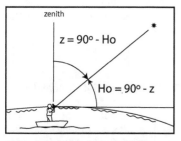

Figure 8.5-2. *Relation between observed height (Ho) and zenith distance (z).*

of the point under the sun (its declination) varies throughout the year as shown in Figure 8.5-1.

If you were standing at the GP of the sun, it would be directly overhead, observed height above the horizon Ho = 90°. Recalling that 1° along a great circle on the earth is 60 nautical miles (see Section 8.2), a second person 180 nmi away from us (3° x 60 nmi/1°), would see the sun at this moment at Ho = 87° high (90° – 3°). The farther you are from the GP, the lower the sun is in the sky. Another person 30° (1800 nmi) away would see the same sun at the same time at Ho = 60°. This is the key principle of celestial navigation: The sextant measures the height of the sun, then 90° minus that height, called the *zenith distance* (z), is the distance to the GP at that moment (Figures 8.5-2). Then we look up the location of that GP at that moment in the almanac, and we know we are somewhere on a circle, centered at the GP with radius equal to the zenith distance.

We can use this principle to find Lat and Lon from the sun at any time of day—it takes more tables than we include here—but the procedure is much simplified if we do this at local apparent noon (LAN) when the sun crosses our meridian at its peak height in the sky (Figure 8.5-3).

The *observed height* (Ho) in this analysis must be the angular height of the center of the sun above the true horizon, independent of our *height of eye* (HE) above the water, and independent of the effects of the atmosphere, which bends the light rays

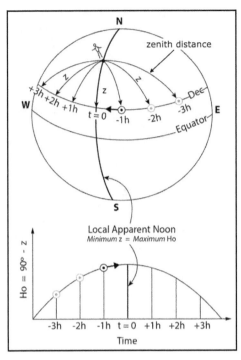

Figure 8.5-3. *As the sun circles the earth at a constant Lat = Dec, the Lon of its GHA increases at 15° per hour (360°/24h). As it gets closer to our meridian, z gets smaller and Ho gets bigger. At LAN, our Lat = z + Dec. Had we been in a south Lat at this moment, our Lat at LAN would be z - Dec. For all cases, Lat is the sum or difference between z and Dec at this special time of LAN.*

slightly due to refraction (Ref). Thus we must make several corrections to the sextant height (Hs) we measure. These corrections are illustrated in Figure 8.5-4 and discussed earlier in the text. For more background and to extend celestial measurements to all bodies at all times, see recommendations in the References.

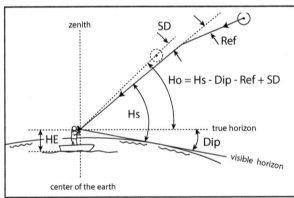

Figure 8.5-4. *Schematic depiction of the corrections to Hs to get Ho. The correction angles are greatly exaggerated. Sunlight bends down as it enters the atmosphere due to refraction (Ref), so we perceive an angle that is slightly too large. Ref is a negative correction. At a height of eye (HE), we see over the true horizon, which makes Hs slightly too large, so the Dip correction is also negative. We need the*

height to the sun's center, but we measure the height to the bottom edge, so we have to add the vertical width of the sun, called its semi-diameter (SD). This varies slightly throughout the year, but we can approximate it as a constant +16'. The Dip and Ref corrections are found from tables included here. Refraction is notably larger at lower Hs values, so in practice it has a larger effect on Polaris sights than it does on LAN sun sights.

8.6 Universal LAN Rule

Latitude at LAN is always the sum or difference between the declination and the zenith distance. By using (±) sign conventions, we can give a general formula that applies in all cases:

$$(Lat) = (Dec) - (z),$$

where the use of ( ) here means we now care about the sign (±) of each term. North latitudes and declinations are positive numbers, and southern values are negative. The sign (±) of z is determined by the direction of the noon sun. If you looked north to the noon sun, then z is positive; if you looked south, z is negative. The parentheses are used in the equation to emphasize that each term must be inserted with the proper algebraic sign (±). If your answer is positive you are north of the equator; if negative, you are south of the equator.

9. GPS BACKUP KIT—THEME AND VARIATIONS

Our guiding principle for this booklet was to provide a means of learning and executing a position fix at sea when a vessel has run out of power and all the batteries have been consumed, so there is no GPS available. We wanted a solution that is compact and inexpensive, using tables and procedures that are easy to learn and use. This goal led to our proposing a minimum kit that mariners would not hesitate to add to their gear to cover the unlikely situation it would actually be needed. Mariners who cross oceans in small boats realize they must be self-reliant and cover all contingencies. To this end, some mariners choose to learn the full range of celestial navigation and invest in a quality metal sextant and related publications and tools. This amounts to roughly a month of study, with a total investment of about $1,000.

To the extent our goal is achieved, the alternative would be less than $100 investment, with no preparatory time required. Namely, purchase or compile this GPS Backup Kit, stow it in a waterproof float bag, and then take it out when needed to learn the process, knowing all the required components are included.

Needless to say, as a marine navigation school dedicated to promoting safe navigation practice and prudent seamanship, we recommend learning the full range of celestial navigation, which includes much more than just finding your Lat and Lon once a day by the sun. But we, as a practical training resource, face the reality that there are an increasing number of mariners who do indeed intend to count on the GPS, along with backup GPS and batteries. It is to these mariners we propose this kit:

- A Davis Mark 3 sextant
- This booklet on how to use that sextant to find Lat and Lon at LAN
- Small magnifier to optimize reading the vernier
- A few universal plotting sheets
- Pencils, sharpener, eraser, ruler, and protractor
- A protective case and waterproof bag for the above

• A waterproof digital quartz watch, with known rate and set date, either in the kit, or on the arm of the navigator at all times. Without accurate time you can find only Lat, not Lon.

That is the theme of this project, but there are many variations. For one, if you already have, or choose to procure, a superior sextant, that could be used in place of the Mark 3. Likewise, if you already have a full *Nautical Almanac* for the time of your voyage, that would offer accurate sun and *Polaris* data. The full printed Almanac is 7" x 10" x 1" in size, weighing about 1.5 lbs.

Alternatively, our Sun Almanac of about 60 half-letter-size pages could be replaced with 2 letter-size pages of Table 4 from Vol 2 or 3 of *Pub. 249, Sight Reduction Tables for Air Navigation*, which is available as a PDF at msi.nga.mil. Table 4 yields more accurate data than our Sun Almanac, but multiple corrections must be applied, which makes it more complex to use, with increased chance of error. The extra accuracy provided, however, is not justified when using a Mark 3 sextant. For those using a more accurate sextant, Table 4 could be printed and used, or consider the small *Long Term Almanac: 2000-2050, Sun and Selected Stars* by Geoffrey Kolbe (Starpath Publications, 2008).

Another variation on just buying or compiling a Mark 3 backup kit and stowing it for use as needed, is to actually read this booklet ahead of time, and practice the use of the Mark 3 along with finding Lat and Lon as described. We are confident you could learn this when needed, but it could be a valuable and enjoyable experience to try it once or twice ahead of time. You would then indeed be doing celestial navigation, which could inspire you to learn more of the practice and expand your navigational skills. See starpath.com/gpsbackup for additional information.

10. FINDING THE UTC OF MERIDIAN PASSAGE (LAN)

Finding Lat and Lon from the height of the sun at local apparent noon (LAN) is quickly solved using our custom Sun Almanac, once the sights are in hand. LAN is also called the sun's meridian passage, or just *meridian passage*. The measurements themselves, however, can take some time, because we must watch the sun rise, peak out, and then descend as it crosses our meridian. Figure 8.5-3 shows how the sun crossing our meridian presents a rising and then falling curve of sextant heights. We can save time by predicting when this peak will occur (called the time of LAN or time of meridian passage) based on our DR-Lon. In lower latitudes, this can be a very hot time of the day, which is another reason to minimize the sight times.

We have two ways to predict the time of meridian passage (mer pass) at our DR-Lon using the tools of this book. One graphic method is a bit quicker and almost always accurate enough to meet practical needs; the second method is all numeric, using the Sun Almanac. Both methods begin by finding the UTC of meridian passage *at the Greenwich meridian* on the day at hand.

Once we know when the sun crosses the Greenwich meridian headed west at a rate of 15° of Lon per hour, we can figure when it will cross our (western) DR-Lon. We just convert our Lon to time with the Arc to Time table and add that time to the mer pass at Greenwich.

Mer pass at DR-Lon W = mer pass at Greenwich + DR-Lon (converted to time)

In eastern longitudes the sun passes us on its way to Greenwich, so the answer then is

Mer pass at DR-Lon E = mer pass at Greenwich - DR-Lon (converted to time)

Then knowing the time of mer pass at our DR-Lon, we can decide how much earlier we need to go on deck for the sights. If we just want Lat, then 10 min or so early should do it; if we also want Lon as well, then we might start 20 min or so before LAN.

10.1 Using the Analemma to Find Mer Pass at Greenwich

Because of the tilt of the earth's axis relative to the plane of its elliptical orbit about the sun (Figure 8.5-1), the UTC of mer pass at Greenwich is not a constant 1200 UTC that we might guess; it actually varies from 1144 to 1214 throughout the year. The difference between 1200 UTC and the actual mer pass time at Greenwich is called the Equation of Time (EqT). A unique plot of the EqT and the sun's declination, called an analemma, can be used to determine the EqT for any date, and from this we find the UTC of mer pass at Greenwich:

$$\text{Mer Pass at Greenwich} = 1200\ \text{UTC} \pm \text{EqT}$$

The full analemma plot is in the Tables Section; an example of it use is shown in Figure 10.1-1 where we determine the mer pass at Greenwich for August 15 and June 1.

Example 1. Find UTC of mer pass on August 15 at 125° 34' W.

From Figure 10.1-1, we see that the sun crosses the Greenwich meridian on August 25 at about 1204 UTC, from which it moves west at 15° per hour. From the Arc to Time table (Tables Section) we see that 125° = 8h 20m and 34' = 2m 16s, which we

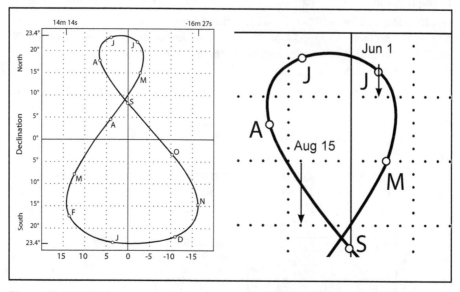

Figure 10.1-1. *Right is a zoomed view of the analemma used to find mer pass at Greenwich on August 15 and June 1. Start by estimating where the 15th is on the curve between August 1 (A) and September 1 (S), and read the EqT from the time scale, which is 1 min per dot. Here we get 4 min, so mer pass at Greenwich is 1204 UTC. On June 1, EqT would be just more than -2m, meaning mer pass would be just less than 1158 UTC.*

round to 2m, for a total DR-Lon time equivalent of 8h 22m. Add this to 1204 to get 2026 UTC for the time of LAN at 125° 34' W on August 15.

These times vary a minute or so within the leap year cycle, but they repeat every 4 years. The precise value in 2001, for example, will be the same in 2005. For practical purposes we can consider these time estimates as independent of the year.

Example 2. Find UTC of mer pass on June 1 at 148° 40' E.

From Figure 10.1-1 we see that the sun crosses the Greenwich meridian on June 1 at about 1158 UTC, and it got there at that time after crossing our meridian of 150° 40' E some time earlier. We figure how much earlier by converting our Lon to time with the Arc to Time table (Tables Section). We find: 148° = 9h 52m and 40' = 2m 40s, which we round to 3m, for a total DR-Lon time equivalent of 9h 55m. Subtract this from 1158 to get 0203 UTC for the time of LAN at 148° 40' E on June 1.

10.2 Using the Sun Almanac to Find Mer Pass at our DR-Lon (see also Section 8.4)

To find the time of mer pass at our DR-Lon using the Sun Almanac we do not need to find the time at Greenwich, nor do we need to covert our Lon to time. We know that the sun crosses our Lon when the GHA of the sun is equal to our Lon, so we just have to look into the Sun Almanac to see when that happens.

It is unlikely that our Lon will be one of the listed GHAs, so we have to interpolate between one before and one after. Redoing Example 1 and 2 with this method illustrates the process.

Example 3. Find UTC of mer pass on August 15 at 125° 34' W using the Sun Almanac.

Referring to Figure 10.2-1, we see that the sun was at Lon 118° 53.6' W at 2000 on August 15 and then at 133° 53.7' W at 2100, so we know the answer is between 2000 and 2100. Recall that in western longitudes there is a one-to-one correspondence between GHA and Lon.

To find the right time, we figure how far the sun must go beyond 118° 53.6' W to get to us at 125° 34' W. This is a difference of 6° 40.4'. In the Arc to Time table we see that 6° is 24m and 40.4' is 2m 41s, which we round to 3m, so the total travel time is 27 min, so the final answer is 2027. We got 2026 from the analemma, so it was pretty close.

If we cared to, we could do the time conversion manually. The base 15° per 60 min is the same as 1° = 4m and 1' = 4s, so 6° 40.4' = 6° × 4m/1° + 40.4' × 4s/1' = 24m 161.6s = 24m + 2.7m = 26.7m.

Hr	GHA		DEC	
19	103°	53.5'	N013°	52.3'
20	118°	53.6'	N013°	51.5'
21	133°	53.7'	N013°	50.7'
22	148°	53.8'	N013°	49.9'
23	163°	54.0'	N013°	49.2'
August 16				
00	178°	54.1'	N013°	48.4'
01	193°	54.2'	N013°	47.6'

Figure 10.2-1. *Section of the Sun Almanac for August 15 and 16. Full Almanac in the Tables Section.*

Example 4. Find UTC of mer pass on June 1 at 148° 40' E using the Sun Almanac.

The first step for eastern Lon solutions is to convert the Lon to an equivalent GHA. The GHA increases to the west from 0° to 360°, so the GHA matches up with west Lon until we get to GHA = 180, after which the GHA of an eastern Lon is 360 - Lon E as shown in Figure 10.2-2.

In our example, 148° 40' E would correspond to a GHA of 360° - 148° 40' = 211° 20'. Now we look into the Sun Almanac on June 1 to see when the sun was at that GHA. Referring to Figure 10.2-2, we see that happened between 0200 and 0300. At 0200 the GHA is 210° 33.1', and then the sun has to go on to our Lon, equivalent to a GHA of 211° 20', which is just another 46.9'. In the Arc to Time table we see that 47' is equal to 3m and 8s, which we round to 3m. The final answer is then 0203 UTC, which is the same we got from the analemma in example 2.

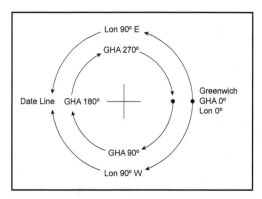

Hr	GHA		DEC	
	June 1			
00	180°	33.3'	N022°	01.3'
01	195°	33.2'	N022°	01.7'
02	210°	33.1'	N022°	02.0'
03	225°	33.0'	N022°	02.4'
04	240°	32.9'	N022°	02.7'
05	255°	32.8'	N022°	03.0'

Figure 10.2-3. *Section of the Sun Almanac for June 1. Full Almanac in the Tables Section.*

Figure 10.2-2. *The relationship between GHA and Lon. In west longitudes they are the same. In east longitudes, the GHA of the sun as it crosses your longitude would be 360° - Lon E.*

11. REFERENCES

Other books on ocean navigation by the author.

- *Celestial Navigation: A complete Home-study Course, 2nd ed.*

- *How to Use Plastic Sextants: With Applications to Metal Sextants and a Review of Sextant Piloting*

- *Hawaii by Sextant: An In-depth Exercise in Celestial Navigation Using Real Sextant Sights and Logbook Entries*

- *Emergency Navigation Card (summary of methods on a waterproof card)*

- *Emergency Navigation: Find Your Position and Shape Your Course at Sea Even If your Instruments Fail, 2nd ed.*

- *www.starpath.com/gpsbackup for resources and news related to this book.*

12. TABLES

Hr	GHA		DEC	
		January 1		
00	179°	10.8'	S023°	01.2'
01	194°	10.5'	S023°	01.0'
02	209°	10.2'	S023°	00.8'
03	224°	09.9'	S023°	00.6'
04	239°	09.6'	S023°	00.4'
05	254°	09.3'	S023°	00.2'
06	269°	09.0'	S022°	60.0'
07	284°	08.7'	S022°	59.8'
08	299°	08.4'	S022°	59.6'
09	314°	08.1'	S022°	59.4'
10	329°	07.8'	S022°	59.2'
11	344°	07.5'	S022°	58.9'
12	359°	07.2'	S022°	58.7'
13	014°	06.9'	S022°	58.5'
14	029°	06.7'	S022°	58.3'
15	044°	06.4'	S022°	58.1'
16	059°	06.1'	S022°	57.9'
17	074°	05.8'	S022°	57.7'
18	089°	05.5'	S022°	57.5'
19	104°	05.2'	S022°	57.2'
20	119°	04.9'	S022°	57.0'
21	134°	04.6'	S022°	56.8'
22	149°	04.3'	S022°	56.6'
23	164°	04.0'	S022°	56.4'
		January 2		
00	179°	03.7'	S022°	56.2'
01	194°	03.4'	S022°	55.9'
02	209°	03.1'	S022°	55.7'
03	224°	02.8'	S022°	55.5'
04	239°	02.6'	S022°	55.3'
05	254°	02.3'	S022°	55.0'
06	269°	02.0'	S022°	54.8'
07	284°	01.7'	S022°	54.6'
08	299°	01.4'	S022°	54.4'
09	314°	01.1'	S022°	54.1'
10	329°	00.8'	S022°	53.9'
11	344°	00.5'	S022°	53.7'
12	359°	00.2'	S022°	53.4'
13	013°	59.9'	S022°	53.2'
14	028°	59.6'	S022°	53.0'
15	043°	59.4'	S022°	52.8'
16	058°	59.1'	S022°	52.5'
17	073°	58.8'	S022°	52.3'
18	088°	58.5'	S022°	52.1'
19	103°	58.2'	S022°	51.8'
20	118°	57.9'	S022°	51.6'
21	133°	57.6'	S022°	51.3'
22	148°	57.3'	S022°	51.1'
23	163°	57.0'	S022°	50.9'
		January 3		
00	178°	56.7'	S022°	50.6'
01	193°	56.5'	S022°	50.4'
02	208°	56.2'	S022°	50.2'
03	223°	55.9'	S022°	49.9'
04	238°	55.6'	S022°	49.7'
05	253°	55.3'	S022°	49.4'
06	268°	55.0'	S022°	49.2'
07	283°	54.7'	S022°	48.9'
08	298°	54.4'	S022°	48.7'
09	313°	54.2'	S022°	48.4'
10	328°	53.9'	S022°	48.2'
11	343°	53.6'	S022°	48.0'
12	358°	53.3'	S022°	47.7'
13	013°	53.0'	S022°	47.5'
14	028°	52.7'	S022°	47.2'
15	043°	52.4'	S022°	47.0'
16	058°	52.1'	S022°	46.7'
17	073°	51.9'	S022°	46.5'
18	088°	51.6'	S022°	46.2'
19	103°	51.3'	S022°	45.9'
20	118°	51.0'	S022°	45.7'
21	133°	50.7'	S022°	45.4'
22	148°	50.4'	S022°	45.2'
23	163°	50.2'	S022°	44.9'
		January 4		
00	178°	49.9'	S022°	44.7'
01	193°	49.6'	S022°	44.4'
02	208°	49.3'	S022°	44.1'
03	223°	49.0'	S022°	43.9'
04	238°	48.7'	S022°	43.6'
05	253°	48.4'	S022°	43.4'
06	268°	48.2'	S022°	43.1'
07	283°	47.9'	S022°	42.8'
08	298°	47.6'	S022°	42.6'
09	313°	47.3'	S022°	42.3'
10	328°	47.0'	S022°	42.0'
11	343°	46.7'	S022°	41.8'
12	358°	46.5'	S022°	41.5'
13	013°	46.2'	S022°	41.2'
14	028°	45.9'	S022°	41.0'
15	043°	45.6'	S022°	40.7'
16	058°	45.3'	S022°	40.4'
17	073°	45.1'	S022°	40.2'
18	088°	44.8'	S022°	39.9'
19	103°	44.5'	S022°	39.6'
20	118°	44.2'	S022°	39.3'
21	133°	43.9'	S022°	39.1'
22	148°	43.6'	S022°	38.8'
23	163°	43.4'	S022°	38.5'
		January 5		
00	178°	43.1'	S022°	38.2'
01	193°	42.8'	S022°	38.0'
02	208°	42.5'	S022°	37.7'
03	223°	42.2'	S022°	37.4'
04	238°	42.0'	S022°	37.1'
05	253°	41.7'	S022°	36.9'
06	268°	41.4'	S022°	36.6'
07	283°	41.1'	S022°	36.3'
08	298°	40.8'	S022°	36.0'
09	313°	40.6'	S022°	35.7'
10	328°	40.3'	S022°	35.4'
11	343°	40.0'	S022°	35.2'
12	358°	39.7'	S022°	34.9'
13	013°	39.5'	S022°	34.6'
14	028°	39.2'	S022°	34.3'
15	043°	38.9'	S022°	34.0'
16	058°	38.6'	S022°	33.7'
17	073°	38.3'	S022°	33.4'
18	088°	38.1'	S022°	33.1'
19	103°	37.8'	S022°	32.8'
20	118°	37.5'	S022°	32.6'
21	133°	37.2'	S022°	32.3'
22	148°	37.0'	S022°	32.0'
23	163°	36.7'	S022°	31.7'
		January 6		
00	178°	36.4'	S022°	31.4'
01	193°	36.1'	S022°	31.1'
02	208°	35.9'	S022°	30.8'
03	223°	35.6'	S022°	30.5'
04	238°	35.3'	S022°	30.2'
05	253°	35.0'	S022°	29.9'
06	268°	34.8'	S022°	29.6'
07	283°	34.5'	S022°	29.3'
08	298°	34.2'	S022°	29.0'
09	313°	33.9'	S022°	28.7'
10	328°	33.7'	S022°	28.4'
11	343°	33.4'	S022°	28.1'
12	358°	33.1'	S022°	27.8'
13	013°	32.8'	S022°	27.5'
14	028°	32.6'	S022°	27.2'
15	043°	32.3'	S022°	26.9'
16	058°	32.0'	S022°	26.5'
17	073°	31.7'	S022°	26.2'
18	088°	31.5'	S022°	25.9'
19	103°	31.2'	S022°	25.6'
20	118°	30.9'	S022°	25.3'
21	133°	30.7'	S022°	25.0'
22	148°	30.4'	S022°	24.7'
23	163°	30.1'	S022°	24.4'
		January 7		
00	178°	29.8'	S022°	24.1'
01	193°	29.6'	S022°	23.7'
02	208°	29.3'	S022°	23.4'
03	223°	29.0'	S022°	23.1'
04	238°	28.8'	S022°	22.8'
05	253°	28.5'	S022°	22.5'
06	268°	28.2'	S022°	22.2'
07	283°	28.0'	S022°	21.8'
08	298°	27.7'	S022°	21.5'
09	313°	27.4'	S022°	21.2'
10	328°	27.1'	S022°	20.9'
11	343°	26.9'	S022°	20.6'
12	358°	26.6'	S022°	20.2'
13	013°	26.3'	S022°	19.9'
14	028°	26.1'	S022°	19.6'
15	043°	25.8'	S022°	19.3'
16	058°	25.5'	S022°	18.9'
17	073°	25.3'	S022°	18.6'
18	088°	25.0'	S022°	18.3'
19	103°	24.7'	S022°	18.0'

Hr	GHA		DEC		Hr	GHA		DEC		Hr	GHA		DEC	
20	118°	24.5'	S022°	17.6'	02	208°	10.4'	S021°	58.8'	09	312°	56.8'	S021°	37.3'
21	133°	24.2'	S022°	17.3'	03	223°	10.1'	S021°	58.4'	10	327°	56.6'	S021°	36.9'
22	148°	23.9'	S022°	17.0'	04	238°	09.9'	S021°	58.0'	11	342°	56.3'	S021°	36.5'
23	163°	23.7'	S022°	16.6'	05	253°	09.6'	S021°	57.6'	12	357°	56.1'	S021°	36.1'
	January 8				06	268°	09.4'	S021°	57.3'	13	012°	55.8'	S021°	35.6'
00	178°	23.4'	S022°	16.3'	07	283°	09.1'	S021°	56.9'	14	027°	55.6'	S021°	35.2'
01	193°	23.1'	S022°	16.0'	08	298°	08.9'	S021°	56.5'	15	042°	55.4'	S021°	34.8'
02	208°	22.9'	S022°	15.6'	09	313°	08.6'	S021°	56.1'	16	057°	55.1'	S021°	34.4'
03	223°	22.6'	S022°	15.3'	10	328°	08.4'	S021°	55.8'	17	072°	54.9'	S021°	34.0'
04	238°	22.3'	S022°	15.0'	11	343°	08.1'	S021°	55.4'	18	087°	54.7'	S021°	33.6'
05	253°	22.1'	S022°	14.6'	12	358°	07.9'	S021°	55.0'	19	102°	54.4'	S021°	33.1'
06	268°	21.8'	S022°	14.3'	13	013°	07.6'	S021°	54.6'	20	117°	54.2'	S021°	32.7'
07	283°	21.5'	S022°	14.0'	14	028°	07.4'	S021°	54.3'	21	132°	53.9'	S021°	32.3'
08	298°	21.3'	S022°	13.6'	15	043°	07.1'	S021°	53.9'	22	147°	53.7'	S021°	31.9'
09	313°	21.0'	S022°	13.3'	16	058°	06.9'	S021°	53.5'	23	162°	53.5'	S021°	31.5'
10	328°	20.8'	S022°	12.9'	17	073°	06.6'	S021°	53.1'		January 13			
11	343°	20.5'	S022°	12.6'	18	088°	06.4'	S021°	52.7'	00	177°	53.2'	S021°	31.1'
12	358°	20.2'	S022°	12.3'	19	103°	06.1'	S021°	52.4'	01	192°	53.0'	S021°	30.6'
13	013°	20.0'	S022°	11.9'	20	118°	05.9'	S021°	52.0'	02	207°	52.8'	S021°	30.2'
14	028°	19.7'	S022°	11.6'	21	133°	05.6'	S021°	51.6'	03	222°	52.5'	S021°	29.8'
15	043°	19.4'	S022°	11.2'	22	148°	05.4'	S021°	51.2'	04	237°	52.3'	S021°	29.4'
16	058°	19.2'	S022°	10.9'	23	163°	05.1'	S021°	50.8'	05	252°	52.1'	S021°	28.9'
17	073°	18.9'	S022°	10.5'		January 11				06	267°	51.8'	S021°	28.5'
18	088°	18.7'	S022°	10.2'	00	178°	04.9'	S021°	50.4'	07	282°	51.6'	S021°	28.1'
19	103°	18.4'	S022°	09.9'	01	193°	04.6'	S021°	50.0'	08	297°	51.3'	S021°	27.7'
20	118°	18.1'	S022°	09.5'	02	208°	04.4'	S021°	49.7'	09	312°	51.1'	S021°	27.2'
21	133°	17.9'	S022°	09.2'	03	223°	04.1'	S021°	49.3'	10	327°	50.9'	S021°	26.8'
22	148°	17.6'	S022°	08.8'	04	238°	03.9'	S021°	48.9'	11	342°	50.6'	S021°	26.4'
23	163°	17.4'	S022°	08.5'	05	253°	03.6'	S021°	48.5'	12	357°	50.4'	S021°	25.9'
	January 9				06	268°	03.4'	S021°	48.1'	13	012°	50.2'	S021°	25.5'
00	178°	17.1'	S022°	08.1'	07	283°	03.1'	S021°	47.7'	14	027°	50.0'	S021°	25.1'
01	193°	16.8'	S022°	07.8'	08	298°	02.9'	S021°	47.3'	15	042°	49.7'	S021°	24.7'
02	208°	16.6'	S022°	07.4'	09	313°	02.6'	S021°	46.9'	16	057°	49.5'	S021°	24.2'
03	223°	16.3'	S022°	07.1'	10	328°	02.4'	S021°	46.5'	17	072°	49.3'	S021°	23.8'
04	238°	16.1'	S022°	06.7'	11	343°	02.1'	S021°	46.1'	18	087°	49.0'	S021°	23.4'
05	253°	15.8'	S022°	06.4'	12	358°	01.9'	S021°	45.7'	19	102°	48.8'	S021°	22.9'
06	268°	15.5'	S022°	06.0'	13	013°	01.7'	S021°	45.3'	20	117°	48.6'	S021°	22.5'
07	283°	15.3'	S022°	05.6'	14	028°	01.4'	S021°	45.0'	21	132°	48.3'	S021°	22.0'
08	298°	15.0'	S022°	05.3'	15	043°	01.2'	S021°	44.6'	22	147°	48.1'	S021°	21.6'
09	313°	14.8'	S022°	04.9'	16	058°	00.9'	S021°	44.2'	23	162°	47.9'	S021°	21.2'
10	328°	14.5'	S022°	04.6'	17	073°	00.7'	S021°	43.8'		January 14			
11	343°	14.2'	S022°	04.2'	18	088°	00.4'	S021°	43.4'	00	177°	47.6'	S021°	20.7'
12	358°	14.0'	S022°	03.9'	19	103°	00.2'	S021°	43.0'	01	192°	47.4'	S021°	20.3'
13	013°	13.7'	S022°	03.5'	20	117°	59.9'	S021°	42.6'	02	207°	47.2'	S021°	19.9'
14	028°	13.5'	S022°	03.1'	21	132°	59.7'	S021°	42.2'	03	222°	47.0'	S021°	19.4'
15	043°	13.2'	S022°	02.8'	22	147°	59.5'	S021°	41.8'	04	237°	46.7'	S021°	19.0'
16	058°	13.0'	S022°	02.4'	23	162°	59.2'	S021°	41.4'	05	252°	46.5'	S021°	18.5'
17	073°	12.7'	S022°	02.0'		January 12				06	267°	46.3'	S021°	18.1'
18	088°	12.4'	S022°	01.7'	00	177°	59.0'	S021°	41.0'	07	282°	46.0'	S021°	17.6'
19	103°	12.2'	S022°	01.3'	01	192°	58.7'	S021°	40.5'	08	297°	45.8'	S021°	17.2'
20	118°	11.9'	S022°	01.0'	02	207°	58.5'	S021°	40.1'	09	312°	45.6'	S021°	16.8'
21	133°	11.7'	S022°	00.6'	03	222°	58.2'	S021°	39.7'	10	327°	45.4'	S021°	16.3'
22	148°	11.4'	S022°	00.2'	04	237°	58.0'	S021°	39.3'	11	342°	45.1'	S021°	15.9'
23	163°	11.2'	S021°	59.9'	05	252°	57.8'	S021°	38.9'	12	357°	44.9'	S021°	15.4'
	January 10				06	267°	57.5'	S021°	38.5'	13	012°	44.7'	S021°	15.0'
00	178°	10.9'	S021°	59.5'	07	282°	57.3'	S021°	38.1'	14	027°	44.5'	S021°	14.5'
01	193°	10.7'	S021°	59.1'	08	297°	57.0'	S021°	37.7'	15	042°	44.2'	S021°	14.1'

Hr	GHA		DEC		Hr	GHA		DEC		Hr	GHA		DEC	
16	057°	44.0'	S021°	13.6'	23	162°	32.1'	S020°	47.8'	05	252°	21.3'	S020°	20.5'
17	072°	43.8'	S021°	13.2'	January 17					06	267°	21.1'	S020°	19.9'
18	087°	43.6'	S021°	12.7'	00	177°	31.9'	S020°	47.3'	07	282°	20.9'	S020°	19.4'
19	102°	43.3'	S021°	12.3'	01	192°	31.7'	S020°	46.8'	08	297°	20.7'	S020°	18.9'
20	117°	43.1'	S021°	11.8'	02	207°	31.4'	S020°	46.4'	09	312°	20.5'	S020°	18.4'
21	132°	42.9'	S021°	11.4'	03	222°	31.2'	S020°	45.9'	10	327°	20.3'	S020°	17.8'
22	147°	42.7'	S021°	10.9'	04	237°	31.0'	S020°	45.4'	11	342°	20.1'	S020°	17.3'
23	162°	42.4'	S021°	10.5'	05	252°	30.8'	S020°	44.9'	12	357°	19.9'	S020°	16.8'
January 15					06	267°	30.6'	S020°	44.4'	13	012°	19.7'	S020°	16.2'
00	177°	42.2'	S021°	10.0'	07	282°	30.4'	S020°	43.9'	14	027°	19.5'	S020°	15.7'
01	192°	42.0'	S021°	09.5'	08	297°	30.2'	S020°	43.4'	15	042°	19.3'	S020°	15.2'
02	207°	41.8'	S021°	09.1'	09	312°	30.0'	S020°	42.9'	16	057°	19.2'	S020°	14.7'
03	222°	41.5'	S021°	08.6'	10	327°	29.8'	S020°	42.4'	17	072°	19.0'	S020°	14.1'
04	237°	41.3'	S021°	08.2'	11	342°	29.6'	S020°	41.9'	18	087°	18.8'	S020°	13.6'
05	252°	41.1'	S021°	07.7'	12	357°	29.4'	S020°	41.4'	19	102°	18.6'	S020°	13.1'
06	267°	40.9'	S021°	07.3'	13	012°	29.2'	S020°	40.9'	20	117°	18.4'	S020°	12.5'
07	282°	40.7'	S021°	06.8'	14	027°	29.0'	S020°	40.4'	21	132°	18.2'	S020°	12.0'
08	297°	40.4'	S021°	06.3'	15	042°	28.8'	S020°	39.9'	22	147°	18.0'	S020°	11.5'
09	312°	40.2'	S021°	05.9'	16	057°	28.6'	S020°	39.4'	23	162°	17.8'	S020°	10.9'
10	327°	40.0'	S021°	05.4'	17	072°	28.4'	S020°	38.9'	January 20				
11	342°	39.8'	S021°	05.0'	18	087°	28.2'	S020°	38.4'	00	177°	17.7'	S020°	10.4'
12	357°	39.6'	S021°	04.5'	19	102°	28.0'	S020°	37.9'	01	192°	17.5'	S020°	09.8'
13	012°	39.3'	S021°	04.0'	20	117°	27.8'	S020°	37.4'	02	207°	17.3'	S020°	09.3'
14	027°	39.1'	S021°	03.6'	21	132°	27.6'	S020°	36.9'	03	222°	17.1'	S020°	08.8'
15	042°	38.9'	S021°	03.1'	22	147°	27.4'	S020°	36.4'	04	237°	16.9'	S020°	08.2'
16	057°	38.7'	S021°	02.6'	23	162°	27.2'	S020°	35.9'	05	252°	16.7'	S020°	07.7'
17	072°	38.5'	S021°	02.2'	January 18					06	267°	16.6'	S020°	07.1'
18	087°	38.3'	S021°	01.7'	00	177°	27.0'	S020°	35.4'	07	282°	16.4'	S020°	06.6'
19	102°	38.0'	S021°	01.2'	01	192°	26.7'	S020°	34.9'	08	297°	16.2'	S020°	06.1'
20	117°	37.8'	S021°	00.8'	02	207°	26.5'	S020°	34.4'	09	312°	16.0'	S020°	05.5'
21	132°	37.6'	S021°	00.3'	03	222°	26.3'	S020°	33.9'	10	327°	15.8'	S020°	05.0'
22	147°	37.4'	S020°	59.8'	04	237°	26.1'	S020°	33.4'	11	342°	15.6'	S020°	04.4'
23	162°	37.2'	S020°	59.3'	05	252°	25.9'	S020°	32.9'	12	357°	15.5'	S020°	03.9'
January 16					06	267°	25.7'	S020°	32.4'	13	012°	15.3'	S020°	03.3'
00	177°	37.0'	S020°	58.9'	07	282°	25.5'	S020°	31.9'	14	027°	15.1'	S020°	02.8'
01	192°	36.7'	S020°	58.4'	08	297°	25.4'	S020°	31.3'	15	042°	14.9'	S020°	02.2'
02	207°	36.5'	S020°	57.9'	09	312°	25.2'	S020°	30.8'	16	057°	14.7'	S020°	01.7'
03	222°	36.3'	S020°	57.5'	10	327°	25.0'	S020°	30.3'	17	072°	14.5'	S020°	01.1'
04	237°	36.1'	S020°	57.0'	11	342°	24.8'	S020°	29.8'	18	087°	14.4'	S020°	00.6'
05	252°	35.9'	S020°	56.5'	12	357°	24.6'	S020°	29.3'	19	102°	14.2'	S020°	00.1'
06	267°	35.7'	S020°	56.0'	13	012°	24.4'	S020°	28.8'	20	117°	14.0'	S019°	59.5'
07	282°	35.5'	S020°	55.5'	14	027°	24.2'	S020°	28.3'	21	132°	13.8'	S019°	59.0'
08	297°	35.2'	S020°	55.1'	15	042°	24.0'	S020°	27.7'	22	147°	13.6'	S019°	58.4'
09	312°	35.0'	S020°	54.6'	16	057°	23.8'	S020°	27.2'	23	162°	13.5'	S019°	57.8'
10	327°	34.8'	S020°	54.1'	17	072°	23.6'	S020°	26.7'	January 21				
11	342°	34.6'	S020°	53.6'	18	087°	23.4'	S020°	26.2'	00	177°	13.3'	S019°	57.3'
12	357°	34.4'	S020°	53.2'	19	102°	23.2'	S020°	25.7'	01	192°	13.1'	S019°	56.7'
13	012°	34.2'	S020°	52.7'	20	117°	23.0'	S020°	25.2'	02	207°	12.9'	S019°	56.2'
14	027°	34.0'	S020°	52.2'	21	132°	22.8'	S020°	24.6'	03	222°	12.8'	S019°	55.6'
15	042°	33.8'	S020°	51.7'	22	147°	22.6'	S020°	24.1'	04	237°	12.6'	S019°	55.1'
16	057°	33.5'	S020°	51.2'	23	162°	22.4'	S020°	23.6'	05	252°	12.4'	S019°	54.5'
17	072°	33.3'	S020°	50.7'	January 19					06	267°	12.2'	S019°	54.0'
18	087°	33.1'	S020°	50.3'	00	177°	22.2'	S020°	23.1'	07	282°	12.1'	S019°	53.4'
19	102°	32.9'	S020°	49.8'	01	192°	22.0'	S020°	22.6'	08	297°	11.9'	S019°	52.8'
20	117°	32.7'	S020°	49.3'	02	207°	21.8'	S020°	22.0'	09	312°	11.7'	S019°	52.3'
21	132°	32.5'	S020°	48.8'	03	222°	21.6'	S020°	21.5'	10	327°	11.5'	S019°	51.7'
22	147°	32.3'	S020°	48.3'	04	237°	21.4'	S020°	21.0'	11	342°	11.4'	S019°	51.2'

Hr	GHA	DEC
12	357° 11.2'	S019° 50.6'
13	012° 11.0'	S019° 50.1'
14	027° 10.8'	S019° 49.5'
15	042° 10.7'	S019° 48.9'
16	057° 10.5'	S019° 48.4'
17	072° 10.3'	S019° 47.8'
18	087° 10.1'	S019° 47.2'
19	102° 10.0'	S019° 46.7'
20	117° 09.8'	S019° 46.1'
21	132° 09.6'	S019° 45.5'
22	147° 09.5'	S019° 45.0'
23	162° 09.3'	S019° 44.4'
January 22		
00	177° 09.1'	S019° 43.8'
01	192° 08.9'	S019° 43.3'
02	207° 08.8'	S019° 42.7'
03	222° 08.6'	S019° 42.1'
04	237° 08.4'	S019° 41.6'
05	252° 08.3'	S019° 41.0'
06	267° 08.1'	S019° 40.4'
07	282° 07.9'	S019° 39.8'
08	297° 07.8'	S019° 39.3'
09	312° 07.6'	S019° 38.7'
10	327° 07.4'	S019° 38.1'
11	342° 07.3'	S019° 37.5'
12	357° 07.1'	S019° 37.0'
13	012° 06.9'	S019° 36.4'
14	027° 06.8'	S019° 35.8'
15	042° 06.6'	S019° 35.2'
16	057° 06.4'	S019° 34.7'
17	072° 06.3'	S019° 34.1'
18	087° 06.1'	S019° 33.5'
19	102° 05.9'	S019° 32.9'
20	117° 05.8'	S019° 32.3'
21	132° 05.6'	S019° 31.8'
22	147° 05.5'	S019° 31.2'
23	162° 05.3'	S019° 30.6'
January 23		
00	177° 05.1'	S019° 30.0'
01	192° 05.0'	S019° 29.4'
02	207° 04.8'	S019° 28.8'
03	222° 04.6'	S019° 28.3'
04	237° 04.5'	S019° 27.7'
05	252° 04.3'	S019° 27.1'
06	267° 04.2'	S019° 26.5'
07	282° 04.0'	S019° 25.9'
08	297° 03.8'	S019° 25.3'
09	312° 03.7'	S019° 24.7'
10	327° 03.5'	S019° 24.1'
11	342° 03.4'	S019° 23.6'
12	357° 03.2'	S019° 23.0'
13	012° 03.0'	S019° 22.4'
14	027° 02.9'	S019° 21.8'
15	042° 02.7'	S019° 21.2'
16	057° 02.6'	S019° 20.6'
17	072° 02.4'	S019° 20.0'
18	087° 02.3'	S019° 19.4'

Hr	GHA	DEC
19	102° 02.1'	S019° 18.8'
20	117° 02.0'	S019° 18.2'
21	132° 01.8'	S019° 17.6'
22	147° 01.6'	S019° 17.0'
23	162° 01.5'	S019° 16.4'
January 24		
00	177° 01.3'	S019° 15.8'
01	192° 01.2'	S019° 15.2'
02	207° 01.0'	S019° 14.6'
03	222° 00.9'	S019° 14.0'
04	237° 00.7'	S019° 13.4'
05	252° 00.6'	S019° 12.8'
06	267° 00.4'	S019° 12.2'
07	282° 00.3'	S019° 11.6'
08	297° 00.1'	S019° 11.0'
09	311° 60.0'	S019° 10.4'
10	326° 59.8'	S019° 09.8'
11	341° 59.7'	S019° 09.2'
12	356° 59.5'	S019° 08.6'
13	011° 59.4'	S019° 08.0'
14	026° 59.2'	S019° 07.4'
15	041° 59.1'	S019° 06.8'
16	056° 58.9'	S019° 06.2'
17	071° 58.8'	S019° 05.6'
18	086° 58.6'	S019° 05.0'
19	101° 58.5'	S019° 04.3'
20	116° 58.3'	S019° 03.7'
21	131° 58.2'	S019° 03.1'
22	146° 58.0'	S019° 02.5'
23	161° 57.9'	S019° 01.9'
January 25		
00	176° 57.7'	S019° 01.3'
01	191° 57.6'	S019° 00.7'
02	206° 57.4'	S019° 00.1'
03	221° 57.3'	S018° 59.4'
04	236° 57.2'	S018° 58.8'
05	251° 57.0'	S018° 58.2'
06	266° 56.9'	S018° 57.6'
07	281° 56.7'	S018° 57.0'
08	296° 56.6'	S018° 56.4'
09	311° 56.4'	S018° 55.7'
10	326° 56.3'	S018° 55.1'
11	341° 56.2'	S018° 54.5'
12	356° 56.0'	S018° 53.9'
13	011° 55.9'	S018° 53.3'
14	026° 55.7'	S018° 52.6'
15	041° 55.6'	S018° 52.0'
16	056° 55.4'	S018° 51.4'
17	071° 55.3'	S018° 50.8'
18	086° 55.2'	S018° 50.2'
19	101° 55.0'	S018° 49.5'
20	116° 54.9'	S018° 48.9'
21	131° 54.8'	S018° 48.3'
22	146° 54.6'	S018° 47.7'
23	161° 54.5'	S018° 47.0'
January 26		
00	176° 54.3'	S018° 46.4'

Hr	GHA	DEC
01	191° 54.2'	S018° 45.8'
02	206° 54.1'	S018° 45.1'
03	221° 53.9'	S018° 44.5'
04	236° 53.8'	S018° 43.9'
05	251° 53.7'	S018° 43.3'
06	266° 53.5'	S018° 42.6'
07	281° 53.4'	S018° 42.0'
08	296° 53.2'	S018° 41.4'
09	311° 53.1'	S018° 40.7'
10	326° 53.0'	S018° 40.1'
11	341° 52.8'	S018° 39.5'
12	356° 52.7'	S018° 38.8'
13	011° 52.6'	S018° 38.2'
14	026° 52.4'	S018° 37.6'
15	041° 52.3'	S018° 36.9'
16	056° 52.2'	S018° 36.3'
17	071° 52.1'	S018° 35.6'
18	086° 51.9'	S018° 35.0'
19	101° 51.8'	S018° 34.4'
20	116° 51.7'	S018° 33.7'
21	131° 51.5'	S018° 33.1'
22	146° 51.4'	S018° 32.5'
23	161° 51.3'	S018° 31.8'
January27		
00	176° 51.1'	S018° 31.2'
01	191° 51.0'	S018° 30.5'
02	206° 50.9'	S018° 29.9'
03	221° 50.8'	S018° 29.2'
04	236° 50.6'	S018° 28.6'
05	251° 50.5'	S018° 28.0'
06	266° 50.4'	S018° 27.3'
07	281° 50.2'	S018° 26.7'
08	296° 50.1'	S018° 26.0'
09	311° 50.0'	S018° 25.4'
10	326° 49.9'	S018° 24.7'
11	341° 49.7'	S018° 24.1'
12	356° 49.6'	S018° 23.4'
13	011° 49.5'	S018° 22.8'
14	026° 49.4'	S018° 22.1'
15	041° 49.2'	S018° 21.5'
16	056° 49.1'	S018° 20.8'
17	071° 49.0'	S018° 20.2'
18	086° 48.9'	S018° 19.5'
19	101° 48.7'	S018° 18.9'
20	116° 48.6'	S018° 18.2'
21	131° 48.5'	S018° 17.6'
22	146° 48.4'	S018° 16.9'
23	161° 48.3'	S018° 16.3'
January 28		
00	176° 48.1'	S018° 15.6'
01	191° 48.0'	S018° 14.9'
02	206° 47.9'	S018° 14.3'
03	221° 47.8'	S018° 13.6'
04	236° 47.7'	S018° 13.0'
05	251° 47.5'	S018° 12.3'
06	266° 47.4'	S018° 11.7'
07	281° 47.3'	S018° 11.0'

Hr	GHA		DEC	
08	296°	47.2'	S018°	10.3'
09	311°	47.1'	S018°	09.7'
10	326°	47.0'	S018°	09.0'
11	341°	46.8'	S018°	08.4'
12	356°	46.7'	S018°	07.7'
13	011°	46.6'	S018°	07.0'
14	026°	46.5'	S018°	06.4'
15	041°	46.4'	S018°	05.7'
16	056°	46.3'	S018°	05.0'
17	071°	46.1'	S018°	04.4'
18	086°	46.0'	S018°	03.7'
19	101°	45.9'	S018°	03.0'
20	116°	45.8'	S018°	02.4'
21	131°	45.7'	S018°	01.7'
22	146°	45.6'	S018°	01.0'
23	161°	45.5'	S018°	00.4'
January 29				
00	176°	45.3'	S017°	59.7'
01	191°	45.2'	S017°	59.0'
02	206°	45.1'	S017°	58.4'
03	221°	45.0'	S017°	57.7'
04	236°	44.9'	S017°	57.0'
05	251°	44.8'	S017°	56.4'
06	266°	44.7'	S017°	55.7'
07	281°	44.6'	S017°	55.0'
08	296°	44.5'	S017°	54.3'
09	311°	44.3'	S017°	53.7'
10	326°	44.2'	S017°	53.0'
11	341°	44.1'	S017°	52.3'
12	356°	44.0'	S017°	51.6'
13	011°	43.9'	S017°	51.0'
14	026°	43.8'	S017°	50.3'
15	041°	43.7'	S017°	49.6'
16	056°	43.6'	S017°	48.9'
17	071°	43.5'	S017°	48.3'
18	086°	43.4'	S017°	47.6'
19	101°	43.3'	S017°	46.9'
20	116°	43.2'	S017°	46.2'
21	131°	43.1'	S017°	45.5'
22	146°	43.0'	S017°	44.9'
23	161°	42.9'	S017°	44.2'
January 30				
00	176°	42.8'	S017°	43.5'
01	191°	42.6'	S017°	42.8'
02	206°	42.5'	S017°	42.1'
03	221°	42.4'	S017°	41.4'
04	236°	42.3'	S017°	40.8'
05	251°	42.2'	S017°	40.1'
06	266°	42.1'	S017°	39.4'
07	281°	42.0'	S017°	38.7'
08	296°	41.9'	S017°	38.0'
09	311°	41.8'	S017°	37.3'
10	326°	41.7'	S017°	36.6'
11	341°	41.6'	S017°	36.0'
12	356°	41.5'	S017°	35.3'
13	011°	41.4'	S017°	34.6'
14	026°	41.3'	S017°	33.9'

Hr	GHA		DEC	
15	041°	41.2'	S017°	33.2'
16	056°	41.1'	S017°	32.5'
17	071°	41.0'	S017°	31.8'
18	086°	40.9'	S017°	31.1'
19	101°	40.8'	S017°	30.4'
20	116°	40.7'	S017°	29.7'
21	131°	40.7'	S017°	29.0'
22	146°	40.6'	S017°	28.3'
23	161°	40.5'	S017°	27.7'
January 31				
00	176°	40.4'	S017°	27.0'
01	191°	40.3'	S017°	26.3'
02	206°	40.2'	S017°	25.6'
03	221°	40.1'	S017°	24.9'
04	236°	40.0'	S017°	24.2'
05	251°	39.9'	S017°	23.5'
06	266°	39.8'	S017°	22.8'
07	281°	39.7'	S017°	22.1'
08	296°	39.6'	S017°	21.4'
09	311°	39.5'	S017°	20.7'
10	326°	39.4'	S017°	20.0'
11	341°	39.3'	S017°	19.3'
12	356°	39.2'	S017°	18.6'
13	011°	39.2'	S017°	17.9'
14	026°	39.1'	S017°	17.2'
15	041°	39.0'	S017°	16.5'
16	056°	38.9'	S017°	15.8'
17	071°	38.8'	S017°	15.1'
18	086°	38.7'	S017°	14.4'
19	101°	38.6'	S017°	13.6'
20	116°	38.5'	S017°	12.9'
21	131°	38.4'	S017°	12.2'
22	146°	38.4'	S017°	11.5'
23	161°	38.3'	S017°	10.8'
February 1				
00	176°	38.2'	S017°	10.1'
01	191°	38.1'	S017°	09.4'
02	206°	38.0'	S017°	08.7'
03	221°	37.9'	S017°	08.0'
04	236°	37.8'	S017°	07.3'
05	251°	37.8'	S017°	06.6'
06	266°	37.7'	S017°	05.9'
07	281°	37.6'	S017°	05.1'
08	296°	37.5'	S017°	04.4'
09	311°	37.4'	S017°	03.7'
10	326°	37.3'	S017°	03.0'
11	341°	37.2'	S017°	02.3'
12	356°	37.2'	S017°	01.6'
13	011°	37.1'	S017°	00.9'
14	026°	37.0'	S017°	00.1'
15	041°	36.9'	S016°	59.4'
16	056°	36.8'	S016°	58.7'
17	071°	36.8'	S016°	58.0'
18	086°	36.7'	S016°	57.3'
19	101°	36.6'	S016°	56.6'
20	116°	36.5'	S016°	55.8'
21	131°	36.4'	S016°	55.1'

Hr	GHA		DEC	
22	146°	36.4'	S016°	54.4'
23	161°	36.3'	S016°	53.7'
February 2				
00	176°	36.2'	S016°	53.0'
01	191°	36.1'	S016°	52.2'
02	206°	36.0'	S016°	51.5'
03	221°	36.0'	S016°	50.8'
04	236°	35.9'	S016°	50.1'
05	251°	35.8'	S016°	49.4'
06	266°	35.7'	S016°	48.6'
07	281°	35.7'	S016°	47.9'
08	296°	35.6'	S016°	47.2'
09	311°	35.5'	S016°	46.5'
10	326°	35.4'	S016°	45.7'
11	341°	35.4'	S016°	45.0'
12	356°	35.3'	S016°	44.3'
13	011°	35.2'	S016°	43.6'
14	026°	35.1'	S016°	42.8'
15	041°	35.1'	S016°	42.1'
16	056°	35.0'	S016°	41.4'
17	071°	34.9'	S016°	40.6'
18	086°	34.8'	S016°	39.9'
19	101°	34.8'	S016°	39.2'
20	116°	34.7'	S016°	38.5'
21	131°	34.6'	S016°	37.7'
22	146°	34.6'	S016°	37.0'
23	161°	34.5'	S016°	36.3'
February 3				
00	176°	34.4'	S016°	35.5'
01	191°	34.4'	S016°	34.8'
02	206°	34.3'	S016°	34.1'
03	221°	34.2'	S016°	33.3'
04	236°	34.1'	S016°	32.6'
05	251°	34.1'	S016°	31.9'
06	266°	34.0'	S016°	31.1'
07	281°	33.9'	S016°	30.4'
08	296°	33.9'	S016°	29.6'
09	311°	33.8'	S016°	28.9'
10	326°	33.7'	S016°	28.2'
11	341°	33.7'	S016°	27.4'
12	356°	33.6'	S016°	26.7'
13	011°	33.5'	S016°	26.0'
14	026°	33.5'	S016°	25.2'
15	041°	33.4'	S016°	24.5'
16	056°	33.4'	S016°	23.7'
17	071°	33.3'	S016°	23.0'
18	086°	33.2'	S016°	22.3'
19	101°	33.2'	S016°	21.5'
20	116°	33.1'	S016°	20.8'
21	131°	33.0'	S016°	20.0'
22	146°	33.0'	S016°	19.3'
23	161°	32.9'	S016°	18.5'
February 4				
00	176°	32.9'	S016°	17.8'
01	191°	32.8'	S016°	17.0'
02	206°	32.7'	S016°	16.3'
03	221°	32.7'	S016°	15.6'

Hr	GHA	DEC
04	236° 32.6'	S016° 14.8'
05	251° 32.5'	S016° 14.1'
06	266° 32.5'	S016° 13.3'
07	281° 32.4'	S016° 12.6'
08	296° 32.4'	S016° 11.8'
09	311° 32.3'	S016° 11.1'
10	326° 32.3'	S016° 10.3'
11	341° 32.2'	S016° 09.6'
12	356° 32.1'	S016° 08.8'
13	011° 32.1'	S016° 08.1'
14	026° 32.0'	S016° 07.3'
15	041° 32.0'	S016° 06.6'
16	056° 31.9'	S016° 05.8'
17	071° 31.9'	S016° 05.1'
18	086° 31.8'	S016° 04.3'
19	101° 31.7'	S016° 03.6'
20	116° 31.7'	S016° 02.8'
21	131° 31.6'	S016° 02.0'
22	146° 31.6'	S016° 01.3'
23	161° 31.5'	S016° 00.5'
February 5		
00	176° 31.5'	S015° 59.8'
01	191° 31.4'	S015° 59.0'
02	206° 31.4'	S015° 58.3'
03	221° 31.3'	S015° 57.5'
04	236° 31.3'	S015° 56.8'
05	251° 31.2'	S015° 56.0'
06	266° 31.2'	S015° 55.2'
07	281° 31.1'	S015° 54.5'
08	296° 31.1'	S015° 53.7'
09	311° 31.0'	S015° 53.0'
10	326° 31.0'	S015° 52.2'
11	341° 30.9'	S015° 51.4'
12	356° 30.9'	S015° 50.7'
13	011° 30.8'	S015° 49.9'
14	026° 30.8'	S015° 49.1'
15	041° 30.7'	S015° 48.4'
16	056° 30.7'	S015° 47.6'
17	071° 30.6'	S015° 46.9'
18	086° 30.6'	S015° 46.1'
19	101° 30.5'	S015° 45.3'
20	116° 30.5'	S015° 44.6'
21	131° 30.4'	S015° 43.8'
22	146° 30.4'	S015° 43.0'
23	161° 30.4'	S015° 42.3'
February 6		
00	176° 30.3'	S015° 41.5'
01	191° 30.3'	S015° 40.7'
02	206° 30.2'	S015° 40.0'
03	221° 30.2'	S015° 39.2'
04	236° 30.1'	S015° 38.4'
05	251° 30.1'	S015° 37.6'
06	266° 30.1'	S015° 36.9'
07	281° 30.0'	S015° 36.1'
08	296° 30.0'	S015° 35.3'
09	311° 29.9'	S015° 34.6'
10	326° 29.9'	S015° 33.8'
11	341° 29.8'	S015° 33.0'
12	356° 29.8'	S015° 32.2'
13	011° 29.8'	S015° 31.5'
14	026° 29.7'	S015° 30.7'
15	041° 29.7'	S015° 29.9'
16	056° 29.6'	S015° 29.1'
17	071° 29.6'	S015° 28.4'
18	086° 29.6'	S015° 27.6'
19	101° 29.5'	S015° 26.8'
20	116° 29.5'	S015° 26.0'
21	131° 29.5'	S015° 25.3'
22	146° 29.4'	S015° 24.5'
23	161° 29.4'	S015° 23.7'
February 7		
00	176° 29.3'	S015° 22.9'
01	191° 29.3'	S015° 22.2'
02	206° 29.3'	S015° 21.4'
03	221° 29.2'	S015° 20.6'
04	236° 29.2'	S015° 19.8'
05	251° 29.2'	S015° 19.0'
06	266° 29.1'	S015° 18.3'
07	281° 29.1'	S015° 17.5'
08	296° 29.1'	S015° 16.7'
09	311° 29.0'	S015° 15.9'
10	326° 29.0'	S015° 15.1'
11	341° 29.0'	S015° 14.3'
12	356° 28.9'	S015° 13.6'
13	011° 28.9'	S015° 12.8'
14	026° 28.9'	S015° 12.0'
15	041° 28.8'	S015° 11.2'
16	056° 28.8'	S015° 10.4'
17	071° 28.8'	S015° 09.6'
18	086° 28.8'	S015° 08.8'
19	101° 28.7'	S015° 08.1'
20	116° 28.7'	S015° 07.3'
21	131° 28.7'	S015° 06.5'
22	146° 28.6'	S015° 05.7'
23	161° 28.6'	S015° 04.9'
February 8		
00	176° 28.6'	S015° 04.1'
01	191° 28.5'	S015° 03.3'
02	206° 28.5'	S015° 02.5'
03	221° 28.5'	S015° 01.7'
04	236° 28.5'	S015° 01.0'
05	251° 28.4'	S015° 00.2'
06	266° 28.4'	S014° 59.4'
07	281° 28.4'	S014° 58.6'
08	296° 28.4'	S014° 57.8'
09	311° 28.3'	S014° 57.0'
10	326° 28.3'	S014° 56.2'
11	341° 28.3'	S014° 55.4'
12	356° 28.3'	S014° 54.6'
13	011° 28.2'	S014° 53.8'
14	026° 28.2'	S014° 53.0'
15	041° 28.2'	S014° 52.2'
16	056° 28.2'	S014° 51.4'
17	071° 28.2'	S014° 50.6'
18	086° 28.1'	S014° 49.8'
19	101° 28.1'	S014° 49.0'
20	116° 28.1'	S014° 48.2'
21	131° 28.1'	S014° 47.4'
22	146° 28.0'	S014° 46.6'
23	161° 28.0'	S014° 45.8'
February 9		
00	176° 28.0'	S014° 45.0'
01	191° 28.0'	S014° 44.2'
02	206° 28.0'	S014° 43.4'
03	221° 27.9'	S014° 42.6'
04	236° 27.9'	S014° 41.8'
05	251° 27.9'	S014° 41.0'
06	266° 27.9'	S014° 40.2'
07	281° 27.9'	S014° 39.4'
08	296° 27.9'	S014° 38.6'
09	311° 27.8'	S014° 37.8'
10	326° 27.8'	S014° 37.0'
11	341° 27.8'	S014° 36.2'
12	356° 27.8'	S014° 35.4'
13	011° 27.8'	S014° 34.6'
14	026° 27.8'	S014° 33.8'
15	041° 27.7'	S014° 33.0'
16	056° 27.7'	S014° 32.2'
17	071° 27.7'	S014° 31.4'
18	086° 27.7'	S014° 30.6'
19	101° 27.7'	S014° 29.8'
20	116° 27.7'	S014° 29.0'
21	131° 27.7'	S014° 28.1'
22	146° 27.7'	S014° 27.3'
23	161° 27.6'	S014° 26.5'
February 10		
00	176° 27.6'	S014° 25.7'
01	191° 27.6'	S014° 24.9'
02	206° 27.6'	S014° 24.1'
03	221° 27.6'	S014° 23.3'
04	236° 27.6'	S014° 22.5'
05	251° 27.6'	S014° 21.7'
06	266° 27.6'	S014° 20.8'
07	281° 27.6'	S014° 20.0'
08	296° 27.6'	S014° 19.2'
09	311° 27.5'	S014° 18.4'
10	326° 27.5'	S014° 17.6'
11	341° 27.5'	S014° 16.8'
12	356° 27.5'	S014° 16.0'
13	011° 27.5'	S014° 15.1'
14	026° 27.5'	S014° 14.3'
15	041° 27.5'	S014° 13.5'
16	056° 27.5'	S014° 12.7'
17	071° 27.5'	S014° 11.9'
18	086° 27.5'	S014° 11.1'
19	101° 27.5'	S014° 10.2'
20	116° 27.5'	S014° 09.4'
21	131° 27.5'	S014° 08.6'
22	146° 27.5'	S014° 07.8'
23	161° 27.5'	S014° 07.0'

Hr	GHA		DEC		Hr	GHA		DEC		Hr	GHA		DEC	
	February 11				06	266°	27.7'	S013°	21.3'	13	011°	29.0'	S012°	34.5'
00	176°	27.5'	S014°	06.2'	07	281°	27.8'	S013°	20.4'	14	026°	29.0'	S012°	33.6'
01	191°	27.4'	S014°	05.3'	08	296°	27.8'	S013°	19.6'	15	041°	29.1'	S012°	32.7'
02	206°	27.4'	S014°	04.5'	09	311°	27.8'	S013°	18.8'	16	056°	29.1'	S012°	31.9'
03	221°	27.4'	S014°	03.7'	10	326°	27.8'	S013°	17.9'	17	071°	29.1'	S012°	31.0'
04	236°	27.4'	S014°	02.9'	11	341°	27.8'	S013°	17.1'	18	086°	29.2'	S012°	30.2'
05	251°	27.4'	S014°	02.0'	12	356°	27.8'	S013°	16.2'	19	101°	29.2'	S012°	29.3'
06	266°	27.4'	S014°	01.2'	13	011°	27.9'	S013°	15.4'	20	116°	29.2'	S012°	28.4'
07	281°	27.4'	S014°	00.4'	14	026°	27.9'	S013°	14.5'	21	131°	29.3'	S012°	27.6'
08	296°	27.4'	S013°	59.6'	15	041°	27.9'	S013°	13.7'	22	146°	29.3'	S012°	26.7'
09	311°	27.4'	S013°	58.8'	16	056°	27.9'	S013°	12.9'	23	161°	29.3'	S012°	25.8'
10	326°	27.4'	S013°	57.9'	17	071°	27.9'	S013°	12.0'		February 16			
11	341°	27.4'	S013°	57.1'	18	086°	27.9'	S013°	11.2'	00	176°	29.4'	S012°	25.0'
12	356°	27.4'	S013°	56.3'	19	101°	28.0'	S013°	10.3'	01	191°	29.4'	S012°	24.1'
13	011°	27.4'	S013°	55.5'	20	116°	28.0'	S013°	09.5'	02	206°	29.5'	S012°	23.2'
14	026°	27.4'	S013°	54.6'	21	131°	28.0'	S013°	08.6'	03	221°	29.5'	S012°	22.4'
15	041°	27.4'	S013°	53.8'	22	146°	28.0'	S013°	07.8'	04	236°	29.5'	S012°	21.5'
16	056°	27.4'	S013°	53.0'	23	161°	28.0'	S013°	06.9'	05	251°	29.6'	S012°	20.6'
17	071°	27.4'	S013°	52.2'		February 14				06	266°	29.6'	S012°	19.8'
18	086°	27.4'	S013°	51.3'	00	176°	28.1'	S013°	06.1'	07	281°	29.6'	S012°	18.9'
19	101°	27.4'	S013°	50.5'	01	191°	28.1'	S013°	05.2'	08	296°	29.7'	S012°	18.0'
20	116°	27.4'	S013°	49.7'	02	206°	28.1'	S013°	04.4'	09	311°	29.7'	S012°	17.2'
21	131°	27.5'	S013°	48.8'	03	221°	28.1'	S013°	03.5'	10	326°	29.7'	S012°	16.3'
22	146°	27.5'	S013°	48.0'	04	236°	28.1'	S013°	02.7'	11	341°	29.8'	S012°	15.4'
23	161°	27.5'	S013°	47.2'	05	251°	28.2'	S013°	01.8'	12	356°	29.8'	S012°	14.6'
	February 12				06	266°	28.2'	S013°	01.0'	13	011°	29.9'	S012°	13.7'
00	176°	27.5'	S013°	46.4'	07	281°	28.2'	S013°	00.1'	14	026°	29.9'	S012°	12.8'
01	191°	27.5'	S013°	45.5'	08	296°	28.2'	S012°	59.3'	15	041°	29.9'	S012°	12.0'
02	206°	27.5'	S013°	44.7'	09	311°	28.2'	S012°	58.4'	16	056°	30.0'	S012°	11.1'
03	221°	27.5'	S013°	43.9'	10	326°	28.3'	S012°	57.6'	17	071°	30.0'	S012°	10.2'
04	236°	27.5'	S013°	43.0'	11	341°	28.3'	S012°	56.7'	18	086°	30.1'	S012°	09.3'
05	251°	27.5'	S013°	42.2'	12	356°	28.3'	S012°	55.9'	19	101°	30.1'	S012°	08.5'
06	266°	27.5'	S013°	41.4'	13	011°	28.3'	S012°	55.0'	20	116°	30.1'	S012°	07.6'
07	281°	27.5'	S013°	40.5'	14	026°	28.4'	S012°	54.2'	21	131°	30.2'	S012°	06.7'
08	296°	27.5'	S013°	39.7'	15	041°	28.4'	S012°	53.3'	22	146°	30.2'	S012°	05.8'
09	311°	27.5'	S013°	38.9'	16	056°	28.4'	S012°	52.5'	23	161°	30.3'	S012°	05.0'
10	326°	27.5'	S013°	38.0'	17	071°	28.4'	S012°	51.6'		February 17			
11	341°	27.5'	S013°	37.2'	18	086°	28.5'	S012°	50.8'	00	176°	30.3'	S012°	04.1'
12	356°	27.5'	S013°	36.4'	19	101°	28.5'	S012°	49.9'	01	191°	30.4'	S012°	03.2'
13	011°	27.5'	S013°	35.5'	20	116°	28.5'	S012°	49.1'	02	206°	30.4'	S012°	02.4'
14	026°	27.6'	S013°	34.7'	21	131°	28.5'	S012°	48.2'	03	221°	30.4'	S012°	01.5'
15	041°	27.6'	S013°	33.9'	22	146°	28.6'	S012°	47.3'	04	236°	30.5'	S012°	00.6'
16	056°	27.6'	S013°	33.0'	23	161°	28.6'	S012°	46.5'	05	251°	30.5'	S011°	59.7'
17	071°	27.6'	S013°	32.2'		February 15				06	266°	30.6'	S011°	58.9'
18	086°	27.6'	S013°	31.4'	00	176°	28.6'	S012°	45.6'	07	281°	30.6'	S011°	58.0'
19	101°	27.6'	S013°	30.5'	01	191°	28.7'	S012°	44.8'	08	296°	30.7'	S011°	57.1'
20	116°	27.6'	S013°	29.7'	02	206°	28.7'	S012°	43.9'	09	311°	30.7'	S011°	56.2'
21	131°	27.6'	S013°	28.8'	03	221°	28.7'	S012°	43.1'	10	326°	30.8'	S011°	55.4'
22	146°	27.6'	S013°	28.0'	04	236°	28.7'	S012°	42.2'	11	341°	30.8'	S011°	54.5'
23	161°	27.7'	S013°	27.2'	05	251°	28.8'	S012°	41.3'	12	356°	30.8'	S011°	53.6'
	February 13				06	266°	28.8'	S012°	40.5'	13	011°	30.9'	S011°	52.7'
00	176°	27.7'	S013°	26.3'	07	281°	28.8'	S012°	39.6'	14	026°	30.9'	S011°	51.8'
01	191°	27.7'	S013°	25.5'	08	296°	28.9'	S012°	38.8'	15	041°	31.0'	S011°	51.0'
02	206°	27.7'	S013°	24.7'	09	311°	28.9'	S012°	37.9'	16	056°	31.0'	S011°	50.1'
03	221°	27.7'	S013°	23.8'	10	326°	28.9'	S012°	37.0'	17	071°	31.1'	S011°	49.2'
04	236°	27.7'	S013°	23.0'	11	341°	28.9'	S012°	36.2'	18	086°	31.1'	S011°	48.3'
05	251°	27.7'	S013°	22.1'	12	356°	29.0'	S012°	35.3'	19	101°	31.2'	S011°	47.5'

Hr	GHA		DEC	
20	116°	31.2'	S011°	46.6'
21	131°	31.3'	S011°	45.7'
22	146°	31.3'	S011°	44.8'
23	161°	31.4'	S011°	43.9'
February 18				
00	176°	31.4'	S011°	43.0'
01	191°	31.5'	S011°	42.2'
02	206°	31.5'	S011°	41.3'
03	221°	31.6'	S011°	40.4'
04	236°	31.6'	S011°	39.5'
05	251°	31.7'	S011°	38.6'
06	266°	31.7'	S011°	37.8'
07	281°	31.8'	S011°	36.9'
08	296°	31.8'	S011°	36.0'
09	311°	31.9'	S011°	35.1'
10	326°	31.9'	S011°	34.2'
11	341°	32.0'	S011°	33.3'
12	356°	32.0'	S011°	32.5'
13	011°	32.1'	S011°	31.6'
14	026°	32.1'	S011°	30.7'
15	041°	32.2'	S011°	29.8'
16	056°	32.3'	S011°	28.9'
17	071°	32.3'	S011°	28.0'
18	086°	32.4'	S011°	27.1'
19	101°	32.4'	S011°	26.2'
20	116°	32.5'	S011°	25.4'
21	131°	32.5'	S011°	24.5'
22	146°	32.6'	S011°	23.6'
23	161°	32.6'	S011°	22.7'
February 19				
00	176°	32.7'	S011°	21.8'
01	191°	32.8'	S011°	20.9'
02	206°	32.8'	S011°	20.0'
03	221°	32.9'	S011°	19.1'
04	236°	32.9'	S011°	18.3'
05	251°	33.0'	S011°	17.4'
06	266°	33.0'	S011°	16.5'
07	281°	33.1'	S011°	15.6'
08	296°	33.2'	S011°	14.7'
09	311°	33.2'	S011°	13.8'
10	326°	33.3'	S011°	12.9'
11	341°	33.3'	S011°	12.0'
12	356°	33.4'	S011°	11.1'
13	011°	33.5'	S011°	10.2'
14	026°	33.5'	S011°	09.3'
15	041°	33.6'	S011°	08.4'
16	056°	33.6'	S011°	07.5'
17	071°	33.7'	S011°	06.7'
18	086°	33.8'	S011°	05.8'
19	101°	33.8'	S011°	04.9'
20	116°	33.9'	S011°	04.0'
21	131°	34.0'	S011°	03.1'
22	146°	34.0'	S011°	02.2'
23	161°	34.1'	S011°	01.3'
February 20				
00	176°	34.1'	S011°	00.4'
01	191°	34.2'	S010°	59.5'

Hr	GHA		DEC	
02	206°	34.3'	S010°	58.6'
03	221°	34.3'	S010°	57.7'
04	236°	34.4'	S010°	56.8'
05	251°	34.5'	S010°	55.9'
06	266°	34.5'	S010°	55.0'
07	281°	34.6'	S010°	54.1'
08	296°	34.7'	S010°	53.2'
09	311°	34.7'	S010°	52.3'
10	326°	34.8'	S010°	51.4'
11	341°	34.9'	S010°	50.5'
12	356°	34.9'	S010°	49.6'
13	011°	35.0'	S010°	48.7'
14	026°	35.1'	S010°	47.8'
15	041°	35.1'	S010°	46.9'
16	056°	35.2'	S010°	46.0'
17	071°	35.3'	S010°	45.1'
18	086°	35.3'	S010°	44.2'
19	101°	35.4'	S010°	43.3'
20	116°	35.5'	S010°	42.4'
21	131°	35.6'	S010°	41.5'
22	146°	35.6'	S010°	40.6'
23	161°	35.7'	S010°	39.7'
February 21				
00	176°	35.8'	S010°	38.8'
01	191°	35.8'	S010°	37.9'
02	206°	35.9'	S010°	37.0'
03	221°	36.0'	S010°	36.1'
04	236°	36.0'	S010°	35.2'
05	251°	36.1'	S010°	34.3'
06	266°	36.2'	S010°	33.4'
07	281°	36.3'	S010°	32.5'
08	296°	36.3'	S010°	31.6'
09	311°	36.4'	S010°	30.7'
10	326°	36.5'	S010°	29.8'
11	341°	36.6'	S010°	28.8'
12	356°	36.6'	S010°	27.9'
13	011°	36.7'	S010°	27.0'
14	026°	36.8'	S010°	26.1'
15	041°	36.9'	S010°	25.2'
16	056°	36.9'	S010°	24.3'
17	071°	37.0'	S010°	23.4'
18	086°	37.1'	S010°	22.5'
19	101°	37.2'	S010°	21.6'
20	116°	37.2'	S010°	20.7'
21	131°	37.3'	S010°	19.8'
22	146°	37.4'	S010°	18.9'
23	161°	37.5'	S010°	18.0'
February 22				
00	176°	37.5'	S010°	17.0'
01	191°	37.6'	S010°	16.1'
02	206°	37.7'	S010°	15.2'
03	221°	37.8'	S010°	14.3'
04	236°	37.8'	S010°	13.4'
05	251°	37.9'	S010°	12.5'
06	266°	38.0'	S010°	11.6'
07	281°	38.1'	S010°	10.7'
08	296°	38.2'	S010°	09.8'

Hr	GHA		DEC	
09	311°	38.2'	S010°	08.8'
10	326°	38.3'	S010°	07.9'
11	341°	38.4'	S010°	07.0'
12	356°	38.5'	S010°	06.1'
13	011°	38.6'	S010°	05.2'
14	026°	38.6'	S010°	04.3'
15	041°	38.7'	S010°	03.4'
16	056°	38.8'	S010°	02.5'
17	071°	38.9'	S010°	01.5'
18	086°	39.0'	S010°	00.6'
19	101°	39.1'	S009°	59.7'
20	116°	39.1'	S009°	58.8'
21	131°	39.2'	S009°	57.9'
22	146°	39.3'	S009°	57.0'
23	161°	39.4'	S009°	56.0'
February 23				
00	176°	39.5'	S009°	55.1'
01	191°	39.6'	S009°	54.2'
02	206°	39.6'	S009°	53.3'
03	221°	39.7'	S009°	52.4'
04	236°	39.8'	S009°	51.5'
05	251°	39.9'	S009°	50.5'
06	266°	40.0'	S009°	49.6'
07	281°	40.1'	S009°	48.7'
08	296°	40.1'	S009°	47.8'
09	311°	40.2'	S009°	46.9'
10	326°	40.3'	S009°	46.0'
11	341°	40.4'	S009°	45.0'
12	356°	40.5'	S009°	44.1'
13	011°	40.6'	S009°	43.2'
14	026°	40.7'	S009°	42.3'
15	041°	40.8'	S009°	41.4'
16	056°	40.8'	S009°	40.4'
17	071°	40.9'	S009°	39.5'
18	086°	41.0'	S009°	38.6'
19	101°	41.1'	S009°	37.7'
20	116°	41.2'	S009°	36.8'
21	131°	41.3'	S009°	35.8'
22	146°	41.4'	S009°	34.9'
23	161°	41.5'	S009°	34.0'
February 24				
00	176°	41.6'	S009°	33.1'
01	191°	41.6'	S009°	32.1'
02	206°	41.7'	S009°	31.2'
03	221°	41.8'	S009°	30.3'
04	236°	41.9'	S009°	29.4'
05	251°	42.0'	S009°	28.5'
06	266°	42.1'	S009°	27.5'
07	281°	42.2'	S009°	26.6'
08	296°	42.3'	S009°	25.7'
09	311°	42.4'	S009°	24.8'
10	326°	42.5'	S009°	23.8'
11	341°	42.6'	S009°	22.9'
12	356°	42.7'	S009°	22.0'
13	011°	42.7'	S009°	21.1'
14	026°	42.8'	S009°	20.1'
15	041°	42.9'	S009°	19.2'

Hr	GHA		DEC	
16	056°	43.0'	S009°	18.3'
17	071°	43.1'	S009°	17.3'
18	086°	43.2'	S009°	16.4'
19	101°	43.3'	S009°	15.5'
20	116°	43.4'	S009°	14.6'
21	131°	43.5'	S009°	13.6'
22	146°	43.6'	S009°	12.7'
23	161°	43.7'	S009°	11.8'
February 25				
00	176°	43.8'	S009°	10.9'
01	191°	43.9'	S009°	09.9'
02	206°	44.0'	S009°	09.0'
03	221°	44.1'	S009°	08.1'
04	236°	44.2'	S009°	07.1'
05	251°	44.3'	S009°	06.2'
06	266°	44.4'	S009°	05.3'
07	281°	44.5'	S009°	04.4'
08	296°	44.6'	S009°	03.4'
09	311°	44.7'	S009°	02.5'
10	326°	44.8'	S009°	01.6'
11	341°	44.9'	S009°	00.6'
12	356°	45.0'	S008°	59.7'
13	011°	45.1'	S008°	58.8'
14	026°	45.2'	S008°	57.8'
15	041°	45.3'	S008°	56.9'
16	056°	45.4'	S008°	56.0'
17	071°	45.5'	S008°	55.0'
18	086°	45.6'	S008°	54.1'
19	101°	45.7'	S008°	53.2'
20	116°	45.8'	S008°	52.2'
21	131°	45.9'	S008°	51.3'
22	146°	46.0'	S008°	50.4'
23	161°	46.1'	S008°	49.4'
February 26				
00	176°	46.2'	S008°	48.5'
01	191°	46.3'	S008°	47.6'
02	206°	46.4'	S008°	46.6'
03	221°	46.5'	S008°	45.7'
04	236°	46.6'	S008°	44.8'
05	251°	46.7'	S008°	43.8'
06	266°	46.8'	S008°	42.9'
07	281°	46.9'	S008°	42.0'
08	296°	47.0'	S008°	41.0'
09	311°	47.1'	S008°	40.1'
10	326°	47.2'	S008°	39.2'
11	341°	47.3'	S008°	38.2'
12	356°	47.4'	S008°	37.3'
13	011°	47.5'	S008°	36.4'
14	026°	47.6'	S008°	35.4'
15	041°	47.7'	S008°	34.5'
16	056°	47.8'	S008°	33.5'
17	071°	47.9'	S008°	32.6'
18	086°	48.1'	S008°	31.7'
19	101°	48.2'	S008°	30.7'
20	116°	48.3'	S008°	29.8'
21	131°	48.4'	S008°	28.8'
22	146°	48.5'	S008°	27.9'

Hr	GHA		DEC	
23	161°	48.6'	S008°	27.0'
February 27				
00	176°	48.7'	S008°	26.0'
01	191°	48.8'	S008°	25.1'
02	206°	48.9'	S008°	24.2'
03	221°	49.0'	S008°	23.2'
04	236°	49.1'	S008°	22.3'
05	251°	49.2'	S008°	21.3'
06	266°	49.3'	S008°	20.4'
07	281°	49.5'	S008°	19.5'
08	296°	49.6'	S008°	18.5'
09	311°	49.7'	S008°	17.6'
10	326°	49.8'	S008°	16.6'
11	341°	49.9'	S008°	15.7'
12	356°	50.0'	S008°	14.7'
13	011°	50.1'	S008°	13.8'
14	026°	50.2'	S008°	12.9'
15	041°	50.3'	S008°	11.9'
16	056°	50.5'	S008°	11.0'
17	071°	50.6'	S008°	10.0'
18	086°	50.7'	S008°	09.1'
19	101°	50.8'	S008°	08.1'
20	116°	50.9'	S008°	07.2'
21	131°	51.0'	S008°	06.3'
22	146°	51.1'	S008°	05.3'
23	161°	51.2'	S008°	04.4'
February 28				
00	176°	51.4'	S008°	03.4'
01	191°	51.5'	S008°	02.5'
02	206°	51.6'	S008°	01.5'
03	221°	51.7'	S008°	00.6'
04	236°	51.8'	S007°	59.7'
05	251°	51.9'	S007°	58.7'
06	266°	52.0'	S007°	57.8'
07	281°	52.2'	S007°	56.8'
08	296°	52.3'	S007°	55.9'
09	311°	52.4'	S007°	54.9'
10	326°	52.5'	S007°	54.0'
11	341°	52.6'	S007°	53.0'
12	356°	52.7'	S007°	52.1'
13	011°	52.8'	S007°	51.1'
14	026°	53.0'	S007°	50.2'
15	041°	53.1'	S007°	49.2'
16	056°	53.2'	S007°	48.3'
17	071°	53.3'	S007°	47.4'
18	086°	53.4'	S007°	46.4'
19	101°	53.6'	S007°	45.5'
20	116°	53.7'	S007°	44.5'
21	131°	53.8'	S007°	43.6'
22	146°	53.9'	S007°	42.6'
23	161°	54.0'	S007°	41.7'
March 1				
00	176°	54.1'	S007°	40.7'
01	191°	54.3'	S007°	39.8'
02	206°	54.4'	S007°	38.8'
03	221°	54.5'	S007°	37.9'
04	236°	54.6'	S007°	36.9'

Hr	GHA		DEC	
05	251°	54.7'	S007°	36.0'
06	266°	54.9'	S007°	35.0'
07	281°	55.0'	S007°	34.1'
08	296°	55.1'	S007°	33.1'
09	311°	55.2'	S007°	32.2'
10	326°	55.3'	S007°	31.2'
11	341°	55.5'	S007°	30.3'
12	356°	55.6'	S007°	29.3'
13	011°	55.7'	S007°	28.4'
14	026°	55.8'	S007°	27.4'
15	041°	56.0'	S007°	26.5'
16	056°	56.1'	S007°	25.5'
17	071°	56.2'	S007°	24.6'
18	086°	56.3'	S007°	23.6'
19	101°	56.4'	S007°	22.6'
20	116°	56.6'	S007°	21.7'
21	131°	56.7'	S007°	20.7'
22	146°	56.8'	S007°	19.8'
23	161°	56.9'	S007°	18.8'
March 2				
00	176°	57.1'	S007°	17.9'
01	191°	57.2'	S007°	16.9'
02	206°	57.3'	S007°	16.0'
03	221°	57.4'	S007°	15.0'
04	236°	57.6'	S007°	14.1'
05	251°	57.7'	S007°	13.1'
06	266°	57.8'	S007°	12.2'
07	281°	57.9'	S007°	11.2'
08	296°	58.1'	S007°	10.2'
09	311°	58.2'	S007°	09.3'
10	326°	58.3'	S007°	08.3'
11	341°	58.4'	S007°	07.4'
12	356°	58.6'	S007°	06.4'
13	011°	58.7'	S007°	05.5'
14	026°	58.8'	S007°	04.5'
15	041°	59.0'	S007°	03.6'
16	056°	59.1'	S007°	02.6'
17	071°	59.2'	S007°	01.6'
18	086°	59.3'	S007°	00.7'
19	101°	59.5'	S006°	59.7'
20	116°	59.6'	S006°	58.8'
21	131°	59.7'	S006°	57.8'
22	146°	59.8'	S006°	56.9'
23	161°	60.0'	S006°	55.9'
March 3				
00	177°	00.1'	S006°	54.9'
01	192°	00.2'	S006°	54.0'
02	207°	00.4'	S006°	53.0'
03	222°	00.5'	S006°	52.1'
04	237°	00.6'	S006°	51.1'
05	252°	00.8'	S006°	50.2'
06	267°	00.9'	S006°	49.2'
07	282°	01.0'	S006°	48.2'
08	297°	01.1'	S006°	47.3'
09	312°	01.3'	S006°	46.3'
10	327°	01.4'	S006°	45.4'
11	342°	01.5'	S006°	44.4'

Hr	GHA		DEC	
12	357°	01.7'	S006°	43.4'
13	012°	01.8'	S006°	42.5'
14	027°	01.9'	S006°	41.5'
15	042°	02.1'	S006°	40.6'
16	057°	02.2'	S006°	39.6'
17	072°	02.3'	S006°	38.6'
18	087°	02.5'	S006°	37.7'
19	102°	02.6'	S006°	36.7'
20	117°	02.7'	S006°	35.8'
21	132°	02.9'	S006°	34.8'
22	147°	03.0'	S006°	33.8'
23	162°	03.1'	S006°	32.9'
March 4				
00	177°	03.3'	S006°	31.9'
01	192°	03.4'	S006°	31.0'
02	207°	03.5'	S006°	30.0'
03	222°	03.7'	S006°	29.0'
04	237°	03.8'	S006°	28.1'
05	252°	03.9'	S006°	27.1'
06	267°	04.1'	S006°	26.1'
07	282°	04.2'	S006°	25.2'
08	297°	04.3'	S006°	24.2'
09	312°	04.5'	S006°	23.3'
10	327°	04.6'	S006°	22.3'
11	342°	04.8'	S006°	21.3'
12	357°	04.9'	S006°	20.4'
13	012°	05.0'	S006°	19.4'
14	027°	05.2'	S006°	18.4'
15	042°	05.3'	S006°	17.5'
16	057°	05.4'	S006°	16.5'
17	072°	05.6'	S006°	15.5'
18	087°	05.7'	S006°	14.6'
19	102°	05.9'	S006°	13.6'
20	117°	06.0'	S006°	12.7'
21	132°	06.1'	S006°	11.7'
22	147°	06.3'	S006°	10.7'
23	162°	06.4'	S006°	09.8'
March 5				
00	177°	06.5'	S006°	08.8'
01	192°	06.7'	S006°	07.8'
02	207°	06.8'	S006°	06.9'
03	222°	07.0'	S006°	05.9'
04	237°	07.1'	S006°	04.9'
05	252°	07.2'	S006°	04.0'
06	267°	07.4'	S006°	03.0'
07	282°	07.5'	S006°	02.0'
08	297°	07.7'	S006°	01.1'
09	312°	07.8'	S006°	00.1'
10	327°	07.9'	S005°	59.1'
11	342°	08.1'	S005°	58.2'
12	357°	08.2'	S005°	57.2'
13	012°	08.4'	S005°	56.2'
14	027°	08.5'	S005°	55.3'
15	042°	08.6'	S005°	54.3'
16	057°	08.8'	S005°	53.3'
17	072°	08.9'	S005°	52.4'
18	087°	09.1'	S005°	51.4'

Hr	GHA		DEC	
19	102°	09.2'	S005°	50.4'
20	117°	09.4'	S005°	49.5'
21	132°	09.5'	S005°	48.5'
22	147°	09.6'	S005°	47.5'
23	162°	09.8'	S005°	46.6'
March 6				
00	177°	09.9'	S005°	45.6'
01	192°	10.1'	S005°	44.6'
02	207°	10.2'	S005°	43.6'
03	222°	10.4'	S005°	42.7'
04	237°	10.5'	S005°	41.7'
05	252°	10.6'	S005°	40.7'
06	267°	10.8'	S005°	39.8'
07	282°	10.9'	S005°	38.8'
08	297°	11.1'	S005°	37.8'
09	312°	11.2'	S005°	36.9'
10	327°	11.4'	S005°	35.9'
11	342°	11.5'	S005°	34.9'
12	357°	11.7'	S005°	33.9'
13	012°	11.8'	S005°	33.0'
14	027°	11.9'	S005°	32.0'
15	042°	12.1'	S005°	31.0'
16	057°	12.2'	S005°	30.1'
17	072°	12.4'	S005°	29.1'
18	087°	12.5'	S005°	28.1'
19	102°	12.7'	S005°	27.2'
20	117°	12.8'	S005°	26.2'
21	132°	13.0'	S005°	25.2'
22	147°	13.1'	S005°	24.2'
23	162°	13.3'	S005°	23.3'
March 7				
00	177°	13.4'	S005°	22.3'
01	192°	13.6'	S005°	21.3'
02	207°	13.7'	S005°	20.4'
03	222°	13.9'	S005°	19.4'
04	237°	14.0'	S005°	18.4'
05	252°	14.2'	S005°	17.4'
06	267°	14.3'	S005°	16.5'
07	282°	14.5'	S005°	15.5'
08	297°	14.6'	S005°	14.5'
09	312°	14.7'	S005°	13.5'
10	327°	14.9'	S005°	12.6'
11	342°	15.0'	S005°	11.6'
12	357°	15.2'	S005°	10.6'
13	012°	15.3'	S005°	09.7'
14	027°	15.5'	S005°	08.7'
15	042°	15.6'	S005°	07.7'
16	057°	15.8'	S005°	06.7'
17	072°	15.9'	S005°	05.8'
18	087°	16.1'	S005°	04.8'
19	102°	16.2'	S005°	03.8'
20	117°	16.4'	S005°	02.8'
21	132°	16.5'	S005°	01.9'
22	147°	16.7'	S005°	00.9'
23	162°	16.9'	S004°	59.9'
March 8				
00	177°	17.0'	S004°	58.9'

Hr	GHA		DEC	
01	192°	17.2'	S004°	58.0'
02	207°	17.3'	S004°	57.0'
03	222°	17.5'	S004°	56.0'
04	237°	17.6'	S004°	55.0'
05	252°	17.8'	S004°	54.1'
06	267°	17.9'	S004°	53.1'
07	282°	18.1'	S004°	52.1'
08	297°	18.2'	S004°	51.1'
09	312°	18.4'	S004°	50.2'
10	327°	18.5'	S004°	49.2'
11	342°	18.7'	S004°	48.2'
12	357°	18.8'	S004°	47.2'
13	012°	19.0'	S004°	46.3'
14	027°	19.1'	S004°	45.3'
15	042°	19.3'	S004°	44.3'
16	057°	19.4'	S004°	43.3'
17	072°	19.6'	S004°	42.4'
18	087°	19.8'	S004°	41.4'
19	102°	19.9'	S004°	40.4'
20	117°	20.1'	S004°	39.4'
21	132°	20.2'	S004°	38.4'
22	147°	20.4'	S004°	37.5'
23	162°	20.5'	S004°	36.5'
March 9				
00	177°	20.7'	S004°	35.5'
01	192°	20.8'	S004°	34.5'
02	207°	21.0'	S004°	33.6'
03	222°	21.2'	S004°	32.6'
04	237°	21.3'	S004°	31.6'
05	252°	21.5'	S004°	30.6'
06	267°	21.6'	S004°	29.6'
07	282°	21.8'	S004°	28.7'
08	297°	21.9'	S004°	27.7'
09	312°	22.1'	S004°	26.7'
10	327°	22.2'	S004°	25.7'
11	342°	22.4'	S004°	24.8'
12	357°	22.6'	S004°	23.8'
13	012°	22.7'	S004°	22.8'
14	027°	22.9'	S004°	21.8'
15	042°	23.0'	S004°	20.8'
16	057°	23.2'	S004°	19.9'
17	072°	23.3'	S004°	18.9'
18	087°	23.5'	S004°	17.9'
19	102°	23.7'	S004°	16.9'
20	117°	23.8'	S004°	15.9'
21	132°	24.0'	S004°	15.0'
22	147°	24.1'	S004°	14.0'
23	162°	24.3'	S004°	13.0'
March 10				
00	177°	24.5'	S004°	12.0'
01	192°	24.6'	S004°	11.1'
02	207°	24.8'	S004°	10.1'
03	222°	24.9'	S004°	09.1'
04	237°	25.1'	S004°	08.1'
05	252°	25.3'	S004°	07.1'
06	267°	25.4'	S004°	06.2'
07	282°	25.6'	S004°	05.2'

Hr	GHA		DEC	
08	297°	25.7'	S004°	04.2'
09	312°	25.9'	S004°	03.2'
10	327°	26.1'	S004°	02.2'
11	342°	26.2'	S004°	01.2'
12	357°	26.4'	S004°	00.3'
13	012°	26.5'	S003°	59.3'
14	027°	26.7'	S003°	58.3'
15	042°	26.9'	S003°	57.3'
16	057°	27.0'	S003°	56.3'
17	072°	27.2'	S003°	55.4'
18	087°	27.3'	S003°	54.4'
19	102°	27.5'	S003°	53.4'
20	117°	27.7'	S003°	52.4'
21	132°	27.8'	S003°	51.4'
22	147°	28.0'	S003°	50.5'
23	162°	28.2'	S003°	49.5'
March 11				
00	177°	28.3'	S003°	48.5'
01	192°	28.5'	S003°	47.5'
02	207°	28.6'	S003°	46.5'
03	222°	28.8'	S003°	45.5'
04	237°	29.0'	S003°	44.6'
05	252°	29.1'	S003°	43.6'
06	267°	29.3'	S003°	42.6'
07	282°	29.5'	S003°	41.6'
08	297°	29.6'	S003°	40.6'
09	312°	29.8'	S003°	39.7'
10	327°	29.9'	S003°	38.7'
11	342°	30.1'	S003°	37.7'
12	357°	30.3'	S003°	36.7'
13	012°	30.4'	S003°	35.7'
14	027°	30.6'	S003°	34.7'
15	042°	30.8'	S003°	33.8'
16	057°	30.9'	S003°	32.8'
17	072°	31.1'	S003°	31.8'
18	087°	31.3'	S003°	30.8'
19	102°	31.4'	S003°	29.8'
20	117°	31.6'	S003°	28.8'
21	132°	31.8'	S003°	27.9'
22	147°	31.9'	S003°	26.9'
23	162°	32.1'	S003°	25.9'
March 12				
00	177°	32.3'	S003°	24.9'
01	192°	32.4'	S003°	23.9'
02	207°	32.6'	S003°	22.9'
03	222°	32.8'	S003°	22.0'
04	237°	32.9'	S003°	21.0'
05	252°	33.1'	S003°	20.0'
06	267°	33.3'	S003°	19.0'
07	282°	33.4'	S003°	18.0'
08	297°	33.6'	S003°	17.0'
09	312°	33.8'	S003°	16.1'
10	327°	33.9'	S003°	15.1'
11	342°	34.1'	S003°	14.1'
12	357°	34.3'	S003°	13.1'
13	012°	34.4'	S003°	12.1'
14	027°	34.6'	S003°	11.1'

Hr	GHA		DEC	
15	042°	34.8'	S003°	10.2'
16	057°	34.9'	S003°	09.2'
17	072°	35.1'	S003°	08.2'
18	087°	35.3'	S003°	07.2'
19	102°	35.4'	S003°	06.2'
20	117°	35.6'	S003°	05.2'
21	132°	35.8'	S003°	04.2'
22	147°	35.9'	S003°	03.3'
23	162°	36.1'	S003°	02.3'
March 13				
00	177°	36.3'	S003°	01.3'
01	192°	36.4'	S003°	00.3'
02	207°	36.6'	S002°	59.3'
03	222°	36.8'	S002°	58.3'
04	237°	36.9'	S002°	57.4'
05	252°	37.1'	S002°	56.4'
06	267°	37.3'	S002°	55.4'
07	282°	37.5'	S002°	54.4'
08	297°	37.6'	S002°	53.4'
09	312°	37.8'	S002°	52.4'
10	327°	38.0'	S002°	51.4'
11	342°	38.1'	S002°	50.5'
12	357°	38.3'	S002°	49.5'
13	012°	38.5'	S002°	48.5'
14	027°	38.6'	S002°	47.5'
15	042°	38.8'	S002°	46.5'
16	057°	39.0'	S002°	45.5'
17	072°	39.2'	S002°	44.5'
18	087°	39.3'	S002°	43.6'
19	102°	39.5'	S002°	42.6'
20	117°	39.7'	S002°	41.6'
21	132°	39.8'	S002°	40.6'
22	147°	40.0'	S002°	39.6'
23	162°	40.2'	S002°	38.6'
March 14				
00	177°	40.3'	S002°	37.6'
01	192°	40.5'	S002°	36.6'
02	207°	40.7'	S002°	35.7'
03	222°	40.9'	S002°	34.7'
04	237°	41.0'	S002°	33.7'
05	252°	41.2'	S002°	32.7'
06	267°	41.4'	S002°	31.7'
07	282°	41.6'	S002°	30.7'
08	297°	41.7'	S002°	29.7'
09	312°	41.9'	S002°	28.8'
10	327°	42.1'	S002°	27.8'
11	342°	42.2'	S002°	26.8'
12	357°	42.4'	S002°	25.8'
13	012°	42.6'	S002°	24.8'
14	027°	42.8'	S002°	23.8'
15	042°	42.9'	S002°	22.8'
16	057°	43.1'	S002°	21.8'
17	072°	43.3'	S002°	20.9'
18	087°	43.5'	S002°	19.9'
19	102°	43.6'	S002°	18.9'
20	117°	43.8'	S002°	17.9'
21	132°	44.0'	S002°	16.9'

Hr	GHA		DEC	
22	147°	44.1'	S002°	15.9'
23	162°	44.3'	S002°	14.9'
March 15				
00	177°	44.5'	S002°	14.0'
01	192°	44.7'	S002°	13.0'
02	207°	44.8'	S002°	12.0'
03	222°	45.0'	S002°	11.0'
04	237°	45.2'	S002°	10.0'
05	252°	45.4'	S002°	09.0'
06	267°	45.5'	S002°	08.0'
07	282°	45.7'	S002°	07.0'
08	297°	45.9'	S002°	06.1'
09	312°	46.1'	S002°	05.1'
10	327°	46.2'	S002°	04.1'
11	342°	46.4'	S002°	03.1'
12	357°	46.6'	S002°	02.1'
13	012°	46.8'	S002°	01.1'
14	027°	46.9'	S002°	00.1'
15	042°	47.1'	S001°	59.1'
16	057°	47.3'	S001°	58.2'
17	072°	47.5'	S001°	57.2'
18	087°	47.6'	S001°	56.2'
19	102°	47.8'	S001°	55.2'
20	117°	48.0'	S001°	54.2'
21	132°	48.2'	S001°	53.2'
22	147°	48.3'	S001°	52.2'
23	162°	48.5'	S001°	51.2'
March 16				
00	177°	48.7'	S001°	50.2'
01	192°	48.9'	S001°	49.3'
02	207°	49.1'	S001°	48.3'
03	222°	49.2'	S001°	47.3'
04	237°	49.4'	S001°	46.3'
05	252°	49.6'	S001°	45.3'
06	267°	49.8'	S001°	44.3'
07	282°	49.9'	S001°	43.3'
08	297°	50.1'	S001°	42.3'
09	312°	50.3'	S001°	41.4'
10	327°	50.5'	S001°	40.4'
11	342°	50.6'	S001°	39.4'
12	357°	50.8'	S001°	38.4'
13	012°	51.0'	S001°	37.4'
14	027°	51.2'	S001°	36.4'
15	042°	51.4'	S001°	35.4'
16	057°	51.5'	S001°	34.4'
17	072°	51.7'	S001°	33.4'
18	087°	51.9'	S001°	32.5'
19	102°	52.1'	S001°	31.5'
20	117°	52.2'	S001°	30.5'
21	132°	52.4'	S001°	29.5'
22	147°	52.6'	S001°	28.5'
23	162°	52.8'	S001°	27.5'
March 17				
00	177°	53.0'	S001°	26.5'
01	192°	53.1'	S001°	25.5'
02	207°	53.3'	S001°	24.6'
03	222°	53.5'	S001°	23.6'

Hr	GHA		DEC	
04	237°	53.7'	S001°	22.6'
05	252°	53.9'	S001°	21.6'
06	267°	54.0'	S001°	20.6'
07	282°	54.2'	S001°	19.6'
08	297°	54.4'	S001°	18.6'
09	312°	54.6'	S001°	17.6'
10	327°	54.8'	S001°	16.6'
11	342°	54.9'	S001°	15.7'
12	357°	55.1'	S001°	14.7'
13	012°	55.3'	S001°	13.7'
14	027°	55.5'	S001°	12.7'
15	042°	55.7'	S001°	11.7'
16	057°	55.8'	S001°	10.7'
17	072°	56.0'	S001°	09.7'
18	087°	56.2'	S001°	08.7'
19	102°	56.4'	S001°	07.7'
20	117°	56.6'	S001°	06.8'
21	132°	56.7'	S001°	05.8'
22	147°	56.9'	S001°	04.8'
23	162°	57.1'	S001°	03.8'
		March 18		
00	177°	57.3'	S001°	02.8'
01	192°	57.5'	S001°	01.8'
02	207°	57.6'	S001°	00.8'
03	222°	57.8'	S000°	59.8'
04	237°	58.0'	S000°	58.8'
05	252°	58.2'	S000°	57.9'
06	267°	58.4'	S000°	56.9'
07	282°	58.5'	S000°	55.9'
08	297°	58.7'	S000°	54.9'
09	312°	58.9'	S000°	53.9'
10	327°	59.1'	S000°	52.9'
11	342°	59.3'	S000°	51.9'
12	357°	59.4'	S000°	50.9'
13	012°	59.6'	S000°	49.9'
14	027°	59.8'	S000°	49.0'
15	042°	60.0'	S000°	48.0'
16	058°	00.2'	S000°	47.0'
17	073°	00.4'	S000°	46.0'
18	088°	00.5'	S000°	45.0'
19	103°	00.7'	S000°	44.0'
20	118°	00.9'	S000°	43.0'
21	133°	01.1'	S000°	42.0'
22	148°	01.3'	S000°	41.0'
23	163°	01.4'	S000°	40.1'
		March 19		
00	178°	01.6'	S000°	39.1'
01	193°	01.8'	S000°	38.1'
02	208°	02.0'	S000°	37.1'
03	223°	02.2'	S000°	36.1'
04	238°	02.4'	S000°	35.1'
05	253°	02.5'	S000°	34.1'
06	268°	02.7'	S000°	33.1'
07	283°	02.9'	S000°	32.1'
08	298°	03.1'	S000°	31.2'
09	313°	03.3'	S000°	30.2'
10	328°	03.5'	S000°	29.2'

Hr	GHA		DEC	
11	343°	03.6'	S000°	28.2'
12	358°	03.8'	S000°	27.2'
13	013°	04.0'	S000°	26.2'
14	028°	04.2'	S000°	25.2'
15	043°	04.4'	S000°	24.2'
16	058°	04.6'	S000°	23.2'
17	073°	04.7'	S000°	22.3'
18	088°	04.9'	S000°	21.3'
19	103°	05.1'	S000°	20.3'
20	118°	05.3'	S000°	19.3'
21	133°	05.5'	S000°	18.3'
22	148°	05.7'	S000°	17.3'
23	163°	05.8'	S000°	16.3'
		March 20		
00	178°	06.0'	S000°	15.3'
01	193°	06.2'	S000°	14.4'
02	208°	06.4'	S000°	13.4'
03	223°	06.6'	S000°	12.4'
04	238°	06.8'	S000°	11.4'
05	253°	06.9'	S000°	10.4'
06	268°	07.1'	S000°	09.4'
07	283°	07.3'	S000°	08.4'
08	298°	07.5'	S000°	07.4'
09	313°	07.7'	S000°	06.4'
10	328°	07.9'	S000°	05.5'
11	343°	08.0'	S000°	04.5'
12	358°	08.2'	S000°	03.5'
13	013°	08.4'	S000°	02.5'
14	028°	08.6'	S000°	01.5'
15	043°	08.8'	S000°	00.5'
16	058°	09.0'	N000°	00.5'
17	073°	09.2'	N000°	01.5'
18	088°	09.3'	N000°	02.4'
19	103°	09.5'	N000°	03.4'
20	118°	09.7'	N000°	04.4'
21	133°	09.9'	N000°	05.4'
22	148°	10.1'	N000°	06.4'
23	163°	10.3'	N000°	07.4'
		March 21		
00	178°	10.4'	N000°	08.4'
01	193°	10.6'	N000°	09.4'
02	208°	10.8'	N000°	10.4'
03	223°	11.0'	N000°	11.3'
04	238°	11.2'	N000°	12.3'
05	253°	11.4'	N000°	13.3'
06	268°	11.6'	N000°	14.3'
07	283°	11.7'	N000°	15.3'
08	298°	11.9'	N000°	16.3'
09	313°	12.1'	N000°	17.3'
10	328°	12.3'	N000°	18.3'
11	343°	12.5'	N000°	19.2'
12	358°	12.7'	N000°	20.2'
13	013°	12.9'	N000°	21.2'
14	028°	13.0'	N000°	22.2'
15	043°	13.2'	N000°	23.2'
16	058°	13.4'	N000°	24.2'
17	073°	13.6'	N000°	25.2'

Hr	GHA		DEC	
18	088°	13.8'	N000°	26.2'
19	103°	14.0'	N000°	27.1'
20	118°	14.2'	N000°	28.1'
21	133°	14.3'	N000°	29.1'
22	148°	14.5'	N000°	30.1'
23	163°	14.7'	N000°	31.1'
		March 22		
00	178°	14.9'	N000°	32.1'
01	193°	15.1'	N000°	33.1'
02	208°	15.3'	N000°	34.1'
03	223°	15.5'	N000°	35.0'
04	238°	15.7'	N000°	36.0'
05	253°	15.8'	N000°	37.0'
06	268°	16.0'	N000°	38.0'
07	283°	16.2'	N000°	39.0'
08	298°	16.4'	N000°	40.0'
09	313°	16.6'	N000°	41.0'
10	328°	16.8'	N000°	42.0'
11	343°	17.0'	N000°	42.9'
12	358°	17.1'	N000°	43.9'
13	013°	17.3'	N000°	44.9'
14	028°	17.5'	N000°	45.9'
15	043°	17.7'	N000°	46.9'
16	058°	17.9'	N000°	47.9'
17	073°	18.1'	N000°	48.9'
18	088°	18.3'	N000°	49.8'
19	103°	18.4'	N000°	50.8'
20	118°	18.6'	N000°	51.8'
21	133°	18.8'	N000°	52.8'
22	148°	19.0'	N000°	53.8'
23	163°	19.2'	N000°	54.8'
		March 23		
00	178°	19.4'	N000°	55.8'
01	193°	19.6'	N000°	56.7'
02	208°	19.8'	N000°	57.7'
03	223°	19.9'	N000°	58.7'
04	238°	20.1'	N000°	59.7'
05	253°	20.3'	N001°	00.7'
06	268°	20.5'	N001°	01.7'
07	283°	20.7'	N001°	02.7'
08	298°	20.9'	N001°	03.6'
09	313°	21.1'	N001°	04.6'
10	328°	21.3'	N001°	05.6'
11	343°	21.4'	N001°	06.6'
12	358°	21.6'	N001°	07.6'
13	013°	21.8'	N001°	08.6'
14	028°	22.0'	N001°	09.6'
15	043°	22.2'	N001°	10.5'
16	058°	22.4'	N001°	11.5'
17	073°	22.6'	N001°	12.5'
18	088°	22.8'	N001°	13.5'
19	103°	22.9'	N001°	14.5'
20	118°	23.1'	N001°	15.5'
21	133°	23.3'	N001°	16.5'
22	148°	23.5'	N001°	17.4'
23	163°	23.7'	N001°	18.4'

Hr	GHA		DEC	
		March 24		
00	178°	23.9'	N001°	19.4'
01	193°	24.1'	N001°	20.4'
02	208°	24.3'	N001°	21.4'
03	223°	24.4'	N001°	22.4'
04	238°	24.6'	N001°	23.4'
05	253°	24.8'	N001°	24.3'
06	268°	25.0'	N001°	25.3'
07	283°	25.2'	N001°	26.3'
08	298°	25.4'	N001°	27.3'
09	313°	25.6'	N001°	28.3'
10	328°	25.8'	N001°	29.3'
11	343°	26.0'	N001°	30.2'
12	358°	26.1'	N001°	31.2'
13	013°	26.3'	N001°	32.2'
14	028°	26.5'	N001°	33.2'
15	043°	26.7'	N001°	34.2'
16	058°	26.9'	N001°	35.2'
17	073°	27.1'	N001°	36.2'
18	088°	27.3'	N001°	37.1'
19	103°	27.5'	N001°	38.1'
20	118°	27.6'	N001°	39.1'
21	133°	27.8'	N001°	40.1'
22	148°	28.0'	N001°	41.1'
23	163°	28.2'	N001°	42.1'
		March 25		
00	178°	28.4'	N001°	43.0'
01	193°	28.6'	N001°	44.0'
02	208°	28.8'	N001°	45.0'
03	223°	29.0'	N001°	46.0'
04	238°	29.1'	N001°	47.0'
05	253°	29.3'	N001°	48.0'
06	268°	29.5'	N001°	48.9'
07	283°	29.7'	N001°	49.9'
08	298°	29.9'	N001°	50.9'
09	313°	30.1'	N001°	51.9'
10	328°	30.3'	N001°	52.9'
11	343°	30.5'	N001°	53.8'
12	358°	30.7'	N001°	54.8'
13	013°	30.8'	N001°	55.8'
14	028°	31.0'	N001°	56.8'
15	043°	31.2'	N001°	57.8'
16	058°	31.4'	N001°	58.8'
17	073°	31.6'	N001°	59.7'
18	088°	31.8'	N002°	00.7'
19	103°	32.0'	N002°	01.7'
20	118°	32.2'	N002°	02.7'
21	133°	32.4'	N002°	03.7'
22	148°	32.5'	N002°	04.7'
23	163°	32.7'	N002°	05.6'
		March 26		
00	178°	32.9'	N002°	06.6'
01	193°	33.1'	N002°	07.6'
02	208°	33.3'	N002°	08.6'
03	223°	33.5'	N002°	09.6'
04	238°	33.7'	N002°	10.5'
05	253°	33.9'	N002°	11.5'
06	268°	34.0'	N002°	12.5'
07	283°	34.2'	N002°	13.5'
08	298°	34.4'	N002°	14.5'
09	313°	34.6'	N002°	15.4'
10	328°	34.8'	N002°	16.4'
11	343°	35.0'	N002°	17.4'
12	358°	35.2'	N002°	18.4'
13	013°	35.4'	N002°	19.4'
14	028°	35.6'	N002°	20.4'
15	043°	35.7'	N002°	21.3'
16	058°	35.9'	N002°	22.3'
17	073°	36.1'	N002°	23.3'
18	088°	36.3'	N002°	24.3'
19	103°	36.5'	N002°	25.3'
20	118°	36.7'	N002°	26.2'
21	133°	36.9'	N002°	27.2'
22	148°	37.1'	N002°	28.2'
23	163°	37.3'	N002°	29.2'
		March 27		
00	178°	37.4'	N002°	30.2'
01	193°	37.6'	N002°	31.1'
02	208°	37.8'	N002°	32.1'
03	223°	38.0'	N002°	33.1'
04	238°	38.2'	N002°	34.1'
05	253°	38.4'	N002°	35.0'
06	268°	38.6'	N002°	36.0'
07	283°	38.8'	N002°	37.0'
08	298°	39.0'	N002°	38.0'
09	313°	39.1'	N002°	39.0'
10	328°	39.3'	N002°	39.9'
11	343°	39.5'	N002°	40.9'
12	358°	39.7'	N002°	41.9'
13	013°	39.9'	N002°	42.9'
14	028°	40.1'	N002°	43.9'
15	043°	40.3'	N002°	44.8'
16	058°	40.5'	N002°	45.8'
17	073°	40.6'	N002°	46.8'
18	088°	40.8'	N002°	47.8'
19	103°	41.0'	N002°	48.7'
20	118°	41.2'	N002°	49.7'
21	133°	41.4'	N002°	50.7'
22	148°	41.6'	N002°	51.7'
23	163°	41.8'	N002°	52.7'
		March 28		
00	178°	42.0'	N002°	53.6'
01	193°	42.2'	N002°	54.6'
02	208°	42.3'	N002°	55.6'
03	223°	42.5'	N002°	56.6'
04	238°	42.7'	N002°	57.5'
05	253°	42.9'	N002°	58.5'
06	268°	43.1'	N002°	59.5'
07	283°	43.3'	N003°	00.5'
08	298°	43.5'	N003°	01.5'
09	313°	43.7'	N003°	02.4'
10	328°	43.8'	N003°	03.4'
11	343°	44.0'	N003°	04.4'
12	358°	44.2'	N003°	05.4'
13	013°	44.4'	N003°	06.3'
14	028°	44.6'	N003°	07.3'
15	043°	44.8'	N003°	08.3'
16	058°	45.0'	N003°	09.3'
17	073°	45.2'	N003°	10.2'
18	088°	45.4'	N003°	11.2'
19	103°	45.5'	N003°	12.2'
20	118°	45.7'	N003°	13.2'
21	133°	45.9'	N003°	14.1'
22	148°	46.1'	N003°	15.1'
23	163°	46.3'	N003°	16.1'
		March 29		
00	178°	46.5'	N003°	17.1'
01	193°	46.7'	N003°	18.0'
02	208°	46.9'	N003°	19.0'
03	223°	47.0'	N003°	20.0'
04	238°	47.2'	N003°	21.0'
05	253°	47.4'	N003°	21.9'
06	268°	47.6'	N003°	22.9'
07	283°	47.8'	N003°	23.9'
08	298°	48.0'	N003°	24.9'
09	313°	48.2'	N003°	25.8'
10	328°	48.4'	N003°	26.8'
11	343°	48.6'	N003°	27.8'
12	358°	48.7'	N003°	28.8'
13	013°	48.9'	N003°	29.7'
14	028°	49.1'	N003°	30.7'
15	043°	49.3'	N003°	31.7'
16	058°	49.5'	N003°	32.6'
17	073°	49.7'	N003°	33.6'
18	088°	49.9'	N003°	34.6'
19	103°	50.1'	N003°	35.6'
20	118°	50.2'	N003°	36.5'
21	133°	50.4'	N003°	37.5'
22	148°	50.6'	N003°	38.5'
23	163°	50.8'	N003°	39.5'
		March 30		
00	178°	51.0'	N003°	40.4'
01	193°	51.2'	N003°	41.4'
02	208°	51.4'	N003°	42.4'
03	223°	51.6'	N003°	43.3'
04	238°	51.7'	N003°	44.3'
05	253°	51.9'	N003°	45.3'
06	268°	52.1'	N003°	46.3'
07	283°	52.3'	N003°	47.2'
08	298°	52.5'	N003°	48.2'
09	313°	52.7'	N003°	49.2'
10	328°	52.9'	N003°	50.1'
11	343°	53.0'	N003°	51.1'
12	358°	53.2'	N003°	52.1'
13	013°	53.4'	N003°	53.1'
14	028°	53.6'	N003°	54.0'
15	043°	53.8'	N003°	55.0'
16	058°	54.0'	N003°	56.0'
17	073°	54.2'	N003°	56.9'
18	088°	54.4'	N003°	57.9'
19	103°	54.5'	N003°	58.9'

Hr	GHA		DEC	
20	118°	54.7'	N003°	59.8'
21	133°	54.9'	N004°	00.8'
22	148°	55.1'	N004°	01.8'
23	163°	55.3'	N004°	02.8'
March 31				
00	178°	55.5'	N004°	03.7'
01	193°	55.7'	N004°	04.7'
02	208°	55.9'	N004°	05.7'
03	223°	56.0'	N004°	06.6'
04	238°	56.2'	N004°	07.6'
05	253°	56.4'	N004°	08.6'
06	268°	56.6'	N004°	09.5'
07	283°	56.8'	N004°	10.5'
08	298°	57.0'	N004°	11.5'
09	313°	57.2'	N004°	12.4'
10	328°	57.3'	N004°	13.4'
11	343°	57.5'	N004°	14.4'
12	358°	57.7'	N004°	15.3'
13	013°	57.9'	N004°	16.3'
14	028°	58.1'	N004°	17.3'
15	043°	58.3'	N004°	18.2'
16	058°	58.5'	N004°	19.2'
17	073°	58.6'	N004°	20.2'
18	088°	58.8'	N004°	21.1'
19	103°	59.0'	N004°	22.1'
20	118°	59.2'	N004°	23.1'
21	133°	59.4'	N004°	24.0'
22	148°	59.6'	N004°	25.0'
23	163°	59.8'	N004°	26.0'
April 1				
00	178°	59.9'	N004°	26.9'
01	194°	00.1'	N004°	27.9'
02	209°	00.3'	N004°	28.9'
03	224°	00.5'	N004°	29.8'
04	239°	00.7'	N004°	30.8'
05	254°	00.9'	N004°	31.8'
06	269°	01.1'	N004°	32.7'
07	284°	01.2'	N004°	33.7'
08	299°	01.4'	N004°	34.7'
09	314°	01.6'	N004°	35.6'
10	329°	01.8'	N004°	36.6'
11	344°	02.0'	N004°	37.6'
12	359°	02.2'	N004°	38.5'
13	014°	02.4'	N004°	39.5'
14	029°	02.5'	N004°	40.5'
15	044°	02.7'	N004°	41.4'
16	059°	02.9'	N004°	42.4'
17	074°	03.1'	N004°	43.3'
18	089°	03.3'	N004°	44.3'
19	104°	03.5'	N004°	45.3'
20	119°	03.7'	N004°	46.2'
21	134°	03.8'	N004°	47.2'
22	149°	04.0'	N004°	48.2'
23	164°	04.2'	N004°	49.1'
April 2				
00	179°	04.4'	N004°	50.1'
01	194°	04.6'	N004°	51.0'

Hr	GHA		DEC	
02	209°	04.8'	N004°	52.0'
03	224°	04.9'	N004°	53.0'
04	239°	05.1'	N004°	53.9'
05	254°	05.3'	N004°	54.9'
06	269°	05.5'	N004°	55.9'
07	284°	05.7'	N004°	56.8'
08	299°	05.9'	N004°	57.8'
09	314°	06.0'	N004°	58.7'
10	329°	06.2'	N004°	59.7'
11	344°	06.4'	N005°	00.7'
12	359°	06.6'	N005°	01.6'
13	014°	06.8'	N005°	02.6'
14	029°	07.0'	N005°	03.5'
15	044°	07.2'	N005°	04.5'
16	059°	07.3'	N005°	05.5'
17	074°	07.5'	N005°	06.4'
18	089°	07.7'	N005°	07.4'
19	104°	07.9'	N005°	08.3'
20	119°	08.1'	N005°	09.3'
21	134°	08.3'	N005°	10.3'
22	149°	08.4'	N005°	11.2'
23	164°	08.6'	N005°	12.2'
April 3				
00	179°	08.8'	N005°	13.1'
01	194°	09.0'	N005°	14.1'
02	209°	09.2'	N005°	15.1'
03	224°	09.4'	N005°	16.0'
04	239°	09.5'	N005°	17.0'
05	254°	09.7'	N005°	17.9'
06	269°	09.9'	N005°	18.9'
07	284°	10.1'	N005°	19.8'
08	299°	10.3'	N005°	20.8'
09	314°	10.4'	N005°	21.8'
10	329°	10.6'	N005°	22.7'
11	344°	10.8'	N005°	23.7'
12	359°	11.0'	N005°	24.6'
13	014°	11.2'	N005°	25.6'
14	029°	11.4'	N005°	26.5'
15	044°	11.5'	N005°	27.5'
16	059°	11.7'	N005°	28.5'
17	074°	11.9'	N005°	29.4'
18	089°	12.1'	N005°	30.4'
19	104°	12.3'	N005°	31.3'
20	119°	12.5'	N005°	32.3'
21	134°	12.6'	N005°	33.2'
22	149°	12.8'	N005°	34.2'
23	164°	13.0'	N005°	35.1'
April 4				
00	179°	13.2'	N005°	36.1'
01	194°	13.4'	N005°	37.1'
02	209°	13.5'	N005°	38.0'
03	224°	13.7'	N005°	39.0'
04	239°	13.9'	N005°	39.9'
05	254°	14.1'	N005°	40.9'
06	269°	14.3'	N005°	41.8'
07	284°	14.4'	N005°	42.8'
08	299°	14.6'	N005°	43.7'

Hr	GHA		DEC	
09	314°	14.8'	N005°	44.7'
10	329°	15.0'	N005°	45.6'
11	344°	15.2'	N005°	46.6'
12	359°	15.4'	N005°	47.5'
13	014°	15.5'	N005°	48.5'
14	029°	15.7'	N005°	49.4'
15	044°	15.9'	N005°	50.4'
16	059°	16.1'	N005°	51.4'
17	074°	16.3'	N005°	52.3'
18	089°	16.4'	N005°	53.3'
19	104°	16.6'	N005°	54.2'
20	119°	16.8'	N005°	55.2'
21	134°	17.0'	N005°	56.1'
22	149°	17.2'	N005°	57.1'
23	164°	17.3'	N005°	58.0'
April 5				
00	179°	17.5'	N005°	59.0'
01	194°	17.7'	N005°	59.9'
02	209°	17.9'	N006°	00.9'
03	224°	18.1'	N006°	01.8'
04	239°	18.2'	N006°	02.8'
05	254°	18.4'	N006°	03.7'
06	269°	18.6'	N006°	04.7'
07	284°	18.8'	N006°	05.6'
08	299°	19.0'	N006°	06.6'
09	314°	19.1'	N006°	07.5'
10	329°	19.3'	N006°	08.5'
11	344°	19.5'	N006°	09.4'
12	359°	19.7'	N006°	10.4'
13	014°	19.8'	N006°	11.3'
14	029°	20.0'	N006°	12.3'
15	044°	20.2'	N006°	13.2'
16	059°	20.4'	N006°	14.1'
17	074°	20.6'	N006°	15.1'
18	089°	20.7'	N006°	16.0'
19	104°	20.9'	N006°	17.0'
20	119°	21.1'	N006°	17.9'
21	134°	21.3'	N006°	18.9'
22	149°	21.5'	N006°	19.8'
23	164°	21.6'	N006°	20.8'
April 6				
00	179°	21.8'	N006°	21.7'
01	194°	22.0'	N006°	22.7'
02	209°	22.2'	N006°	23.6'
03	224°	22.3'	N006°	24.6'
04	239°	22.5'	N006°	25.5'
05	254°	22.7'	N006°	26.4'
06	269°	22.9'	N006°	27.4'
07	284°	23.0'	N006°	28.3'
08	299°	23.2'	N006°	29.3'
09	314°	23.4'	N006°	30.2'
10	329°	23.6'	N006°	31.2'
11	344°	23.8'	N006°	32.1'
12	359°	23.9'	N006°	33.1'
13	014°	24.1'	N006°	34.0'
14	029°	24.3'	N006°	34.9'
15	044°	24.5'	N006°	35.9'

Hr	GHA		DEC		Hr	GHA		DEC		Hr	GHA		DEC	
16	059°	24.6'	N006°	36.8'	23	164°	34.2'	N007°	28.4'	05	254°	43.3'	N008°	18.4'
17	074°	24.8'	N006°	37.8'		April 9				06	269°	43.4'	N008°	19.3'
18	089°	25.0'	N006°	38.7'	00	179°	34.4'	N007°	29.3'	07	284°	43.6'	N008°	20.2'
19	104°	25.2'	N006°	39.7'	01	194°	34.5'	N007°	30.2'	08	299°	43.8'	N008°	21.1'
20	119°	25.3'	N006°	40.6'	02	209°	34.7'	N007°	31.2'	09	314°	43.9'	N008°	22.0'
21	134°	25.5'	N006°	41.5'	03	224°	34.9'	N007°	32.1'	10	329°	44.1'	N008°	23.0'
22	149°	25.7'	N006°	42.5'	04	239°	35.0'	N007°	33.0'	11	344°	44.2'	N008°	23.9'
23	164°	25.9'	N006°	43.4'	05	254°	35.2'	N007°	34.0'	12	359°	44.4'	N008°	24.8'
	April 7				06	269°	35.4'	N007°	34.9'	13	014°	44.6'	N008°	25.7'
00	179°	26.0'	N006°	44.4'	07	284°	35.6'	N007°	35.8'	14	029°	44.7'	N008°	26.6'
01	194°	26.2'	N006°	45.3'	08	299°	35.7'	N007°	36.8'	15	044°	44.9'	N008°	27.5'
02	209°	26.4'	N006°	46.3'	09	314°	35.9'	N007°	37.7'	16	059°	45.1'	N008°	28.5'
03	224°	26.6'	N006°	47.2'	10	329°	36.1'	N007°	38.6'	17	074°	45.2'	N008°	29.4'
04	239°	26.8'	N006°	48.1'	11	344°	36.2'	N007°	39.5'	18	089°	45.4'	N008°	30.3'
05	254°	26.9'	N006°	49.1'	12	359°	36.4'	N007°	40.5'	19	104°	45.6'	N008°	31.2'
06	269°	27.1'	N006°	50.0'	13	014°	36.6'	N007°	41.4'	20	119°	45.7'	N008°	32.1'
07	284°	27.3'	N006°	51.0'	14	029°	36.7'	N007°	42.3'	21	134°	45.9'	N008°	33.0'
08	299°	27.5'	N006°	51.9'	15	044°	36.9'	N007°	43.3'	22	149°	46.0'	N008°	33.9'
09	314°	27.6'	N006°	52.8'	16	059°	37.1'	N007°	44.2'	23	164°	46.2'	N008°	34.9'
10	329°	27.8'	N006°	53.8'	17	074°	37.3'	N007°	45.1'		April 12			
11	344°	28.0'	N006°	54.7'	18	089°	37.4'	N007°	46.0'	00	179°	46.4'	N008°	35.8'
12	359°	28.1'	N006°	55.7'	19	104°	37.6'	N007°	47.0'	01	194°	46.5'	N008°	36.7'
13	014°	28.3'	N006°	56.6'	20	119°	37.8'	N007°	47.9'	02	209°	46.7'	N008°	37.6'
14	029°	28.5'	N006°	57.5'	21	134°	37.9'	N007°	48.8'	03	224°	46.9'	N008°	38.5'
15	044°	28.7'	N006°	58.5'	22	149°	38.1'	N007°	49.8'	04	239°	47.0'	N008°	39.4'
16	059°	28.8'	N006°	59.4'	23	164°	38.3'	N007°	50.7'	05	254°	47.2'	N008°	40.3'
17	074°	29.0'	N007°	00.3'		April 10				06	269°	47.3'	N008°	41.3'
18	089°	29.2'	N007°	01.3'	00	179°	38.4'	N007°	51.6'	07	284°	47.5'	N008°	42.2'
19	104°	29.4'	N007°	02.2'	01	194°	38.6'	N007°	52.5'	08	299°	47.7'	N008°	43.1'
20	119°	29.5'	N007°	03.2'	02	209°	38.8'	N007°	53.5'	09	314°	47.8'	N008°	44.0'
21	134°	29.7'	N007°	04.1'	03	224°	38.9'	N007°	54.4'	10	329°	48.0'	N008°	44.9'
22	149°	29.9'	N007°	05.0'	04	239°	39.1'	N007°	55.3'	11	344°	48.1'	N008°	45.8'
23	164°	30.1'	N007°	06.0'	05	254°	39.3'	N007°	56.2'	12	359°	48.3'	N008°	46.7'
	April 8				06	269°	39.4'	N007°	57.2'	13	014°	48.5'	N008°	47.6'
00	179°	30.2'	N007°	06.9'	07	284°	39.6'	N007°	58.1'	14	029°	48.6'	N008°	48.6'
01	194°	30.4'	N007°	07.8'	08	299°	39.8'	N007°	59.0'	15	044°	48.8'	N008°	49.5'
02	209°	30.6'	N007°	08.8'	09	314°	39.9'	N007°	59.9'	16	059°	48.9'	N008°	50.4'
03	224°	30.8'	N007°	09.7'	10	329°	40.1'	N008°	00.9'	17	074°	49.1'	N008°	51.3'
04	239°	30.9'	N007°	10.6'	11	344°	40.3'	N008°	01.8'	18	089°	49.3'	N008°	52.2'
05	254°	31.1'	N007°	11.6'	12	359°	40.4'	N008°	02.7'	19	104°	49.4'	N008°	53.1'
06	269°	31.3'	N007°	12.5'	13	014°	40.6'	N008°	03.6'	20	119°	49.6'	N008°	54.0'
07	284°	31.4'	N007°	13.5'	14	029°	40.8'	N008°	04.5'	21	134°	49.7'	N008°	54.9'
08	299°	31.6'	N007°	14.4'	15	044°	40.9'	N008°	05.5'	22	149°	49.9'	N008°	55.8'
09	314°	31.8'	N007°	15.3'	16	059°	41.1'	N008°	06.4'	23	164°	50.1'	N008°	56.7'
10	329°	32.0'	N007°	16.3'	17	074°	41.3'	N008°	07.3'		April 13			
11	344°	32.1'	N007°	17.2'	18	089°	41.4'	N008°	08.2'	00	179°	50.2'	N008°	57.7'
12	359°	32.3'	N007°	18.1'	19	104°	41.6'	N008°	09.2'	01	194°	50.4'	N008°	58.6'
13	014°	32.5'	N007°	19.1'	20	119°	41.8'	N008°	10.1'	02	209°	50.5'	N008°	59.5'
14	029°	32.7'	N007°	20.0'	21	134°	41.9'	N008°	11.0'	03	224°	50.7'	N009°	00.4'
15	044°	32.8'	N007°	20.9'	22	149°	42.1'	N008°	11.9'	04	239°	50.9'	N009°	01.3'
16	059°	33.0'	N007°	21.9'	23	164°	42.3'	N008°	12.8'	05	254°	51.0'	N009°	02.2'
17	074°	33.2'	N007°	22.8'		April 11				06	269°	51.2'	N009°	03.1'
18	089°	33.3'	N007°	23.7'	00	179°	42.4'	N008°	13.8'	07	284°	51.3'	N009°	04.0'
19	104°	33.5'	N007°	24.7'	01	194°	42.6'	N008°	14.7'	08	299°	51.5'	N009°	04.9'
20	119°	33.7'	N007°	25.6'	02	209°	42.8'	N008°	15.6'	09	314°	51.6'	N009°	05.8'
21	134°	33.9'	N007°	26.5'	03	224°	42.9'	N008°	16.5'	10	329°	51.8'	N009°	06.7'
22	149°	34.0'	N007°	27.5'	04	239°	43.1'	N008°	17.4'	11	344°	52.0'	N009°	07.6'

Hr	GHA		DEC		Hr	GHA		DEC		Hr	GHA		DEC	
12	359°	52.1'	N009°	08.5'	19	105°	00.5'	N009°	57.9'	01	195°	08.4'	N010°	45.5'
13	014°	52.3'	N009°	09.4'	20	120°	00.7'	N009°	58.8'	02	210°	08.5'	N010°	46.4'
14	029°	52.4'	N009°	10.3'	21	135°	00.8'	N009°	59.7'	03	225°	08.6'	N010°	47.3'
15	044°	52.6'	N009°	11.2'	22	150°	01.0'	N010°	00.6'	04	240°	08.8'	N010°	48.2'
16	059°	52.7'	N009°	12.1'	23	165°	01.1'	N010°	01.5'	05	255°	08.9'	N010°	49.0'
17	074°	52.9'	N009°	13.1'	April 16					06	270°	09.1'	N010°	49.9'
18	089°	53.1'	N009°	14.0'	00	180°	01.3'	N010°	02.4'	07	285°	09.2'	N010°	50.8'
19	104°	53.2'	N009°	14.9'	01	195°	01.4'	N010°	03.2'	08	300°	09.3'	N010°	51.6'
20	119°	53.4'	N009°	15.8'	02	210°	01.6'	N010°	04.1'	09	315°	09.5'	N010°	52.5'
21	134°	53.5'	N009°	16.7'	03	225°	01.7'	N010°	05.0'	10	330°	09.6'	N010°	53.4'
22	149°	53.7'	N009°	17.6'	04	240°	01.9'	N010°	05.9'	11	345°	09.8'	N010°	54.3'
23	164°	53.8'	N009°	18.5'	05	255°	02.0'	N010°	06.8'	12	000°	09.9'	N010°	55.1'
April 14					06	270°	02.2'	N010°	07.7'	13	015°	10.0'	N010°	56.0'
00	179°	54.0'	N009°	19.4'	07	285°	02.3'	N010°	08.6'	14	030°	10.2'	N010°	56.9'
01	194°	54.2'	N009°	20.3'	08	300°	02.5'	N010°	09.5'	15	045°	10.3'	N010°	57.7'
02	209°	54.3'	N009°	21.2'	09	315°	02.6'	N010°	10.3'	16	060°	10.4'	N010°	58.6'
03	224°	54.5'	N009°	22.1'	10	330°	02.8'	N010°	11.2'	17	075°	10.6'	N010°	59.5'
04	239°	54.6'	N009°	23.0'	11	345°	02.9'	N010°	12.1'	18	090°	10.7'	N011°	00.4'
05	254°	54.8'	N009°	23.9'	12	000°	03.1'	N010°	13.0'	19	105°	10.9'	N011°	01.2'
06	269°	54.9'	N009°	24.8'	13	015°	03.2'	N010°	13.9'	20	120°	11.0'	N011°	02.1'
07	284°	55.1'	N009°	25.7'	14	030°	03.4'	N010°	14.8'	21	135°	11.1'	N011°	03.0'
08	299°	55.2'	N009°	26.6'	15	045°	03.5'	N010°	15.6'	22	150°	11.3'	N011°	03.8'
09	314°	55.4'	N009°	27.5'	16	060°	03.6'	N010°	16.5'	23	165°	11.4'	N011°	04.7'
10	329°	55.5'	N009°	28.4'	17	075°	03.8'	N010°	17.4'	April 19				
11	344°	55.7'	N009°	29.3'	18	090°	03.9'	N010°	18.3'	00	180°	11.5'	N011°	05.6'
12	359°	55.9'	N009°	30.2'	19	105°	04.1'	N010°	19.2'	01	195°	11.7'	N011°	06.4'
13	014°	56.0'	N009°	31.1'	20	120°	04.2'	N010°	20.1'	02	210°	11.8'	N011°	07.3'
14	029°	56.2'	N009°	32.0'	21	135°	04.4'	N010°	20.9'	03	225°	12.0'	N011°	08.2'
15	044°	56.3'	N009°	32.9'	22	150°	04.5'	N010°	21.8'	04	240°	12.1'	N011°	09.0'
16	059°	56.5'	N009°	33.8'	23	165°	04.7'	N010°	22.7'	05	255°	12.2'	N011°	09.9'
17	074°	56.6'	N009°	34.7'	April 17					06	270°	12.4'	N011°	10.8'
18	089°	56.8'	N009°	35.6'	00	180°	04.8'	N010°	23.6'	07	285°	12.5'	N011°	11.6'
19	104°	56.9'	N009°	36.5'	01	195°	04.9'	N010°	24.5'	08	300°	12.6'	N011°	12.5'
20	119°	57.1'	N009°	37.4'	02	210°	05.1'	N010°	25.4'	09	315°	12.8'	N011°	13.3'
21	134°	57.2'	N009°	38.3'	03	225°	05.2'	N010°	26.2'	10	330°	12.9'	N011°	14.2'
22	149°	57.4'	N009°	39.2'	04	240°	05.4'	N010°	27.1'	11	345°	13.0'	N011°	15.1'
23	164°	57.5'	N009°	40.0'	05	255°	05.5'	N010°	28.0'	12	000°	13.2'	N011°	15.9'
April 15					06	270°	05.7'	N010°	28.9'	13	015°	13.3'	N011°	16.8'
00	179°	57.7'	N009°	40.9'	07	285°	05.8'	N010°	29.8'	14	030°	13.4'	N011°	17.7'
01	194°	57.8'	N009°	41.8'	08	300°	06.0'	N010°	30.6'	15	045°	13.6'	N011°	18.5'
02	209°	58.0'	N009°	42.7'	09	315°	06.1'	N010°	31.5'	16	060°	13.7'	N011°	19.4'
03	224°	58.1'	N009°	43.6'	10	330°	06.2'	N010°	32.4'	17	075°	13.8'	N011°	20.2'
04	239°	58.3'	N009°	44.5'	11	345°	06.4'	N010°	33.3'	18	090°	14.0'	N011°	21.1'
05	254°	58.4'	N009°	45.4'	12	000°	06.5'	N010°	34.2'	19	105°	14.1'	N011°	22.0'
06	269°	58.6'	N009°	46.3'	13	015°	06.7'	N010°	35.0'	20	120°	14.2'	N011°	22.8'
07	284°	58.7'	N009°	47.2'	14	030°	06.8'	N010°	35.9'	21	135°	14.4'	N011°	23.7'
08	299°	58.9'	N009°	48.1'	15	045°	07.0'	N010°	36.8'	22	150°	14.5'	N011°	24.5'
09	314°	59.0'	N009°	49.0'	16	060°	07.1'	N010°	37.7'	23	165°	14.6'	N011°	25.4'
10	329°	59.2'	N009°	49.9'	17	075°	07.2'	N010°	38.5'	April 20				
11	344°	59.3'	N009°	50.8'	18	090°	07.4'	N010°	39.4'	00	180°	14.8'	N011°	26.3'
12	359°	59.5'	N009°	51.7'	19	105°	07.5'	N010°	40.3'	01	195°	14.9'	N011°	27.1'
13	014°	59.7'	N009°	52.6'	20	120°	07.7'	N010°	41.2'	02	210°	15.0'	N011°	28.0'
14	029°	59.8'	N009°	53.5'	21	135°	07.9'	N010°	42.0'	03	225°	15.2'	N011°	28.8'
15	044°	59.9'	N009°	54.3'	22	150°	07.9'	N010°	42.9'	04	240°	15.3'	N011°	29.7'
16	060°	00.1'	N009°	55.2'	23	165°	08.1'	N010°	43.8'	05	255°	15.4'	N011°	30.6'
17	075°	00.2'	N009°	56.1'	April 18					06	270°	15.6'	N011°	31.4'
18	090°	00.4'	N009°	57.0'	00	180°	08.2'	N010°	44.7'	07	285°	15.7'	N011°	32.3'

Hr	GHA		DEC	
08	300°	15.8'	N011°	33.1'
09	315°	15.9'	N011°	34.0'
10	330°	16.1'	N011°	34.8'
11	345°	16.2'	N011°	35.7'
12	000°	16.3'	N011°	36.6'
13	015°	16.5'	N011°	37.4'
14	030°	16.6'	N011°	38.3'
15	045°	16.7'	N011°	39.1'
16	060°	16.9'	N011°	40.0'
17	075°	17.0'	N011°	40.8'
18	090°	17.1'	N011°	41.7'
19	105°	17.2'	N011°	42.5'
20	120°	17.4'	N011°	43.4'
21	135°	17.5'	N011°	44.2'
22	150°	17.6'	N011°	45.1'
23	165°	17.7'	N011°	45.9'
April 21				
00	180°	17.9'	N011°	46.8'
01	195°	18.0'	N011°	47.6'
02	210°	18.1'	N011°	48.5'
03	225°	18.3'	N011°	49.3'
04	240°	18.4'	N011°	50.2'
05	255°	18.5'	N011°	51.0'
06	270°	18.6'	N011°	51.9'
07	285°	18.8'	N011°	52.7'
08	300°	18.9'	N011°	53.6'
09	315°	19.0'	N011°	54.4'
10	330°	19.1'	N011°	55.3'
11	345°	19.3'	N011°	56.1'
12	000°	19.4'	N011°	57.0'
13	015°	19.5'	N011°	57.8'
14	030°	19.6'	N011°	58.7'
15	045°	19.8'	N011°	59.5'
16	060°	19.9'	N012°	00.4'
17	075°	20.0'	N012°	01.2'
18	090°	20.1'	N012°	02.1'
19	105°	20.3'	N012°	02.9'
20	120°	20.4'	N012°	03.7'
21	135°	20.5'	N012°	04.6'
22	150°	20.6'	N012°	05.4'
23	165°	20.8'	N012°	06.3'
April 22				
00	180°	20.9'	N012°	07.1'
01	195°	21.0'	N012°	08.0'
02	210°	21.1'	N012°	08.8'
03	225°	21.3'	N012°	09.6'
04	240°	21.4'	N012°	10.5'
05	255°	21.5'	N012°	11.3'
06	270°	21.6'	N012°	12.2'
07	285°	21.7'	N012°	13.0'
08	300°	21.9'	N012°	13.8'
09	315°	22.0'	N012°	14.7'
10	330°	22.1'	N012°	15.5'
11	345°	22.2'	N012°	16.4'
12	000°	22.3'	N012°	17.2'
13	015°	22.5'	N012°	18.0'
14	030°	22.6'	N012°	18.9'

Hr	GHA		DEC	
15	045°	22.7'	N012°	19.7'
16	060°	22.8'	N012°	20.6'
17	075°	22.9'	N012°	21.4'
18	090°	23.1'	N012°	22.2'
19	105°	23.2'	N012°	23.1'
20	120°	23.3'	N012°	23.9'
21	135°	23.4'	N012°	24.7'
22	150°	23.5'	N012°	25.6'
23	165°	23.7'	N012°	26.4'
April 23				
00	180°	23.8'	N012°	27.2'
01	195°	23.9'	N012°	28.1'
02	210°	24.0'	N012°	28.9'
03	225°	24.1'	N012°	29.7'
04	240°	24.2'	N012°	30.6'
05	255°	24.4'	N012°	31.4'
06	270°	24.5'	N012°	32.2'
07	285°	24.6'	N012°	33.1'
08	300°	24.7'	N012°	33.9'
09	315°	24.8'	N012°	34.7'
10	330°	24.9'	N012°	35.6'
11	345°	25.1'	N012°	36.4'
12	000°	25.2'	N012°	37.2'
13	015°	25.3'	N012°	38.1'
14	030°	25.4'	N012°	38.9'
15	045°	25.5'	N012°	39.7'
16	060°	25.6'	N012°	40.5'
17	075°	25.8'	N012°	41.4'
18	090°	25.9'	N012°	42.2'
19	105°	26.0'	N012°	43.0'
20	120°	26.1'	N012°	43.9'
21	135°	26.2'	N012°	44.7'
22	150°	26.3'	N012°	45.5'
23	165°	26.4'	N012°	46.3'
April 24				
00	180°	26.6'	N012°	47.2'
01	195°	26.7'	N012°	48.0'
02	210°	26.8'	N012°	48.8'
03	225°	26.9'	N012°	49.6'
04	240°	27.0'	N012°	50.5'
05	255°	27.1'	N012°	51.3'
06	270°	27.2'	N012°	52.1'
07	285°	27.3'	N012°	52.9'
08	300°	27.5'	N012°	53.8'
09	315°	27.6'	N012°	54.6'
10	330°	27.7'	N012°	55.4'
11	345°	27.8'	N012°	56.2'
12	000°	27.9'	N012°	57.0'
13	015°	28.0'	N012°	57.9'
14	030°	28.1'	N012°	58.7'
15	045°	28.2'	N012°	59.5'
16	060°	28.3'	N013°	00.3'
17	075°	28.5'	N013°	01.2'
18	090°	28.6'	N013°	02.0'
19	105°	28.7'	N013°	02.8'
20	120°	28.8'	N013°	03.6'
21	135°	28.9'	N013°	04.4'

Hr	GHA		DEC	
22	150°	29.0'	N013°	05.2'
23	165°	29.1'	N013°	06.1'
April 25				
00	180°	29.2'	N013°	06.9'
01	195°	29.3'	N013°	07.7'
02	210°	29.4'	N013°	08.5'
03	225°	29.5'	N013°	09.3'
04	240°	29.7'	N013°	10.1'
05	255°	29.8'	N013°	11.0'
06	270°	29.9'	N013°	11.8'
07	285°	30.0'	N013°	12.6'
08	300°	30.1'	N013°	13.4'
09	315°	30.2'	N013°	14.2'
10	330°	30.3'	N013°	15.0'
11	345°	30.4'	N013°	15.8'
12	000°	30.5'	N013°	16.7'
13	015°	30.6'	N013°	17.5'
14	030°	30.7'	N013°	18.3'
15	045°	30.8'	N013°	19.1'
16	060°	30.9'	N013°	19.9'
17	075°	31.0'	N013°	20.7'
18	090°	31.1'	N013°	21.5'
19	105°	31.2'	N013°	22.3'
20	120°	31.3'	N013°	23.1'
21	135°	31.5'	N013°	24.0'
22	150°	31.6'	N013°	24.8'
23	165°	31.7'	N013°	25.6'
April 26				
00	180°	31.8'	N013°	26.4'
01	195°	31.9'	N013°	27.2'
02	210°	32.0'	N013°	28.0'
03	225°	32.1'	N013°	28.8'
04	240°	32.2'	N013°	29.6'
05	255°	32.3'	N013°	30.4'
06	270°	32.4'	N013°	31.2'
07	285°	32.5'	N013°	32.0'
08	300°	32.6'	N013°	32.8'
09	315°	32.7'	N013°	33.6'
10	330°	32.8'	N013°	34.4'
11	345°	32.9'	N013°	35.2'
12	000°	33.0'	N013°	36.0'
13	015°	33.1'	N013°	36.8'
14	030°	33.2'	N013°	37.6'
15	045°	33.3'	N013°	38.4'
16	060°	33.4'	N013°	39.3'
17	075°	33.5'	N013°	40.1'
18	090°	33.6'	N013°	40.9'
19	105°	33.7'	N013°	41.7'
20	120°	33.8'	N013°	42.5'
21	135°	33.9'	N013°	43.3'
22	150°	34.0'	N013°	44.1'
23	165°	34.1'	N013°	44.9'
April 27				
00	180°	34.2'	N013°	45.7'
01	195°	34.3'	N013°	46.4'
02	210°	34.4'	N013°	47.2'
03	225°	34.5'	N013°	48.0'

Hr	GHA		DEC	
04	240°	34.6'	N013°	48.8'
05	255°	34.7'	N013°	49.6'
06	270°	34.8'	N013°	50.4'
07	285°	34.9'	N013°	51.2'
08	300°	35.0'	N013°	52.0'
09	315°	35.1'	N013°	52.8'
10	330°	35.2'	N013°	53.6'
11	345°	35.2'	N013°	54.4'
12	000°	35.3'	N013°	55.2'
13	015°	35.4'	N013°	56.0'
14	030°	35.5'	N013°	56.8'
15	045°	35.6'	N013°	57.6'
16	060°	35.7'	N013°	58.4'
17	075°	35.8'	N013°	59.2'
18	090°	35.9'	N013°	60.0'
19	105°	36.0'	N014°	00.8'
20	120°	36.1'	N014°	01.5'
21	135°	36.2'	N014°	02.3'
22	150°	36.3'	N014°	03.1'
23	165°	36.4'	N014°	03.9'
April 28				
00	180°	36.5'	N014°	04.7'
01	195°	36.6'	N014°	05.5'
02	210°	36.7'	N014°	06.3'
03	225°	36.8'	N014°	07.1'
04	240°	36.8'	N014°	07.9'
05	255°	36.9'	N014°	08.6'
06	270°	37.0'	N014°	09.4'
07	285°	37.1'	N014°	10.2'
08	300°	37.2'	N014°	11.0'
09	315°	37.3'	N014°	11.8'
10	330°	37.4'	N014°	12.6'
11	345°	37.5'	N014°	13.4'
12	000°	37.6'	N014°	14.1'
13	015°	37.7'	N014°	14.9'
14	030°	37.8'	N014°	15.7'
15	045°	37.8'	N014°	16.5'
16	060°	37.9'	N014°	17.3'
17	075°	38.0'	N014°	18.1'
18	090°	38.1'	N014°	18.8'
19	105°	38.2'	N014°	19.6'
20	120°	38.3'	N014°	20.4'
21	135°	38.4'	N014°	21.2'
22	150°	38.5'	N014°	22.0'
23	165°	38.6'	N014°	22.7'
April 29				
00	180°	38.6'	N014°	23.5'
01	195°	38.7'	N014°	24.3'
02	210°	38.8'	N014°	25.1'
03	225°	38.9'	N014°	25.9'
04	240°	39.0'	N014°	26.6'
05	255°	39.1'	N014°	27.4'
06	270°	39.2'	N014°	28.2'
07	285°	39.3'	N014°	29.0'
08	300°	39.3'	N014°	29.7'
09	315°	39.4'	N014°	30.5'
10	330°	39.5'	N014°	31.3'

Hr	GHA		DEC	
11	345°	39.6'	N014°	32.1'
12	000°	39.7'	N014°	32.8'
13	015°	39.8'	N014°	33.6'
14	030°	39.8'	N014°	34.4'
15	045°	39.9'	N014°	35.2'
16	060°	40.0'	N014°	35.9'
17	075°	40.1'	N014°	36.7'
18	090°	40.2'	N014°	37.5'
19	105°	40.3'	N014°	38.2'
20	120°	40.3'	N014°	39.0'
21	135°	40.4'	N014°	39.8'
22	150°	40.5'	N014°	40.6'
23	165°	40.6'	N014°	41.3'
April 30				
00	180°	40.7'	N014°	42.1'
01	195°	40.7'	N014°	42.9'
02	210°	40.8'	N014°	43.6'
03	225°	40.9'	N014°	44.4'
04	240°	41.0'	N014°	45.2'
05	255°	41.1'	N014°	45.9'
06	270°	41.2'	N014°	46.7'
07	285°	41.2'	N014°	47.5'
08	300°	41.3'	N014°	48.2'
09	315°	41.4'	N014°	49.0'
10	330°	41.5'	N014°	49.8'
11	345°	41.6'	N014°	50.5'
12	000°	41.6'	N014°	51.3'
13	015°	41.7'	N014°	52.1'
14	030°	41.8'	N014°	52.8'
15	045°	41.9'	N014°	53.6'
16	060°	42.0'	N014°	54.3'
17	075°	42.0'	N014°	55.1'
18	090°	42.1'	N014°	55.9'
19	105°	42.2'	N014°	56.6'
20	120°	42.3'	N014°	57.4'
21	135°	42.4'	N014°	58.2'
22	150°	42.4'	N014°	58.9'
23	165°	42.5'	N014°	59.7'
May 1				
00	180°	42.6'	N015°	00.4'
01	195°	42.7'	N015°	01.2'
02	210°	42.7'	N015°	01.9'
03	225°	42.8'	N015°	02.7'
04	240°	42.9'	N015°	03.5'
05	255°	43.0'	N015°	04.2'
06	270°	43.0'	N015°	05.0'
07	285°	43.1'	N015°	05.7'
08	300°	43.2'	N015°	06.5'
09	315°	43.3'	N015°	07.2'
10	330°	43.3'	N015°	08.0'
11	345°	43.4'	N015°	08.8'
12	000°	43.5'	N015°	09.5'
13	015°	43.6'	N015°	10.3'
14	030°	43.6'	N015°	11.0'
15	045°	43.7'	N015°	11.8'
16	060°	43.8'	N015°	12.5'
17	075°	43.9'	N015°	13.3'

Hr	GHA		DEC	
18	090°	43.9'	N015°	14.0'
19	105°	44.0'	N015°	14.8'
20	120°	44.1'	N015°	15.5'
21	135°	44.1'	N015°	16.3'
22	150°	44.2'	N015°	17.0'
23	165°	44.3'	N015°	17.8'
May 2				
00	180°	44.4'	N015°	18.5'
01	195°	44.4'	N015°	19.3'
02	210°	44.5'	N015°	20.0'
03	225°	44.6'	N015°	20.8'
04	240°	44.6'	N015°	21.5'
05	255°	44.7'	N015°	22.3'
06	270°	44.8'	N015°	23.0'
07	285°	44.8'	N015°	23.7'
08	300°	44.9'	N015°	24.5'
09	315°	45.0'	N015°	25.2'
10	330°	45.1'	N015°	26.0'
11	345°	45.1'	N015°	26.7'
12	000°	45.2'	N015°	27.5'
13	015°	45.3'	N015°	28.2'
14	030°	45.3'	N015°	29.0'
15	045°	45.4'	N015°	29.7'
16	060°	45.5'	N015°	30.4'
17	075°	45.5'	N015°	31.2'
18	090°	45.6'	N015°	31.9'
19	105°	45.7'	N015°	32.7'
20	120°	45.7'	N015°	33.4'
21	135°	45.8'	N015°	34.1'
22	150°	45.9'	N015°	34.9'
23	165°	45.9'	N015°	35.6'
May 3				
00	180°	46.0'	N015°	36.4'
01	195°	46.1'	N015°	37.1'
02	210°	46.1'	N015°	37.8'
03	225°	46.2'	N015°	38.6'
04	240°	46.3'	N015°	39.3'
05	255°	46.3'	N015°	40.0'
06	270°	46.4'	N015°	40.8'
07	285°	46.4'	N015°	41.5'
08	300°	46.5'	N015°	42.2'
09	315°	46.6'	N015°	43.0'
10	330°	46.6'	N015°	43.7'
11	345°	46.7'	N015°	44.4'
12	000°	46.8'	N015°	45.2'
13	015°	46.8'	N015°	45.9'
14	030°	46.9'	N015°	46.6'
15	045°	46.9'	N015°	47.4'
16	060°	47.0'	N015°	48.1'
17	075°	47.1'	N015°	48.8'
18	090°	47.1'	N015°	49.6'
19	105°	47.2'	N015°	50.3'
20	120°	47.3'	N015°	51.0'
21	135°	47.3'	N015°	51.7'
22	150°	47.4'	N015°	52.5'
23	165°	47.4'	N015°	53.2'

Hr	GHA		DEC		Hr	GHA		DEC		Hr	GHA		DEC	
May 4					06	270°	50.4'	N016°	32.5'	13	015°	52.5'	N017°	10.4'
00	180°	47.5'	N015°	53.9'	07	285°	50.4'	N016°	33.2'	14	030°	52.6'	N017°	11.0'
01	195°	47.6'	N015°	54.7'	08	300°	50.5'	N016°	33.9'	15	045°	52.6'	N017°	11.7'
02	210°	47.6'	N015°	55.4'	09	315°	50.5'	N016°	34.6'	16	060°	52.6'	N017°	12.4'
03	225°	47.7'	N015°	56.1'	10	330°	50.5'	N016°	35.3'	17	075°	52.7'	N017°	13.1'
04	240°	47.7'	N015°	56.8'	11	345°	50.6'	N016°	36.0'	18	090°	52.7'	N017°	13.7'
05	255°	47.8'	N015°	57.6'	12	000°	50.6'	N016°	36.7'	19	105°	52.7'	N017°	14.4'
06	270°	47.8'	N015°	58.3'	13	015°	50.7'	N016°	37.4'	20	120°	52.8'	N017°	15.1'
07	285°	47.9'	N015°	59.0'	14	030°	50.7'	N016°	38.1'	21	135°	52.8'	N017°	15.7'
08	300°	48.0'	N015°	59.7'	15	045°	50.8'	N016°	38.8'	22	150°	52.8'	N017°	16.4'
09	315°	48.0'	N016°	00.5'	16	060°	50.8'	N016°	39.5'	23	165°	52.9'	N017°	17.1'
10	330°	48.1'	N016°	01.2'	17	075°	50.9'	N016°	40.2'	May 9				
11	345°	48.1'	N016°	01.9'	18	090°	50.9'	N016°	40.9'	00	180°	52.9'	N017°	17.7'
12	000°	48.2'	N016°	02.6'	19	105°	50.9'	N016°	41.6'	01	195°	52.9'	N017°	18.4'
13	015°	48.2'	N016°	03.3'	20	120°	51.0'	N016°	42.3'	02	210°	53.0'	N017°	19.1'
14	030°	48.3'	N016°	04.1'	21	135°	51.0'	N016°	43.0'	03	225°	53.0'	N017°	19.8'
15	045°	48.4'	N016°	04.8'	22	150°	51.1'	N016°	43.7'	04	240°	53.0'	N017°	20.4'
16	060°	48.4'	N016°	05.5'	23	165°	51.1'	N016°	44.4'	05	255°	53.0'	N017°	21.1'
17	075°	48.5'	N016°	06.2'	May 7					06	270°	53.1'	N017°	21.8'
18	090°	48.5'	N016°	06.9'	00	180°	51.2'	N016°	45.1'	07	285°	53.1'	N017°	22.4'
19	105°	48.6'	N016°	07.7'	01	195°	51.2'	N016°	45.7'	08	300°	53.1'	N017°	23.1'
20	120°	48.6'	N016°	08.4'	02	210°	51.2'	N016°	46.4'	09	315°	53.2'	N017°	23.8'
21	135°	48.7'	N016°	09.1'	03	225°	51.3'	N016°	47.1'	10	330°	53.2'	N017°	24.4'
22	150°	48.7'	N016°	09.8'	04	240°	51.3'	N016°	47.8'	11	345°	53.2'	N017°	25.1'
23	165°	48.8'	N016°	10.5'	05	255°	51.4'	N016°	48.5'	12	000°	53.2'	N017°	25.7'
May 5					06	270°	51.4'	N016°	49.2'	13	015°	53.3'	N017°	26.4'
00	180°	48.9'	N016°	11.2'	07	285°	51.4'	N016°	49.9'	14	030°	53.3'	N017°	27.1'
01	195°	48.9'	N016°	12.0'	08	300°	51.5'	N016°	50.6'	15	045°	53.3'	N017°	27.7'
02	210°	49.0'	N016°	12.7'	09	315°	51.5'	N016°	51.3'	16	060°	53.3'	N017°	28.4'
03	225°	49.0'	N016°	13.4'	10	330°	51.6'	N016°	52.0'	17	075°	53.4'	N017°	29.1'
04	240°	49.1'	N016°	14.1'	11	345°	51.6'	N016°	52.6'	18	090°	53.4'	N017°	29.7'
05	255°	49.1'	N016°	14.8'	12	000°	51.6'	N016°	53.3'	19	105°	53.4'	N017°	30.4'
06	270°	49.2'	N016°	15.5'	13	015°	51.7'	N016°	54.0'	20	120°	53.5'	N017°	31.0'
07	285°	49.2'	N016°	16.2'	14	030°	51.7'	N016°	54.7'	21	135°	53.5'	N017°	31.7'
08	300°	49.3'	N016°	17.0'	15	045°	51.8'	N016°	55.4'	22	150°	53.5'	N017°	32.3'
09	315°	49.3'	N016°	17.7'	16	060°	51.8'	N016°	56.1'	23	165°	53.5'	N017°	33.0'
10	330°	49.4'	N016°	18.4'	17	075°	51.8'	N016°	56.8'	May 10				
11	345°	49.4'	N016°	19.1'	18	090°	51.9'	N016°	57.4'	00	180°	53.6'	N017°	33.7'
12	000°	49.5'	N016°	19.8'	19	105°	51.9'	N016°	58.1'	01	195°	53.6'	N017°	34.3'
13	015°	49.5'	N016°	20.5'	20	120°	52.0'	N016°	58.8'	02	210°	53.6'	N017°	35.0'
14	030°	49.6'	N016°	21.2'	21	135°	52.0'	N016°	59.5'	03	225°	53.6'	N017°	35.6'
15	045°	49.6'	N016°	21.9'	22	150°	52.0'	N017°	00.2'	04	240°	53.6'	N017°	36.3'
16	060°	49.7'	N016°	22.6'	23	165°	52.1'	N017°	00.9'	05	255°	53.7'	N017°	36.9'
17	075°	49.7'	N016°	23.3'	May 8					06	270°	53.7'	N017°	37.6'
18	090°	49.8'	N016°	24.0'	00	180°	52.1'	N017°	01.5'	07	285°	53.7'	N017°	38.3'
19	105°	49.8'	N016°	24.8'	01	195°	52.1'	N017°	02.2'	08	300°	53.7'	N017°	38.9'
20	120°	49.9'	N016°	25.5'	02	210°	52.2'	N017°	02.9'	09	315°	53.8'	N017°	39.6'
21	135°	49.9'	N016°	26.2'	03	225°	52.2'	N017°	03.6'	10	330°	53.8'	N017°	40.2'
22	150°	50.0'	N016°	26.9'	04	240°	52.2'	N017°	04.3'	11	345°	53.8'	N017°	40.9'
23	165°	50.0'	N016°	27.6'	05	255°	52.3'	N017°	04.9'	12	000°	53.8'	N017°	41.5'
May 6					06	270°	52.3'	N017°	05.6'	13	015°	53.8'	N017°	42.2'
00	180°	50.1'	N016°	28.3'	07	285°	52.3'	N017°	06.3'	14	030°	53.9'	N017°	42.8'
01	195°	50.1'	N016°	29.0'	08	300°	52.4'	N017°	07.0'	15	045°	53.9'	N017°	43.5'
02	210°	50.2'	N016°	29.7'	09	315°	52.4'	N017°	07.7'	16	060°	53.9'	N017°	44.1'
03	225°	50.2'	N016°	30.4'	10	330°	52.4'	N017°	08.3'	17	075°	53.9'	N017°	44.8'
04	240°	50.3'	N016°	31.1'	11	345°	52.5'	N017°	09.0'	18	090°	53.9'	N017°	45.4'
05	255°	50.3'	N016°	31.8'	12	000°	52.5'	N017°	09.7'	19	105°	54.0'	N017°	46.1'

Hr	GHA		DEC	
20	120°	54.0'	N017°	46.7'
21	135°	54.0'	N017°	47.4'
22	150°	54.0'	N017°	48.0'
23	165°	54.0'	N017°	48.6'
May 11				
00	180°	54.1'	N017°	49.3'
01	195°	54.1'	N017°	49.9'
02	210°	54.1'	N017°	50.6'
03	225°	54.1'	N017°	51.2'
04	240°	54.1'	N017°	51.9'
05	255°	54.2'	N017°	52.5'
06	270°	54.2'	N017°	53.1'
07	285°	54.2'	N017°	53.8'
08	300°	54.2'	N017°	54.4'
09	315°	54.2'	N017°	55.1'
10	330°	54.2'	N017°	55.7'
11	345°	54.3'	N017°	56.3'
12	000°	54.3'	N017°	57.0'
13	015°	54.3'	N017°	57.6'
14	030°	54.3'	N017°	58.3'
15	045°	54.3'	N017°	58.9'
16	060°	54.3'	N017°	59.5'
17	075°	54.3'	N018°	00.2'
18	090°	54.4'	N018°	00.8'
19	105°	54.4'	N018°	01.4'
20	120°	54.4'	N018°	02.1'
21	135°	54.4'	N018°	02.7'
22	150°	54.4'	N018°	03.3'
23	165°	54.4'	N018°	04.0'
May 12				
00	180°	54.4'	N018°	04.6'
01	195°	54.4'	N018°	05.2'
02	210°	54.5'	N018°	05.9'
03	225°	54.5'	N018°	06.5'
04	240°	54.5'	N018°	07.1'
05	255°	54.5'	N018°	07.8'
06	270°	54.5'	N018°	08.4'
07	285°	54.5'	N018°	09.0'
08	300°	54.5'	N018°	09.6'
09	315°	54.5'	N018°	10.3'
10	330°	54.5'	N018°	10.9'
11	345°	54.6'	N018°	11.5'
12	000°	54.6'	N018°	12.2'
13	015°	54.6'	N018°	12.8'
14	030°	54.6'	N018°	13.4'
15	045°	54.6'	N018°	14.0'
16	060°	54.6'	N018°	14.7'
17	075°	54.6'	N018°	15.3'
18	090°	54.6'	N018°	15.9'
19	105°	54.6'	N018°	16.5'
20	120°	54.6'	N018°	17.1'
21	135°	54.6'	N018°	17.8'
22	150°	54.6'	N018°	18.4'
23	165°	54.7'	N018°	19.0'
May 13				
00	180°	54.7'	N018°	19.6'
01	195°	54.7'	N018°	20.2'

Hr	GHA		DEC	
02	210°	54.7'	N018°	20.9'
03	225°	54.7'	N018°	21.5'
04	240°	54.7'	N018°	22.1'
05	255°	54.7'	N018°	22.7'
06	270°	54.7'	N018°	23.3'
07	285°	54.7'	N018°	24.0'
08	300°	54.7'	N018°	24.6'
09	315°	54.7'	N018°	25.2'
10	330°	54.7'	N018°	25.8'
11	345°	54.7'	N018°	26.4'
12	000°	54.7'	N018°	27.0'
13	015°	54.7'	N018°	27.6'
14	030°	54.7'	N018°	28.2'
15	045°	54.7'	N018°	28.9'
16	060°	54.7'	N018°	29.5'
17	075°	54.7'	N018°	30.1'
18	090°	54.7'	N018°	30.7'
19	105°	54.7'	N018°	31.3'
20	120°	54.7'	N018°	31.9'
21	135°	54.7'	N018°	32.5'
22	150°	54.7'	N018°	33.1'
23	165°	54.7'	N018°	33.7'
May 14				
00	180°	54.7'	N018°	34.3'
01	195°	54.7'	N018°	34.9'
02	210°	54.7'	N018°	35.6'
03	225°	54.7'	N018°	36.2'
04	240°	54.7'	N018°	36.8'
05	255°	54.7'	N018°	37.4'
06	270°	54.7'	N018°	38.0'
07	285°	54.7'	N018°	38.6'
08	300°	54.7'	N018°	39.2'
09	315°	54.7'	N018°	39.8'
10	330°	54.7'	N018°	40.4'
11	345°	54.7'	N018°	41.0'
12	000°	54.7'	N018°	41.6'
13	015°	54.7'	N018°	42.2'
14	030°	54.7'	N018°	42.8'
15	045°	54.7'	N018°	43.4'
16	060°	54.7'	N018°	44.0'
17	075°	54.7'	N018°	44.6'
18	090°	54.7'	N018°	45.2'
19	105°	54.7'	N018°	45.8'
20	120°	54.7'	N018°	46.4'
21	135°	54.7'	N018°	47.0'
22	150°	54.7'	N018°	47.5'
23	165°	54.7'	N018°	48.1'
May 15				
00	180°	54.7'	N018°	48.7'
01	195°	54.7'	N018°	49.3'
02	210°	54.7'	N018°	49.9'
03	225°	54.7'	N018°	50.5'
04	240°	54.7'	N018°	51.1'
05	255°	54.7'	N018°	51.7'
06	270°	54.6'	N018°	52.3'
07	285°	54.6'	N018°	52.9'
08	300°	54.6'	N018°	53.5'

Hr	GHA		DEC	
09	315°	54.6'	N018°	54.1'
10	330°	54.6'	N018°	54.6'
11	345°	54.6'	N018°	55.2'
12	000°	54.6'	N018°	55.8'
13	015°	54.6'	N018°	56.4'
14	030°	54.6'	N018°	57.0'
15	045°	54.6'	N018°	57.6'
16	060°	54.6'	N018°	58.2'
17	075°	54.6'	N018°	58.7'
18	090°	54.5'	N018°	59.3'
19	105°	54.5'	N018°	59.9'
20	120°	54.5'	N019°	00.5'
21	135°	54.5'	N019°	01.1'
22	150°	54.5'	N019°	01.7'
23	165°	54.5'	N019°	02.2'
May 16				
00	180°	54.5'	N019°	02.8'
01	195°	54.5'	N019°	03.4'
02	210°	54.5'	N019°	04.0'
03	225°	54.4'	N019°	04.6'
04	240°	54.4'	N019°	05.1'
05	255°	54.4'	N019°	05.7'
06	270°	54.4'	N019°	06.3'
07	285°	54.4'	N019°	06.9'
08	300°	54.4'	N019°	07.4'
09	315°	54.4'	N019°	08.0'
10	330°	54.4'	N019°	08.6'
11	345°	54.3'	N019°	09.2'
12	000°	54.3'	N019°	09.7'
13	015°	54.3'	N019°	10.3'
14	030°	54.3'	N019°	10.9'
15	045°	54.3'	N019°	11.5'
16	060°	54.3'	N019°	12.0'
17	075°	54.3'	N019°	12.6'
18	090°	54.2'	N019°	13.2'
19	105°	54.2'	N019°	13.7'
20	120°	54.2'	N019°	14.3'
21	135°	54.2'	N019°	14.9'
22	150°	54.2'	N019°	15.4'
23	165°	54.2'	N019°	16.0'
May 17				
00	180°	54.1'	N019°	16.6'
01	195°	54.1'	N019°	17.1'
02	210°	54.1'	N019°	17.7'
03	225°	54.1'	N019°	18.3'
04	240°	54.1'	N019°	18.8'
05	255°	54.1'	N019°	19.4'
06	270°	54.0'	N019°	20.0'
07	285°	54.0'	N019°	20.5'
08	300°	54.0'	N019°	21.1'
09	315°	54.0'	N019°	21.6'
10	330°	54.0'	N019°	22.2'
11	345°	53.9'	N019°	22.8'
12	000°	53.9'	N019°	23.3'
13	015°	53.9'	N019°	23.9'
14	030°	53.9'	N019°	24.4'
15	045°	53.9'	N019°	25.0'

Hr	GHA		DEC	
16	060°	53.8'	N019°	25.6'
17	075°	53.8'	N019°	26.1'
18	090°	53.8'	N019°	26.7'
19	105°	53.8'	N019°	27.2'
20	120°	53.7'	N019°	27.8'
21	135°	53.7'	N019°	28.3'
22	150°	53.7'	N019°	28.9'
23	165°	53.7'	N019°	29.4'
May 18				
00	180°	53.7'	N019°	30.0'
01	195°	53.6'	N019°	30.6'
02	210°	53.6'	N019°	31.1'
03	225°	53.6'	N019°	31.7'
04	240°	53.6'	N019°	32.2'
05	255°	53.5'	N019°	32.8'
06	270°	53.5'	N019°	33.3'
07	285°	53.5'	N019°	33.9'
08	300°	53.5'	N019°	34.4'
09	315°	53.4'	N019°	35.0'
10	330°	53.4'	N019°	35.5'
11	345°	53.4'	N019°	36.0'
12	000°	53.4'	N019°	36.6'
13	015°	53.3'	N019°	37.1'
14	030°	53.3'	N019°	37.7'
15	045°	53.3'	N019°	38.2'
16	060°	53.3'	N019°	38.8'
17	075°	53.2'	N019°	39.3'
18	090°	53.2'	N019°	39.9'
19	105°	53.2'	N019°	40.4'
20	120°	53.2'	N019°	40.9'
21	135°	53.1'	N019°	41.5'
22	150°	53.1'	N019°	42.0'
23	165°	53.1'	N019°	42.6'
May 19				
00	180°	53.0'	N019°	43.1'
01	195°	53.0'	N019°	43.6'
02	210°	53.0'	N019°	44.2'
03	225°	53.0'	N019°	44.7'
04	240°	52.9'	N019°	45.2'
05	255°	52.9'	N019°	45.8'
06	270°	52.9'	N019°	46.3'
07	285°	52.8'	N019°	46.9'
08	300°	52.8'	N019°	47.4'
09	315°	52.8'	N019°	47.9'
10	330°	52.7'	N019°	48.5'
11	345°	52.7'	N019°	49.0'
12	000°	52.7'	N019°	49.5'
13	015°	52.6'	N019°	50.1'
14	030°	52.6'	N019°	50.6'
15	045°	52.6'	N019°	51.1'
16	060°	52.6'	N019°	51.6'
17	075°	52.5'	N019°	52.2'
18	090°	52.5'	N019°	52.7'
19	105°	52.5'	N019°	53.2'
20	120°	52.4'	N019°	53.8'
21	135°	52.4'	N019°	54.3'
22	150°	52.4'	N019°	54.8'

Hr	GHA		DEC	
23	165°	52.3'	N019°	55.3'
May 20				
00	180°	52.3'	N019°	55.9'
01	195°	52.2'	N019°	56.4'
02	210°	52.2'	N019°	56.9'
03	225°	52.2'	N019°	57.4'
04	240°	52.1'	N019°	58.0'
05	255°	52.1'	N019°	58.5'
06	270°	52.1'	N019°	59.0'
07	285°	52.0'	N019°	59.5'
08	300°	52.0'	N020°	00.0'
09	315°	52.0'	N020°	00.6'
10	330°	51.9'	N020°	01.1'
11	345°	51.9'	N020°	01.6'
12	000°	51.9'	N020°	02.1'
13	015°	51.8'	N020°	02.6'
14	030°	51.8'	N020°	03.1'
15	045°	51.7'	N020°	03.7'
16	060°	51.7'	N020°	04.2'
17	075°	51.7'	N020°	04.7'
18	090°	51.6'	N020°	05.2'
19	105°	51.6'	N020°	05.7'
20	120°	51.5'	N020°	06.2'
21	135°	51.5'	N020°	06.7'
22	150°	51.5'	N020°	07.3'
23	165°	51.4'	N020°	07.8'
May 21				
00	180°	51.4'	N020°	08.3'
01	195°	51.4'	N020°	08.8'
02	210°	51.3'	N020°	09.3'
03	225°	51.3'	N020°	09.8'
04	240°	51.2'	N020°	10.3'
05	255°	51.2'	N020°	10.8'
06	270°	51.1'	N020°	11.3'
07	285°	51.1'	N020°	11.8'
08	300°	51.1'	N020°	12.3'
09	315°	51.0'	N020°	12.8'
10	330°	51.0'	N020°	13.4'
11	345°	50.9'	N020°	13.9'
12	000°	50.9'	N020°	14.4'
13	015°	50.9'	N020°	14.9'
14	030°	50.8'	N020°	15.4'
15	045°	50.8'	N020°	15.9'
16	060°	50.7'	N020°	16.4'
17	075°	50.7'	N020°	16.9'
18	090°	50.6'	N020°	17.4'
19	105°	50.6'	N020°	17.9'
20	120°	50.5'	N020°	18.4'
21	135°	50.5'	N020°	18.9'
22	150°	50.5'	N020°	19.4'
23	165°	50.4'	N020°	19.9'
May 22				
00	180°	50.4'	N020°	20.4'
01	195°	50.3'	N020°	20.9'
02	210°	50.3'	N020°	21.3'
03	225°	50.2'	N020°	21.8'
04	240°	50.2'	N020°	22.3'

Hr	GHA		DEC	
05	255°	50.1'	N020°	22.8'
06	270°	50.1'	N020°	23.3'
07	285°	50.0'	N020°	23.8'
08	300°	50.0'	N020°	24.3'
09	315°	49.9'	N020°	24.8'
10	330°	49.9'	N020°	25.3'
11	345°	49.9'	N020°	25.8'
12	000°	49.8'	N020°	26.3'
13	015°	49.8'	N020°	26.8'
14	030°	49.7'	N020°	27.2'
15	045°	49.7'	N020°	27.7'
16	060°	49.6'	N020°	28.2'
17	075°	49.6'	N020°	28.7'
18	090°	49.5'	N020°	29.2'
19	105°	49.5'	N020°	29.7'
20	120°	49.4'	N020°	30.2'
21	135°	49.4'	N020°	30.6'
22	150°	49.3'	N020°	31.1'
23	165°	49.3'	N020°	31.6'
May 23				
00	180°	49.2'	N020°	32.1'
01	195°	49.2'	N020°	32.6'
02	210°	49.1'	N020°	33.0'
03	225°	49.1'	N020°	33.5'
04	240°	49.0'	N020°	34.0'
05	255°	49.0'	N020°	34.5'
06	270°	48.9'	N020°	35.0'
07	285°	48.8'	N020°	35.4'
08	300°	48.8'	N020°	35.9'
09	315°	48.7'	N020°	36.4'
10	330°	48.7'	N020°	36.9'
11	345°	48.6'	N020°	37.3'
12	000°	48.6'	N020°	37.8'
13	015°	48.5'	N020°	38.3'
14	030°	48.5'	N020°	38.8'
15	045°	48.4'	N020°	39.2'
16	060°	48.4'	N020°	39.7'
17	075°	48.3'	N020°	40.2'
18	090°	48.3'	N020°	40.7'
19	105°	48.2'	N020°	41.1'
20	120°	48.1'	N020°	41.6'
21	135°	48.1'	N020°	42.1'
22	150°	48.0'	N020°	42.5'
23	165°	48.0'	N020°	43.0'
May 24				
00	180°	47.9'	N020°	43.5'
01	195°	47.9'	N020°	43.9'
02	210°	47.8'	N020°	44.4'
03	225°	47.8'	N020°	44.9'
04	240°	47.7'	N020°	45.3'
05	255°	47.6'	N020°	45.8'
06	270°	47.6'	N020°	46.3'
07	285°	47.5'	N020°	46.7'
08	300°	47.5'	N020°	47.2'
09	315°	47.4'	N020°	47.6'
10	330°	47.3'	N020°	48.1'
11	345°	47.3'	N020°	48.6'

Sun Almanac

Hr	GHA		DEC	
12	000°	47.2'	N020°	49.0'
13	015°	47.2'	N020°	49.5'
14	030°	47.1'	N020°	49.9'
15	045°	47.1'	N020°	50.4'
16	060°	47.0'	N020°	50.8'
17	075°	46.9'	N020°	51.3'
18	090°	46.9'	N020°	51.8'
19	105°	46.8'	N020°	52.2'
20	120°	46.8'	N020°	52.7'
21	135°	46.7'	N020°	53.1'
22	150°	46.6'	N020°	53.6'
23	165°	46.6'	N020°	54.0'
		May 25		
00	180°	46.5'	N020°	54.5'
01	195°	46.4'	N020°	54.9'
02	210°	46.4'	N020°	55.4'
03	225°	46.3'	N020°	55.8'
04	240°	46.3'	N020°	56.3'
05	255°	46.2'	N020°	56.7'
06	270°	46.1'	N020°	57.2'
07	285°	46.1'	N020°	57.6'
08	300°	46.0'	N020°	58.1'
09	315°	45.9'	N020°	58.5'
10	330°	45.9'	N020°	59.0'
11	345°	45.8'	N020°	59.4'
12	000°	45.8'	N020°	59.9'
13	015°	45.7'	N021°	00.3'
14	030°	45.6'	N021°	00.7'
15	045°	45.6'	N021°	01.2'
16	060°	45.5'	N021°	01.6'
17	075°	45.4'	N021°	02.1'
18	090°	45.4'	N021°	02.5'
19	105°	45.3'	N021°	03.0'
20	120°	45.2'	N021°	03.4'
21	135°	45.2'	N021°	03.8'
22	150°	45.1'	N021°	04.3'
23	165°	45.0'	N021°	04.7'
		May 26		
00	180°	45.0'	N021°	05.1'
01	195°	44.9'	N021°	05.6'
02	210°	44.8'	N021°	06.0'
03	225°	44.8'	N021°	06.4'
04	240°	44.7'	N021°	06.9'
05	255°	44.6'	N021°	07.3'
06	270°	44.6'	N021°	07.7'
07	285°	44.5'	N021°	08.2'
08	300°	44.4'	N021°	08.6'
09	315°	44.4'	N021°	09.0'
10	330°	44.3'	N021°	09.5'
11	345°	44.2'	N021°	09.9'
12	000°	44.2'	N021°	10.3'
13	015°	44.1'	N021°	10.8'
14	030°	44.0'	N021°	11.2'
15	045°	44.0'	N021°	11.6'
16	060°	43.9'	N021°	12.0'
17	075°	43.8'	N021°	12.5'
18	090°	43.7'	N021°	12.9'

Hr	GHA		DEC	
19	105°	43.7'	N021°	13.3'
20	120°	43.6'	N021°	13.7'
21	135°	43.5'	N021°	14.2'
22	150°	43.5'	N021°	14.6'
23	165°	43.4'	N021°	15.0'
		May 27		
00	180°	43.3'	N021°	15.4'
01	195°	43.2'	N021°	15.9'
02	210°	43.2'	N021°	16.3'
03	225°	43.1'	N021°	16.7'
04	240°	43.0'	N021°	17.1'
05	255°	43.0'	N021°	17.5'
06	270°	42.9'	N021°	18.0'
07	285°	42.8'	N021°	18.4'
08	300°	42.7'	N021°	18.8'
09	315°	42.7'	N021°	19.2'
10	330°	42.6'	N021°	19.6'
11	345°	42.5'	N021°	20.0'
12	000°	42.4'	N021°	20.4'
13	015°	42.4'	N021°	20.9'
14	030°	42.3'	N021°	21.3'
15	045°	42.2'	N021°	21.7'
16	060°	42.1'	N021°	22.1'
17	075°	42.1'	N021°	22.5'
18	090°	42.0'	N021°	22.9'
19	105°	41.9'	N021°	23.3'
20	120°	41.8'	N021°	23.7'
21	135°	41.8'	N021°	24.1'
22	150°	41.7'	N021°	24.6'
23	165°	41.6'	N021°	25.0'
		May 28		
00	180°	41.5'	N021°	25.4'
01	195°	41.5'	N021°	25.8'
02	210°	41.4'	N021°	26.2'
03	225°	41.3'	N021°	26.6'
04	240°	41.2'	N021°	27.0'
05	255°	41.2'	N021°	27.4'
06	270°	41.1'	N021°	27.8'
07	285°	41.0'	N021°	28.2'
08	300°	40.9'	N021°	28.6'
09	315°	40.8'	N021°	29.0'
10	330°	40.8'	N021°	29.4'
11	345°	40.7'	N021°	29.8'
12	000°	40.6'	N021°	30.2'
13	015°	40.5'	N021°	30.6'
14	030°	40.5'	N021°	31.0'
15	045°	40.4'	N021°	31.4'
16	060°	40.3'	N021°	31.8'
17	075°	40.2'	N021°	32.2'
18	090°	40.1'	N021°	32.6'
19	105°	40.1'	N021°	33.0'
20	120°	40.0'	N021°	33.4'
21	135°	39.9'	N021°	33.7'
22	150°	39.8'	N021°	34.1'
23	165°	39.7'	N021°	34.5'
		May 29		
00	180°	39.6'	N021°	34.9'

Hr	GHA		DEC	
01	195°	39.6'	N021°	35.3'
02	210°	39.5'	N021°	35.7'
03	225°	39.4'	N021°	36.1'
04	240°	39.3'	N021°	36.5'
05	255°	39.2'	N021°	36.9'
06	270°	39.2'	N021°	37.3'
07	285°	39.1'	N021°	37.6'
08	300°	39.0'	N021°	38.0'
09	315°	38.9'	N021°	38.4'
10	330°	38.8'	N021°	38.8'
11	345°	38.7'	N021°	39.2'
12	000°	38.7'	N021°	39.6'
13	015°	38.6'	N021°	39.9'
14	030°	38.5'	N021°	40.3'
15	045°	38.4'	N021°	40.7'
16	060°	38.3'	N021°	41.1'
17	075°	38.2'	N021°	41.5'
18	090°	38.2'	N021°	41.8'
19	105°	38.1'	N021°	42.2'
20	120°	38.0'	N021°	42.6'
21	135°	37.9'	N021°	43.0'
22	150°	37.8'	N021°	43.4'
23	165°	37.7'	N021°	43.7'
		May 30		
00	180°	37.6'	N021°	44.1'
01	195°	37.6'	N021°	44.5'
02	210°	37.5'	N021°	44.9'
03	225°	37.4'	N021°	45.2'
04	240°	37.3'	N021°	45.6'
05	255°	37.2'	N021°	46.0'
06	270°	37.1'	N021°	46.3'
07	285°	37.0'	N021°	46.7'
08	300°	37.0'	N021°	47.1'
09	315°	36.9'	N021°	47.5'
10	330°	36.8'	N021°	47.8'
11	345°	36.7'	N021°	48.2'
12	000°	36.6'	N021°	48.6'
13	015°	36.5'	N021°	48.9'
14	030°	36.4'	N021°	49.3'
15	045°	36.3'	N021°	49.7'
16	060°	36.3'	N021°	50.0'
17	075°	36.2'	N021°	50.4'
18	090°	36.1'	N021°	50.7'
19	105°	36.0'	N021°	51.1'
20	120°	35.9'	N021°	51.5'
21	135°	35.8'	N021°	51.8'
22	150°	35.7'	N021°	52.2'
23	165°	35.6'	N021°	52.5'
		May 31		
00	180°	35.5'	N021°	52.9'
01	195°	35.4'	N021°	53.3'
02	210°	35.4'	N021°	53.6'
03	225°	35.3'	N021°	54.0'
04	240°	35.2'	N021°	54.3'
05	255°	35.1'	N021°	54.7'
06	270°	35.0'	N021°	55.1'
07	285°	34.9'	N021°	55.4'

Hr	GHA		DEC	
08	300°	34.8'	N021°	55.8'
09	315°	34.7'	N021°	56.1'
10	330°	34.6'	N021°	56.5'
11	345°	34.5'	N021°	56.8'
12	000°	34.4'	N021°	57.2'
13	015°	34.3'	N021°	57.5'
14	030°	34.3'	N021°	57.9'
15	045°	34.2'	N021°	58.2'
16	060°	34.1'	N021°	58.6'
17	075°	34.0'	N021°	58.9'
18	090°	33.9'	N021°	59.3'
19	105°	33.8'	N021°	59.6'
20	120°	33.7'	N021°	60.0'
21	135°	33.6'	N022°	00.3'
22	150°	33.5'	N022°	00.6'
23	165°	33.4'	N022°	01.0'
June 1				
00	180°	33.3'	N022°	01.3'
01	195°	33.2'	N022°	01.7'
02	210°	33.1'	N022°	02.0'
03	225°	33.0'	N022°	02.4'
04	240°	32.9'	N022°	02.7'
05	255°	32.8'	N022°	03.0'
06	270°	32.8'	N022°	03.4'
07	285°	32.7'	N022°	03.7'
08	300°	32.6'	N022°	04.1'
09	315°	32.5'	N022°	04.4'
10	330°	32.4'	N022°	04.7'
11	345°	32.3'	N022°	05.1'
12	000°	32.2'	N022°	05.4'
13	015°	32.1'	N022°	05.7'
14	030°	32.0'	N022°	06.1'
15	045°	31.9'	N022°	06.4'
16	060°	31.8'	N022°	06.7'
17	075°	31.7'	N022°	07.1'
18	090°	31.6'	N022°	07.4'
19	105°	31.5'	N022°	07.7'
20	120°	31.4'	N022°	08.1'
21	135°	31.3'	N022°	08.4'
22	150°	31.2'	N022°	08.7'
23	165°	31.1'	N022°	09.0'
June 2				
00	180°	31.0'	N022°	09.4'
01	195°	30.9'	N022°	09.7'
02	210°	30.8'	N022°	10.0'
03	225°	30.7'	N022°	10.4'
04	240°	30.6'	N022°	10.7'
05	255°	30.5'	N022°	11.0'
06	270°	30.4'	N022°	11.3'
07	285°	30.3'	N022°	11.6'
08	300°	30.2'	N022°	12.0'
09	315°	30.1'	N022°	12.3'
10	330°	30.0'	N022°	12.6'
11	345°	29.9'	N022°	12.9'
12	000°	29.8'	N022°	13.2'
13	015°	29.7'	N022°	13.6'
14	030°	29.6'	N022°	13.9'
15	045°	29.5'	N022°	14.2'
16	060°	29.4'	N022°	14.5'
17	075°	29.3'	N022°	14.8'
18	090°	29.2'	N022°	15.2'
19	105°	29.1'	N022°	15.5'
20	120°	29.0'	N022°	15.8'
21	135°	28.9'	N022°	16.1'
22	150°	28.8'	N022°	16.4'
23	165°	28.7'	N022°	16.7'
June 3				
00	180°	28.6'	N022°	17.0'
01	195°	28.5'	N022°	17.3'
02	210°	28.4'	N022°	17.6'
03	225°	28.3'	N022°	18.0'
04	240°	28.2'	N022°	18.3'
05	255°	28.1'	N022°	18.6'
06	270°	28.0'	N022°	18.9'
07	285°	27.9'	N022°	19.2'
08	300°	27.8'	N022°	19.5'
09	315°	27.7'	N022°	19.8'
10	330°	27.6'	N022°	20.1'
11	345°	27.5'	N022°	20.4'
12	000°	27.4'	N022°	20.7'
13	015°	27.3'	N022°	21.0'
14	030°	27.2'	N022°	21.3'
15	045°	27.0'	N022°	21.6'
16	060°	26.9'	N022°	21.9'
17	075°	26.8'	N022°	22.2'
18	090°	26.7'	N022°	22.5'
19	105°	26.6'	N022°	22.8'
20	120°	26.5'	N022°	23.1'
21	135°	26.4'	N022°	23.4'
22	150°	26.3'	N022°	23.7'
23	165°	26.2'	N022°	24.0'
June 4				
00	180°	26.1'	N022°	24.3'
01	195°	26.0'	N022°	24.6'
02	210°	25.9'	N022°	24.9'
03	225°	25.8'	N022°	25.2'
04	240°	25.7'	N022°	25.5'
05	255°	25.6'	N022°	25.8'
06	270°	25.5'	N022°	26.0'
07	285°	25.4'	N022°	26.3'
08	300°	25.2'	N022°	26.6'
09	315°	25.1'	N022°	26.9'
10	330°	25.0'	N022°	27.2'
11	345°	24.9'	N022°	27.5'
12	000°	24.8'	N022°	27.8'
13	015°	24.7'	N022°	28.1'
14	030°	24.6'	N022°	28.3'
15	045°	24.5'	N022°	28.6'
16	060°	24.4'	N022°	28.9'
17	075°	24.3'	N022°	29.2'
18	090°	24.2'	N022°	29.5'
19	105°	24.1'	N022°	29.8'
20	120°	23.9'	N022°	30.0'
21	135°	23.8'	N022°	30.3'
22	150°	23.7'	N022°	30.6'
23	165°	23.6'	N022°	30.9'
June 5				
00	180°	23.5'	N022°	31.2'
01	195°	23.4'	N022°	31.4'
02	210°	23.3'	N022°	31.7'
03	225°	23.2'	N022°	32.0'
04	240°	23.1'	N022°	32.3'
05	255°	23.0'	N022°	32.5'
06	270°	22.8'	N022°	32.8'
07	285°	22.7'	N022°	33.1'
08	300°	22.6'	N022°	33.4'
09	315°	22.5'	N022°	33.6'
10	330°	22.4'	N022°	33.9'
11	345°	22.3'	N022°	34.2'
12	000°	22.2'	N022°	34.5'
13	015°	22.1'	N022°	34.7'
14	030°	22.0'	N022°	35.0'
15	045°	21.8'	N022°	35.3'
16	060°	21.7'	N022°	35.5'
17	075°	21.6'	N022°	35.8'
18	090°	21.5'	N022°	36.1'
19	105°	21.4'	N022°	36.3'
20	120°	21.3'	N022°	36.6'
21	135°	21.2'	N022°	36.9'
22	150°	21.1'	N022°	37.1'
23	165°	21.0'	N022°	37.4'
June 6				
00	180°	20.8'	N022°	37.6'
01	195°	20.7'	N022°	37.9'
02	210°	20.6'	N022°	38.2'
03	225°	20.5'	N022°	38.4'
04	240°	20.4'	N022°	38.7'
05	255°	20.3'	N022°	38.9'
06	270°	20.2'	N022°	39.2'
07	285°	20.0'	N022°	39.5'
08	300°	19.9'	N022°	39.7'
09	315°	19.8'	N022°	40.0'
10	330°	19.7'	N022°	40.2'
11	345°	19.6'	N022°	40.5'
12	000°	19.5'	N022°	40.7'
13	015°	19.4'	N022°	41.0'
14	030°	19.2'	N022°	41.2'
15	045°	19.1'	N022°	41.5'
16	060°	19.0'	N022°	41.7'
17	075°	18.9'	N022°	42.0'
18	090°	18.8'	N022°	42.2'
19	105°	18.7'	N022°	42.5'
20	120°	18.6'	N022°	42.7'
21	135°	18.4'	N022°	43.0'
22	150°	18.3'	N022°	43.2'
23	165°	18.2'	N022°	43.5'
June 7				
00	180°	18.1'	N022°	43.7'
01	195°	18.0'	N022°	44.0'
02	210°	17.9'	N022°	44.2'
03	225°	17.7'	N022°	44.5'

Hr	GHA		DEC		Hr	GHA		DEC		Hr	GHA		DEC	
04	240°	17.6'	N022°	44.7'	11	345°	11.0'	N022°	57.0'	18	090°	04.1'	N023°	07.1'
05	255°	17.5'	N022°	44.9'	12	000°	10.9'	N022°	57.2'	19	105°	04.0'	N023°	07.3'
06	270°	17.4'	N022°	45.2'	13	015°	10.8'	N022°	57.4'	20	120°	03.9'	N023°	07.5'
07	285°	17.3'	N022°	45.4'	14	030°	10.7'	N022°	57.6'	21	135°	03.7'	N023°	07.6'
08	300°	17.2'	N022°	45.7'	15	045°	10.5'	N022°	57.8'	22	150°	03.6'	N023°	07.8'
09	315°	17.0'	N022°	45.9'	16	060°	10.4'	N022°	58.0'	23	165°	03.5'	N023°	07.9'
10	330°	16.9'	N022°	46.1'	17	075°	10.3'	N022°	58.2'		June 12			
11	345°	16.8'	N022°	46.4'	18	090°	10.2'	N022°	58.4'	00	180°	03.4'	N023°	08.1'
12	000°	16.7'	N022°	46.6'	19	105°	10.0'	N022°	58.6'	01	195°	03.2'	N023°	08.3'
13	015°	16.6'	N022°	46.9'	20	120°	09.9'	N022°	58.8'	02	210°	03.1'	N023°	08.4'
14	030°	16.5'	N022°	47.1'	21	135°	09.8'	N022°	59.0'	03	225°	03.0'	N023°	08.6'
15	045°	16.3'	N022°	47.3'	22	150°	09.7'	N022°	59.2'	04	240°	02.8'	N023°	08.7'
16	060°	16.2'	N022°	47.6'	23	165°	09.6'	N022°	59.4'	05	255°	02.7'	N023°	08.9'
17	075°	16.1'	N022°	47.8'		June 10				06	270°	02.6'	N023°	09.1'
18	090°	16.0'	N022°	48.0'	00	180°	09.4'	N022°	59.6'	07	285°	02.5'	N023°	09.2'
19	105°	15.9'	N022°	48.3'	01	195°	09.3'	N022°	59.8'	08	300°	02.3'	N023°	09.4'
20	120°	15.7'	N022°	48.5'	02	210°	09.2'	N022°	60.0'	09	315°	02.2'	N023°	09.5'
21	135°	15.6'	N022°	48.7'	03	225°	09.1'	N023°	00.1'	10	330°	02.1'	N023°	09.7'
22	150°	15.5'	N022°	48.9'	04	240°	08.9'	N023°	00.3'	11	345°	01.9'	N023°	09.8'
23	165°	15.4'	N022°	49.2'	05	255°	08.8'	N023°	00.5'	12	000°	01.8'	N023°	10.0'
	June 8				06	270°	08.7'	N023°	00.7'	13	015°	01.7'	N023°	10.1'
00	180°	15.3'	N022°	49.4'	07	285°	08.6'	N023°	00.9'	14	030°	01.6'	N023°	10.3'
01	195°	15.2'	N022°	49.6'	08	300°	08.4'	N023°	01.1'	15	045°	01.4'	N023°	10.4'
02	210°	15.0'	N022°	49.9'	09	315°	08.3'	N023°	01.3'	16	060°	01.3'	N023°	10.6'
03	225°	14.9'	N022°	50.1'	10	330°	08.2'	N023°	01.5'	17	075°	01.2'	N023°	10.7'
04	240°	14.8'	N022°	50.3'	11	345°	08.1'	N023°	01.7'	18	090°	01.0'	N023°	10.9'
05	255°	14.7'	N022°	50.5'	12	000°	07.9'	N023°	01.9'	19	105°	00.9'	N023°	11.0'
06	270°	14.6'	N022°	50.8'	13	015°	07.8'	N023°	02.0'	20	120°	00.8'	N023°	11.2'
07	285°	14.4'	N022°	51.0'	14	030°	07.7'	N023°	02.2'	21	135°	00.6'	N023°	11.3'
08	300°	14.3'	N022°	51.2'	15	045°	07.6'	N023°	02.4'	22	150°	00.5'	N023°	11.5'
09	315°	14.2'	N022°	51.4'	16	060°	07.4'	N023°	02.6'	23	165°	00.4'	N023°	11.6'
10	330°	14.1'	N022°	51.7'	17	075°	07.3'	N023°	02.8'		June 13			
11	345°	14.0'	N022°	51.9'	18	090°	07.2'	N023°	03.0'	00	180°	00.3'	N023°	11.8'
12	000°	13.8'	N022°	52.1'	19	105°	07.1'	N023°	03.1'	01	195°	00.1'	N023°	11.9'
13	015°	13.7'	N022°	52.3'	20	120°	06.9'	N023°	03.3'	02	209°	60.0'	N023°	12.1'
14	030°	13.6'	N022°	52.5'	21	135°	06.8'	N023°	03.5'	03	224°	59.9'	N023°	12.2'
15	045°	13.5'	N022°	52.8'	22	150°	06.7'	N023°	03.7'	04	239°	59.7'	N023°	12.3'
16	060°	13.4'	N022°	53.0'	23	165°	06.5'	N023°	03.9'	05	254°	59.6'	N023°	12.5'
17	075°	13.2'	N022°	53.2'		June 11				06	269°	59.5'	N023°	12.6'
18	090°	13.1'	N022°	53.4'	00	180°	06.4'	N023°	04.0'	07	284°	59.3'	N023°	12.8'
19	105°	13.0'	N022°	53.6'	01	195°	06.3'	N023°	04.2'	08	299°	59.2'	N023°	12.9'
20	120°	12.9'	N022°	53.8'	02	210°	06.2'	N023°	04.4'	09	314°	59.1'	N023°	13.0'
21	135°	12.7'	N022°	54.0'	03	225°	06.0'	N023°	04.6'	10	329°	58.9'	N023°	13.2'
22	150°	12.6'	N022°	54.3'	04	240°	05.9'	N023°	04.7'	11	344°	58.8'	N023°	13.3'
23	165°	12.5'	N022°	54.5'	05	255°	05.8'	N023°	04.9'	12	359°	58.7'	N023°	13.4'
	June 9				06	270°	05.7'	N023°	05.1'	13	014°	58.6'	N023°	13.6'
00	180°	12.4'	N022°	54.7'	07	285°	05.5'	N023°	05.3'	14	029°	58.4'	N023°	13.7'
01	195°	12.3'	N022°	54.9'	08	300°	05.4'	N023°	05.4'	15	044°	58.3'	N023°	13.8'
02	210°	12.1'	N022°	55.1'	09	315°	05.3'	N023°	05.6'	16	059°	58.2'	N023°	14.0'
03	225°	12.0'	N022°	55.3'	10	330°	05.2'	N023°	05.8'	17	074°	58.0'	N023°	14.1'
04	240°	11.9'	N022°	55.5'	11	345°	05.0'	N023°	06.0'	18	089°	57.9'	N023°	14.2'
05	255°	11.8'	N022°	55.7'	12	000°	04.9'	N023°	06.1'	19	104°	57.8'	N023°	14.4'
06	270°	11.6'	N022°	55.9'	13	015°	04.8'	N023°	06.3'	20	119°	57.6'	N023°	14.5'
07	285°	11.5'	N022°	56.2'	14	030°	04.6'	N023°	06.5'	21	134°	57.5'	N023°	14.6'
08	300°	11.4'	N022°	56.4'	15	045°	04.5'	N023°	06.6'	22	149°	57.4'	N023°	14.8'
09	315°	11.3'	N022°	56.6'	16	060°	04.4'	N023°	06.8'	23	164°	57.2'	N023°	14.9'
10	330°	11.2'	N022°	56.8'	17	075°	04.3'	N023°	07.0'					

Hr	GHA		DEC	
June 14				
00	179°	57.1'	N023°	15.0'
01	194°	57.0'	N023°	15.1'
02	209°	56.8'	N023°	15.3'
03	224°	56.7'	N023°	15.4'
04	239°	56.6'	N023°	15.5'
05	254°	56.4'	N023°	15.6'
06	269°	56.3'	N023°	15.8'
07	284°	56.2'	N023°	15.9'
08	299°	56.1'	N023°	16.0'
09	314°	55.9'	N023°	16.1'
10	329°	55.8'	N023°	16.2'
11	344°	55.7'	N023°	16.4'
12	359°	55.5'	N023°	16.5'
13	014°	55.4'	N023°	16.6'
14	029°	55.3'	N023°	16.7'
15	044°	55.1'	N023°	16.8'
16	059°	55.0'	N023°	17.0'
17	074°	54.9'	N023°	17.1'
18	089°	54.7'	N023°	17.2'
19	104°	54.6'	N023°	17.3'
20	119°	54.5'	N023°	17.4'
21	134°	54.3'	N023°	17.5'
22	149°	54.2'	N023°	17.6'
23	164°	54.1'	N023°	17.7'
June 15				
00	179°	53.9'	N023°	17.9'
01	194°	53.8'	N023°	18.0'
02	209°	53.7'	N023°	18.1'
03	224°	53.5'	N023°	18.2'
04	239°	53.4'	N023°	18.3'
05	254°	53.3'	N023°	18.4'
06	269°	53.1'	N023°	18.5'
07	284°	53.0'	N023°	18.6'
08	299°	52.9'	N023°	18.7'
09	314°	52.7'	N023°	18.8'
10	329°	52.6'	N023°	18.9'
11	344°	52.5'	N023°	19.0'
12	359°	52.3'	N023°	19.1'
13	014°	52.2'	N023°	19.2'
14	029°	52.1'	N023°	19.3'
15	044°	51.9'	N023°	19.4'
16	059°	51.8'	N023°	19.5'
17	074°	51.7'	N023°	19.6'
18	089°	51.5'	N023°	19.7'
19	104°	51.4'	N023°	19.8'
20	119°	51.3'	N023°	19.9'
21	134°	51.1'	N023°	20.0'
22	149°	51.0'	N023°	20.1'
23	164°	50.8'	N023°	20.2'
June 16				
00	179°	50.7'	N023°	20.3'
01	194°	50.6'	N023°	20.4'
02	209°	50.4'	N023°	20.5'
03	224°	50.3'	N023°	20.6'
04	239°	50.2'	N023°	20.6'
05	254°	50.0'	N023°	20.7'

Hr	GHA		DEC	
06	269°	49.9'	N023°	20.8'
07	284°	49.8'	N023°	20.9'
08	299°	49.6'	N023°	21.0'
09	314°	49.5'	N023°	21.1'
10	329°	49.4'	N023°	21.2'
11	344°	49.2'	N023°	21.3'
12	359°	49.1'	N023°	21.3'
13	014°	49.0'	N023°	21.4'
14	029°	48.8'	N023°	21.5'
15	044°	48.7'	N023°	21.6'
16	059°	48.6'	N023°	21.7'
17	074°	48.4'	N023°	21.8'
18	089°	48.3'	N023°	21.8'
19	104°	48.2'	N023°	21.9'
20	119°	48.0'	N023°	22.0'
21	134°	47.9'	N023°	22.1'
22	149°	47.8'	N023°	22.1'
23	164°	47.6'	N023°	22.2'
June 17				
00	179°	47.5'	N023°	22.3'
01	194°	47.3'	N023°	22.4'
02	209°	47.2'	N023°	22.5'
03	224°	47.1'	N023°	22.5'
04	239°	46.9'	N023°	22.6'
05	254°	46.8'	N023°	22.7'
06	269°	46.7'	N023°	22.7'
07	284°	46.5'	N023°	22.8'
08	299°	46.4'	N023°	22.9'
09	314°	46.3'	N023°	23.0'
10	329°	46.1'	N023°	23.0'
11	344°	46.0'	N023°	23.1'
12	359°	45.9'	N023°	23.2'
13	014°	45.7'	N023°	23.2'
14	029°	45.6'	N023°	23.3'
15	044°	45.4'	N023°	23.4'
16	059°	45.3'	N023°	23.4'
17	074°	45.2'	N023°	23.5'
18	089°	45.0'	N023°	23.5'
19	104°	44.9'	N023°	23.6'
20	119°	44.8'	N023°	23.7'
21	134°	44.6'	N023°	23.7'
22	149°	44.5'	N023°	23.8'
23	164°	44.4'	N023°	23.8'
June 18				
00	179°	44.2'	N023°	23.9'
01	194°	44.1'	N023°	24.0'
02	209°	44.0'	N023°	24.0'
03	224°	43.8'	N023°	24.1'
04	239°	43.7'	N023°	24.1'
05	254°	43.5'	N023°	24.2'
06	269°	43.4'	N023°	24.2'
07	284°	43.3'	N023°	24.3'
08	299°	43.1'	N023°	24.3'
09	314°	43.0'	N023°	24.4'
10	329°	42.9'	N023°	24.5'
11	344°	42.7'	N023°	24.5'
12	359°	42.6'	N023°	24.6'

Hr	GHA		DEC	
13	014°	42.5'	N023°	24.6'
14	029°	42.3'	N023°	24.7'
15	044°	42.2'	N023°	24.7'
16	059°	42.1'	N023°	24.7'
17	074°	41.9'	N023°	24.8'
18	089°	41.8'	N023°	24.8'
19	104°	41.6'	N023°	24.9'
20	119°	41.5'	N023°	24.9'
21	134°	41.4'	N023°	25.0'
22	149°	41.2'	N023°	25.0'
23	164°	41.1'	N023°	25.1'
June 19				
00	179°	41.0'	N023°	25.1'
01	194°	40.8'	N023°	25.1'
02	209°	40.7'	N023°	25.2'
03	224°	40.6'	N023°	25.2'
04	239°	40.4'	N023°	25.3'
05	254°	40.3'	N023°	25.3'
06	269°	40.1'	N023°	25.3'
07	284°	40.0'	N023°	25.4'
08	299°	39.9'	N023°	25.4'
09	314°	39.7'	N023°	25.4'
10	329°	39.6'	N023°	25.5'
11	344°	39.5'	N023°	25.5'
12	359°	39.3'	N023°	25.5'
13	014°	39.2'	N023°	25.6'
14	029°	39.1'	N023°	25.6'
15	044°	38.9'	N023°	25.6'
16	059°	38.8'	N023°	25.7'
17	074°	38.6'	N023°	25.7'
18	089°	38.5'	N023°	25.7'
19	104°	38.4'	N023°	25.7'
20	119°	38.2'	N023°	25.8'
21	134°	38.1'	N023°	25.8'
22	149°	38.0'	N023°	25.8'
23	164°	37.8'	N023°	25.9'
June 20				
00	179°	37.7'	N023°	25.9'
01	194°	37.6'	N023°	25.9'
02	209°	37.4'	N023°	25.9'
03	224°	37.3'	N023°	25.9'
04	239°	37.1'	N023°	26.0'
05	254°	37.0'	N023°	26.0'
06	269°	36.9'	N023°	26.0'
07	284°	36.7'	N023°	26.0'
08	299°	36.6'	N023°	26.0'
09	314°	36.5'	N023°	26.1'
10	329°	36.3'	N023°	26.1'
11	344°	36.2'	N023°	26.1'
12	359°	36.1'	N023°	26.1'
13	014°	35.9'	N023°	26.1'
14	029°	35.8'	N023°	26.1'
15	044°	35.6'	N023°	26.2'
16	059°	35.5'	N023°	26.2'
17	074°	35.4'	N023°	26.2'
18	089°	35.2'	N023°	26.2'
19	104°	35.1'	N023°	26.2'

Hr	GHA		DEC	
20	119°	35.0'	N023°	26.2'
21	134°	34.8'	N023°	26.2'
22	149°	34.7'	N023°	26.2'
23	164°	34.6'	N023°	26.2'
June 21				
00	179°	34.4'	N023°	26.2'
01	194°	34.3'	N023°	26.2'
02	209°	34.2'	N023°	26.3'
03	224°	34.0'	N023°	26.3'
04	239°	33.9'	N023°	26.3'
05	254°	33.7'	N023°	26.3'
06	269°	33.6'	N023°	26.3'
07	284°	33.5'	N023°	26.3'
08	299°	33.3'	N023°	26.3'
09	314°	33.2'	N023°	26.3'
10	329°	33.1'	N023°	26.3'
11	344°	32.9'	N023°	26.3'
12	359°	32.8'	N023°	26.3'
13	014°	32.7'	N023°	26.3'
14	029°	32.5'	N023°	26.3'
15	044°	32.4'	N023°	26.3'
16	059°	32.2'	N023°	26.3'
17	074°	32.1'	N023°	26.2'
18	089°	32.0'	N023°	26.2'
19	104°	31.8'	N023°	26.2'
20	119°	31.7'	N023°	26.2'
21	134°	31.6'	N023°	26.2'
22	149°	31.4'	N023°	26.2'
23	164°	31.3'	N023°	26.2'
June 22				
00	179°	31.2'	N023°	26.2'
01	194°	31.0'	N023°	26.2'
02	209°	30.9'	N023°	26.2'
03	224°	30.8'	N023°	26.2'
04	239°	30.6'	N023°	26.1'
05	254°	30.5'	N023°	26.1'
06	269°	30.3'	N023°	26.1'
07	284°	30.2'	N023°	26.1'
08	299°	30.1'	N023°	26.1'
09	314°	29.9'	N023°	26.1'
10	329°	29.8'	N023°	26.1'
11	344°	29.7'	N023°	26.0'
12	359°	29.5'	N023°	26.0'
13	014°	29.4'	N023°	26.0'
14	029°	29.3'	N023°	26.0'
15	044°	29.1'	N023°	26.0'
16	059°	29.0'	N023°	25.9'
17	074°	28.9'	N023°	25.9'
18	089°	28.7'	N023°	25.9'
19	104°	28.6'	N023°	25.9'
20	119°	28.4'	N023°	25.8'
21	134°	28.3'	N023°	25.8'
22	149°	28.2'	N023°	25.8'
23	164°	28.0'	N023°	25.8'
June 23				
00	179°	27.9'	N023°	25.7'
01	194°	27.8'	N023°	25.7'
02	209°	27.6'	N023°	25.7'
03	224°	27.5'	N023°	25.6'
04	239°	27.4'	N023°	25.6'
05	254°	27.2'	N023°	25.6'
06	269°	27.1'	N023°	25.6'
07	284°	27.0'	N023°	25.5'
08	299°	26.8'	N023°	25.5'
09	314°	26.7'	N023°	25.5'
10	329°	26.6'	N023°	25.4'
11	344°	26.4'	N023°	25.4'
12	359°	26.3'	N023°	25.3'
13	014°	26.2'	N023°	25.3'
14	029°	26.0'	N023°	25.3'
15	044°	25.9'	N023°	25.2'
16	059°	25.7'	N023°	25.2'
17	074°	25.6'	N023°	25.2'
18	089°	25.5'	N023°	25.1'
19	104°	25.3'	N023°	25.1'
20	119°	25.2'	N023°	25.0'
21	134°	25.1'	N023°	25.0'
22	149°	24.9'	N023°	24.9'
23	164°	24.8'	N023°	24.9'
June 24				
00	179°	24.7'	N023°	24.9'
01	194°	24.5'	N023°	24.8'
02	209°	24.4'	N023°	24.8'
03	224°	24.3'	N023°	24.7'
04	239°	24.1'	N023°	24.7'
05	254°	24.0'	N023°	24.6'
06	269°	23.9'	N023°	24.6'
07	284°	23.7'	N023°	24.5'
08	299°	23.6'	N023°	24.5'
09	314°	23.5'	N023°	24.4'
10	329°	23.3'	N023°	24.4'
11	344°	23.2'	N023°	24.3'
12	359°	23.1'	N023°	24.3'
13	014°	22.9'	N023°	24.2'
14	029°	22.8'	N023°	24.2'
15	044°	22.7'	N023°	24.1'
16	059°	22.5'	N023°	24.0'
17	074°	22.4'	N023°	24.0'
18	089°	22.3'	N023°	23.9'
19	104°	22.1'	N023°	23.9'
20	119°	22.0'	N023°	23.8'
21	134°	21.9'	N023°	23.8'
22	149°	21.7'	N023°	23.7'
23	164°	21.6'	N023°	23.6'
June 25				
00	179°	21.5'	N023°	23.6'
01	194°	21.3'	N023°	23.5'
02	209°	21.2'	N023°	23.4'
03	224°	21.1'	N023°	23.4'
04	239°	20.9'	N023°	23.3'
05	254°	20.8'	N023°	23.2'
06	269°	20.7'	N023°	23.2'
07	284°	20.5'	N023°	23.1'
08	299°	20.4'	N023°	23.0'
09	314°	20.3'	N023°	23.0'
10	329°	20.1'	N023°	22.9'
11	344°	20.0'	N023°	22.8'
12	359°	19.9'	N023°	22.8'
13	014°	19.7'	N023°	22.7'
14	029°	19.6'	N023°	22.6'
15	044°	19.5'	N023°	22.6'
16	059°	19.3'	N023°	22.5'
17	074°	19.2'	N023°	22.4'
18	089°	19.1'	N023°	22.3'
19	104°	18.9'	N023°	22.3'
20	119°	18.8'	N023°	22.2'
21	134°	18.7'	N023°	22.1'
22	149°	18.5'	N023°	22.0'
23	164°	18.4'	N023°	21.9'
June 26				
00	179°	18.3'	N023°	21.9'
01	194°	18.1'	N023°	21.8'
02	209°	18.0'	N023°	21.7'
03	224°	17.9'	N023°	21.6'
04	239°	17.8'	N023°	21.5'
05	254°	17.6'	N023°	21.5'
06	269°	17.5'	N023°	21.4'
07	284°	17.4'	N023°	21.3'
08	299°	17.2'	N023°	21.2'
09	314°	17.1'	N023°	21.1'
10	329°	17.0'	N023°	21.0'
11	344°	16.8'	N023°	21.0'
12	359°	16.7'	N023°	20.9'
13	014°	16.6'	N023°	20.8'
14	029°	16.4'	N023°	20.7'
15	044°	16.3'	N023°	20.6'
16	059°	16.2'	N023°	20.5'
17	074°	16.0'	N023°	20.4'
18	089°	15.9'	N023°	20.3'
19	104°	15.8'	N023°	20.2'
20	119°	15.7'	N023°	20.1'
21	134°	15.5'	N023°	20.0'
22	149°	15.4'	N023°	20.0'
23	164°	15.3'	N023°	19.9'
June 27				
00	179°	15.1'	N023°	19.8'
01	194°	15.0'	N023°	19.7'
02	209°	14.9'	N023°	19.6'
03	224°	14.7'	N023°	19.5'
04	239°	14.6'	N023°	19.4'
05	254°	14.5'	N023°	19.3'
06	269°	14.4'	N023°	19.2'
07	284°	14.2'	N023°	19.1'
08	299°	14.1'	N023°	19.0'
09	314°	14.0'	N023°	18.9'
10	329°	13.8'	N023°	18.8'
11	344°	13.7'	N023°	18.7'
12	359°	13.6'	N023°	18.6'
13	014°	13.4'	N023°	18.4'
14	029°	13.3'	N023°	18.3'
15	044°	13.2'	N023°	18.2'

Hr	GHA		DEC	
16	059°	13.1'	N023°	18.1'
17	074°	12.9'	N023°	18.0'
18	089°	12.8'	N023°	17.9'
19	104°	12.7'	N023°	17.8'
20	119°	12.5'	N023°	17.7'
21	134°	12.4'	N023°	17.6'
22	149°	12.3'	N023°	17.5'
23	164°	12.2'	N023°	17.4'
June 28				
00	179°	12.0'	N023°	17.2'
01	194°	11.9'	N023°	17.1'
02	209°	11.8'	N023°	17.0'
03	224°	11.6'	N023°	16.9'
04	239°	11.5'	N023°	16.8'
05	254°	11.4'	N023°	16.7'
06	269°	11.3'	N023°	16.5'
07	284°	11.1'	N023°	16.4'
08	299°	11.0'	N023°	16.3'
09	314°	10.9'	N023°	16.2'
10	329°	10.7'	N023°	16.1'
11	344°	10.6'	N023°	16.0'
12	359°	10.5'	N023°	15.8'
13	014°	10.4'	N023°	15.7'
14	029°	10.2'	N023°	15.6'
15	044°	10.1'	N023°	15.5'
16	059°	10.0'	N023°	15.3'
17	074°	09.9'	N023°	15.2'
18	089°	09.7'	N023°	15.1'
19	104°	09.6'	N023°	15.0'
20	119°	09.5'	N023°	14.8'
21	134°	09.4'	N023°	14.7'
22	149°	09.2'	N023°	14.6'
23	164°	09.1'	N023°	14.4'
June 29				
00	179°	09.0'	N023°	14.3'
01	194°	08.8'	N023°	14.2'
02	209°	08.7'	N023°	14.1'
03	224°	08.6'	N023°	13.9'
04	239°	08.5'	N023°	13.8'
05	254°	08.3'	N023°	13.7'
06	269°	08.2'	N023°	13.5'
07	284°	08.1'	N023°	13.4'
08	299°	08.0'	N023°	13.2'
09	314°	07.8'	N023°	13.1'
10	329°	07.7'	N023°	13.0'
11	344°	07.6'	N023°	12.8'
12	359°	07.5'	N023°	12.7'
13	014°	07.3'	N023°	12.6'
14	029°	07.2'	N023°	12.4'
15	044°	07.1'	N023°	12.3'
16	059°	07.0'	N023°	12.1'
17	074°	06.8'	N023°	12.0'
18	089°	06.7'	N023°	11.9'
19	104°	06.6'	N023°	11.7'
20	119°	06.5'	N023°	11.6'
21	134°	06.3'	N023°	11.4'
22	149°	06.2'	N023°	11.3'
23	164°	06.1'	N023°	11.1'
June 30				
00	179°	06.0'	N023°	11.0'
01	194°	05.8'	N023°	10.8'
02	209°	05.7'	N023°	10.7'
03	224°	05.6'	N023°	10.5'
04	239°	05.5'	N023°	10.4'
05	254°	05.3'	N023°	10.2'
06	269°	05.2'	N023°	10.1'
07	284°	05.1'	N023°	09.9'
08	299°	05.0'	N023°	09.8'
09	314°	04.9'	N023°	09.6'
10	329°	04.7'	N023°	09.5'
11	344°	04.6'	N023°	09.3'
12	359°	04.5'	N023°	09.2'
13	014°	04.4'	N023°	09.0'
14	029°	04.2'	N023°	08.8'
15	044°	04.1'	N023°	08.7'
16	059°	04.0'	N023°	08.5'
17	074°	03.9'	N023°	08.4'
18	089°	03.7'	N023°	08.2'
19	104°	03.6'	N023°	08.0'
20	119°	03.5'	N023°	07.9'
21	134°	03.4'	N023°	07.7'
22	149°	03.3'	N023°	07.6'
23	164°	03.1'	N023°	07.4'
July 1				
00	179°	03.0'	N023°	07.2'
01	194°	02.9'	N023°	07.1'
02	209°	02.8'	N023°	06.9'
03	224°	02.7'	N023°	06.7'
04	239°	02.5'	N023°	06.6'
05	254°	02.4'	N023°	06.4'
06	269°	02.3'	N023°	06.2'
07	284°	02.2'	N023°	06.1'
08	299°	02.0'	N023°	05.9'
09	314°	01.9'	N023°	05.7'
10	329°	01.8'	N023°	05.6'
11	344°	01.7'	N023°	05.4'
12	359°	01.6'	N023°	05.2'
13	014°	01.4'	N023°	05.0'
14	029°	01.3'	N023°	04.9'
15	044°	01.2'	N023°	04.7'
16	059°	01.1'	N023°	04.5'
17	074°	01.0'	N023°	04.3'
18	089°	00.8'	N023°	04.2'
19	104°	00.7'	N023°	04.0'
20	119°	00.6'	N023°	03.8'
21	134°	00.5'	N023°	03.6'
22	149°	00.4'	N023°	03.5'
23	164°	00.3'	N023°	03.3'
July 2				
00	179°	00.1'	N023°	03.1'
01	194°	00.0'	N023°	02.9'
02	208°	59.9'	N023°	02.7'
03	223°	59.8'	N023°	02.5'
04	238°	59.7'	N023°	02.4'
05	253°	59.5'	N023°	02.2'
06	268°	59.4'	N023°	02.0'
07	283°	59.3'	N023°	01.8'
08	298°	59.2'	N023°	01.6'
09	313°	59.1'	N023°	01.4'
10	328°	59.0'	N023°	01.2'
11	343°	58.8'	N023°	01.1'
12	358°	58.7'	N023°	00.9'
13	013°	58.6'	N023°	00.7'
14	028°	58.5'	N023°	00.5'
15	043°	58.4'	N023°	00.3'
16	058°	58.2'	N023°	00.1'
17	073°	58.1'	N022°	59.9'
18	088°	58.0'	N022°	59.7'
19	103°	57.9'	N022°	59.5'
20	118°	57.8'	N022°	59.3'
21	133°	57.7'	N022°	59.1'
22	148°	57.6'	N022°	58.9'
23	163°	57.4'	N022°	58.7'
July 3				
00	178°	57.3'	N022°	58.5'
01	193°	57.2'	N022°	58.3'
02	208°	57.1'	N022°	58.1'
03	223°	57.0'	N022°	57.9'
04	238°	56.9'	N022°	57.7'
05	253°	56.7'	N022°	57.5'
06	268°	56.6'	N022°	57.3'
07	283°	56.5'	N022°	57.1'
08	298°	56.4'	N022°	56.9'
09	313°	56.3'	N022°	56.7'
10	328°	56.2'	N022°	56.5'
11	343°	56.1'	N022°	56.3'
12	358°	55.9'	N022°	56.1'
13	013°	55.8'	N022°	55.9'
14	028°	55.7'	N022°	55.7'
15	043°	55.6'	N022°	55.5'
16	058°	55.5'	N022°	55.3'
17	073°	55.4'	N022°	55.1'
18	088°	55.3'	N022°	54.9'
19	103°	55.1'	N022°	54.7'
20	118°	55.0'	N022°	54.4'
21	133°	54.9'	N022°	54.2'
22	148°	54.8'	N022°	54.0'
23	163°	54.7'	N022°	53.8'
July 4				
00	178°	54.6'	N022°	53.6'
01	193°	54.5'	N022°	53.4'
02	208°	54.4'	N022°	53.2'
03	223°	54.2'	N022°	52.9'
04	238°	54.1'	N022°	52.7'
05	253°	54.0'	N022°	52.5'
06	268°	53.9'	N022°	52.3'
07	283°	53.8'	N022°	52.1'
08	298°	53.7'	N022°	51.9'
09	313°	53.6'	N022°	51.6'
10	328°	53.5'	N022°	51.4'
11	343°	53.3'	N022°	51.2'

Hr	GHA		DEC	
12	358°	53.2'	N022°	51.0'
13	013°	53.1'	N022°	50.7'
14	028°	53.0'	N022°	50.5'
15	043°	52.9'	N022°	50.3'
16	058°	52.8'	N022°	50.1'
17	073°	52.7'	N022°	49.8'
18	088°	52.6'	N022°	49.6'
19	103°	52.5'	N022°	49.4'
20	118°	52.4'	N022°	49.2'
21	133°	52.2'	N022°	48.9'
22	148°	52.1'	N022°	48.7'
23	163°	52.0'	N022°	48.5'
July 5				
00	178°	51.9'	N022°	48.2'
01	193°	51.8'	N022°	48.0'
02	208°	51.7'	N022°	47.8'
03	223°	51.6'	N022°	47.5'
04	238°	51.5'	N022°	47.3'
05	253°	51.4'	N022°	47.1'
06	268°	51.3'	N022°	46.8'
07	283°	51.2'	N022°	46.6'
08	298°	51.0'	N022°	46.4'
09	313°	50.9'	N022°	46.1'
10	328°	50.8'	N022°	45.9'
11	343°	50.7'	N022°	45.7'
12	358°	50.6'	N022°	45.4'
13	013°	50.5'	N022°	45.2'
14	028°	50.4'	N022°	44.9'
15	043°	50.3'	N022°	44.7'
16	058°	50.2'	N022°	44.5'
17	073°	50.1'	N022°	44.2'
18	088°	50.0'	N022°	44.0'
19	103°	49.9'	N022°	43.7'
20	118°	49.8'	N022°	43.5'
21	133°	49.7'	N022°	43.2'
22	148°	49.5'	N022°	43.0'
23	163°	49.4'	N022°	42.7'
July 6				
00	178°	49.3'	N022°	42.5'
01	193°	49.2'	N022°	42.3'
02	208°	49.1'	N022°	42.0'
03	223°	49.0'	N022°	41.8'
04	238°	48.9'	N022°	41.5'
05	253°	48.8'	N022°	41.3'
06	268°	48.7'	N022°	41.0'
07	283°	48.6'	N022°	40.8'
08	298°	48.5'	N022°	40.5'
09	313°	48.4'	N022°	40.2'
10	328°	48.3'	N022°	40.0'
11	343°	48.2'	N022°	39.7'
12	358°	48.1'	N022°	39.5'
13	013°	48.0'	N022°	39.2'
14	028°	47.9'	N022°	39.0'
15	043°	47.8'	N022°	38.7'
16	058°	47.7'	N022°	38.5'
17	073°	47.6'	N022°	38.2'
18	088°	47.5'	N022°	37.9'

Hr	GHA		DEC	
19	103°	47.4'	N022°	37.7'
20	118°	47.3'	N022°	37.4'
21	133°	47.2'	N022°	37.2'
22	148°	47.1'	N022°	36.9'
23	163°	46.9'	N022°	36.6'
July 7				
00	178°	46.8'	N022°	36.4'
01	193°	46.7'	N022°	36.1'
02	208°	46.6'	N022°	35.8'
03	223°	46.5'	N022°	35.6'
04	238°	46.4'	N022°	35.3'
05	253°	46.3'	N022°	35.0'
06	268°	46.2'	N022°	34.8'
07	283°	46.1'	N022°	34.5'
08	298°	46.0'	N022°	34.2'
09	313°	45.9'	N022°	34.0'
10	328°	45.8'	N022°	33.7'
11	343°	45.7'	N022°	33.4'
12	358°	45.6'	N022°	33.1'
13	013°	45.5'	N022°	32.9'
14	028°	45.4'	N022°	32.6'
15	043°	45.3'	N022°	32.3'
16	058°	45.2'	N022°	32.1'
17	073°	45.1'	N022°	31.8'
18	088°	45.0'	N022°	31.5'
19	103°	44.9'	N022°	31.2'
20	118°	44.8'	N022°	30.9'
21	133°	44.7'	N022°	30.7'
22	148°	44.6'	N022°	30.4'
23	163°	44.5'	N022°	30.1'
July 8				
00	178°	44.5'	N022°	29.8'
01	193°	44.4'	N022°	29.6'
02	208°	44.3'	N022°	29.3'
03	223°	44.2'	N022°	29.0'
04	238°	44.1'	N022°	28.7'
05	253°	44.0'	N022°	28.4'
06	268°	43.9'	N022°	28.1'
07	283°	43.8'	N022°	27.9'
08	298°	43.7'	N022°	27.6'
09	313°	43.6'	N022°	27.3'
10	328°	43.5'	N022°	27.0'
11	343°	43.4'	N022°	26.7'
12	358°	43.3'	N022°	26.4'
13	013°	43.2'	N022°	26.1'
14	028°	43.1'	N022°	25.8'
15	043°	43.0'	N022°	25.6'
16	058°	42.9'	N022°	25.3'
17	073°	42.8'	N022°	25.0'
18	088°	42.7'	N022°	24.7'
19	103°	42.6'	N022°	24.4'
20	118°	42.5'	N022°	24.1'
21	133°	42.4'	N022°	23.8'
22	148°	42.3'	N022°	23.5'
23	163°	42.2'	N022°	23.2'
July 9				
00	178°	42.2'	N022°	22.9'

Hr	GHA		DEC	
01	193°	42.1'	N022°	22.6'
02	208°	42.0'	N022°	22.3'
03	223°	41.9'	N022°	22.0'
04	238°	41.8'	N022°	21.7'
05	253°	41.7'	N022°	21.4'
06	268°	41.6'	N022°	21.1'
07	283°	41.5'	N022°	20.8'
08	298°	41.4'	N022°	20.5'
09	313°	41.3'	N022°	20.2'
10	328°	41.2'	N022°	19.9'
11	343°	41.1'	N022°	19.6'
12	358°	41.0'	N022°	19.3'
13	013°	41.0'	N022°	19.0'
14	028°	40.9'	N022°	18.7'
15	043°	40.8'	N022°	18.4'
16	058°	40.7'	N022°	18.1'
17	073°	40.6'	N022°	17.8'
18	088°	40.5'	N022°	17.5'
19	103°	40.4'	N022°	17.2'
20	118°	40.3'	N022°	16.9'
21	133°	40.2'	N022°	16.5'
22	148°	40.1'	N022°	16.2'
23	163°	40.0'	N022°	15.9'
July 10				
00	178°	40.0'	N022°	15.6'
01	193°	39.9'	N022°	15.3'
02	208°	39.8'	N022°	15.0'
03	223°	39.7'	N022°	14.7'
04	238°	39.6'	N022°	14.4'
05	253°	39.5'	N022°	14.0'
06	268°	39.4'	N022°	13.7'
07	283°	39.3'	N022°	13.4'
08	298°	39.3'	N022°	13.1'
09	313°	39.2'	N022°	12.8'
10	328°	39.1'	N022°	12.5'
11	343°	39.0'	N022°	12.1'
12	358°	38.9'	N022°	11.8'
13	013°	38.8'	N022°	11.5'
14	028°	38.7'	N022°	11.2'
15	043°	38.6'	N022°	10.8'
16	058°	38.6'	N022°	10.5'
17	073°	38.5'	N022°	10.2'
18	088°	38.4'	N022°	09.9'
19	103°	38.3'	N022°	09.6'
20	118°	38.2'	N022°	09.2'
21	133°	38.1'	N022°	08.9'
22	148°	38.0'	N022°	08.6'
23	163°	38.0'	N022°	08.2'
July 11				
00	178°	37.9'	N022°	07.9'
01	193°	37.8'	N022°	07.6'
02	208°	37.7'	N022°	07.3'
03	223°	37.6'	N022°	06.9'
04	238°	37.5'	N022°	06.6'
05	253°	37.4'	N022°	06.3'
06	268°	37.4'	N022°	05.9'
07	283°	37.3'	N022°	05.6'

Hr	GHA		DEC	
08	298°	37.2'	N022°	05.3'
09	313°	37.1'	N022°	04.9'
10	328°	37.0'	N022°	04.6'
11	343°	36.9'	N022°	04.3'
12	358°	36.9'	N022°	03.9'
13	013°	36.8'	N022°	03.6'
14	028°	36.7'	N022°	03.3'
15	043°	36.6'	N022°	02.9'
16	058°	36.5'	N022°	02.6'
17	073°	36.5'	N022°	02.2'
18	088°	36.4'	N022°	01.9'
19	103°	36.3'	N022°	01.6'
20	118°	36.2'	N022°	01.2'
21	133°	36.1'	N022°	00.9'
22	148°	36.1'	N022°	00.5'
23	163°	36.0'	N022°	00.2'
July 12				
00	178°	35.9'	N021°	59.9'
01	193°	35.8'	N021°	59.5'
02	208°	35.7'	N021°	59.2'
03	223°	35.7'	N021°	58.8'
04	238°	35.6'	N021°	58.5'
05	253°	35.5'	N021°	58.1'
06	268°	35.4'	N021°	57.8'
07	283°	35.3'	N021°	57.4'
08	298°	35.3'	N021°	57.1'
09	313°	35.2'	N021°	56.7'
10	328°	35.1'	N021°	56.4'
11	343°	35.0'	N021°	56.0'
12	358°	34.9'	N021°	55.7'
13	013°	34.9'	N021°	55.3'
14	028°	34.8'	N021°	55.0'
15	043°	34.7'	N021°	54.6'
16	058°	34.6'	N021°	54.3'
17	073°	34.6'	N021°	53.9'
18	088°	34.5'	N021°	53.6'
19	103°	34.4'	N021°	53.2'
20	118°	34.3'	N021°	52.8'
21	133°	34.3'	N021°	52.5'
22	148°	34.2'	N021°	52.1'
23	163°	34.1'	N021°	51.8'
July 13				
00	178°	34.0'	N021°	51.4'
01	193°	34.0'	N021°	51.0'
02	208°	33.9'	N021°	50.7'
03	223°	33.8'	N021°	50.3'
04	238°	33.7'	N021°	50.0'
05	253°	33.7'	N021°	49.6'
06	268°	33.6'	N021°	49.2'
07	283°	33.5'	N021°	48.9'
08	298°	33.4'	N021°	48.5'
09	313°	33.4'	N021°	48.1'
10	328°	33.3'	N021°	47.8'
11	343°	33.2'	N021°	47.4'
12	358°	33.1'	N021°	47.0'
13	013°	33.1'	N021°	46.7'
14	028°	33.0'	N021°	46.3'
15	043°	32.9'	N021°	45.9'
16	058°	32.9'	N021°	45.6'
17	073°	32.8'	N021°	45.2'
18	088°	32.7'	N021°	44.8'
19	103°	32.6'	N021°	44.5'
20	118°	32.6'	N021°	44.1'
21	133°	32.5'	N021°	43.7'
22	148°	32.4'	N021°	43.3'
23	163°	32.4'	N021°	43.0'
July 14				
00	178°	32.3'	N021°	42.6'
01	193°	32.2'	N021°	42.2'
02	208°	32.1'	N021°	41.8'
03	223°	32.1'	N021°	41.5'
04	238°	32.0'	N021°	41.1'
05	253°	31.9'	N021°	40.7'
06	268°	31.9'	N021°	40.3'
07	283°	31.8'	N021°	39.9'
08	298°	31.7'	N021°	39.6'
09	313°	31.7'	N021°	39.2'
10	328°	31.6'	N021°	38.8'
11	343°	31.5'	N021°	38.4'
12	358°	31.5'	N021°	38.0'
13	013°	31.4'	N021°	37.7'
14	028°	31.3'	N021°	37.3'
15	043°	31.3'	N021°	36.9'
16	058°	31.2'	N021°	36.5'
17	073°	31.1'	N021°	36.1'
18	088°	31.1'	N021°	35.7'
19	103°	31.0'	N021°	35.3'
20	118°	30.9'	N021°	35.0'
21	133°	30.9'	N021°	34.6'
22	148°	30.8'	N021°	34.2'
23	163°	30.7'	N021°	33.8'
July 15				
00	178°	30.7'	N021°	33.4'
01	193°	30.6'	N021°	33.0'
02	208°	30.5'	N021°	32.6'
03	223°	30.5'	N021°	32.2'
04	238°	30.4'	N021°	31.8'
05	253°	30.3'	N021°	31.4'
06	268°	30.3'	N021°	31.0'
07	283°	30.2'	N021°	30.6'
08	298°	30.2'	N021°	30.3'
09	313°	30.1'	N021°	29.9'
10	328°	30.0'	N021°	29.5'
11	343°	30.0'	N021°	29.1'
12	358°	29.9'	N021°	28.7'
13	013°	29.8'	N021°	28.3'
14	028°	29.8'	N021°	27.9'
15	043°	29.7'	N021°	27.5'
16	058°	29.7'	N021°	27.1'
17	073°	29.6'	N021°	26.7'
18	088°	29.5'	N021°	26.3'
19	103°	29.5'	N021°	25.9'
20	118°	29.4'	N021°	25.5'
21	133°	29.3'	N021°	25.1'
22	148°	29.3'	N021°	24.7'
23	163°	29.2'	N021°	24.2'
July 16				
00	178°	29.2'	N021°	23.8'
01	193°	29.1'	N021°	23.4'
02	208°	29.0'	N021°	23.0'
03	223°	29.0'	N021°	22.6'
04	238°	28.9'	N021°	22.2'
05	253°	28.9'	N021°	21.8'
06	268°	28.8'	N021°	21.4'
07	283°	28.8'	N021°	21.0'
08	298°	28.7'	N021°	20.6'
09	313°	28.6'	N021°	20.2'
10	328°	28.6'	N021°	19.8'
11	343°	28.5'	N021°	19.3'
12	358°	28.5'	N021°	18.9'
13	013°	28.4'	N021°	18.5'
14	028°	28.4'	N021°	18.1'
15	043°	28.3'	N021°	17.7'
16	058°	28.2'	N021°	17.3'
17	073°	28.2'	N021°	16.9'
18	088°	28.1'	N021°	16.4'
19	103°	28.1'	N021°	16.0'
20	118°	28.0'	N021°	15.6'
21	133°	28.0'	N021°	15.2'
22	148°	27.9'	N021°	14.8'
23	163°	27.9'	N021°	14.3'
July 17				
00	178°	27.8'	N021°	13.9'
01	193°	27.7'	N021°	13.5'
02	208°	27.7'	N021°	13.1'
03	223°	27.6'	N021°	12.7'
04	238°	27.6'	N021°	12.2'
05	253°	27.5'	N021°	11.8'
06	268°	27.5'	N021°	11.4'
07	283°	27.4'	N021°	11.0'
08	298°	27.4'	N021°	10.5'
09	313°	27.3'	N021°	10.1'
10	328°	27.3'	N021°	09.7'
11	343°	27.2'	N021°	09.3'
12	358°	27.2'	N021°	08.8'
13	013°	27.1'	N021°	08.4'
14	028°	27.1'	N021°	08.0'
15	043°	27.0'	N021°	07.5'
16	058°	27.0'	N021°	07.1'
17	073°	26.9'	N021°	06.7'
18	088°	26.9'	N021°	06.2'
19	103°	26.8'	N021°	05.8'
20	118°	26.8'	N021°	05.4'
21	133°	26.7'	N021°	04.9'
22	148°	26.7'	N021°	04.5'
23	163°	26.6'	N021°	04.1'
July 18				
00	178°	26.6'	N021°	03.6'
01	193°	26.5'	N021°	03.2'
02	208°	26.5'	N021°	02.8'
03	223°	26.4'	N021°	02.3'

Hr	GHA		DEC	
04	238°	26.4'	N021°	01.9'
05	253°	26.3'	N021°	01.5'
06	268°	26.3'	N021°	01.0'
07	283°	26.2'	N021°	00.6'
08	298°	26.2'	N021°	00.1'
09	313°	26.1'	N020°	59.7'
10	328°	26.1'	N020°	59.3'
11	343°	26.0'	N020°	58.8'
12	358°	26.0'	N020°	58.4'
13	013°	25.9'	N020°	57.9'
14	028°	25.9'	N020°	57.5'
15	043°	25.9'	N020°	57.0'
16	058°	25.8'	N020°	56.6'
17	073°	25.8'	N020°	56.1'
18	088°	25.7'	N020°	55.7'
19	103°	25.7'	N020°	55.3'
20	118°	25.6'	N020°	54.8'
21	133°	25.6'	N020°	54.4'
22	148°	25.5'	N020°	53.9'
23	163°	25.5'	N020°	53.5'
July 19				
00	178°	25.5'	N020°	53.0'
01	193°	25.4'	N020°	52.6'
02	208°	25.4'	N020°	52.1'
03	223°	25.3'	N020°	51.7'
04	238°	25.3'	N020°	51.2'
05	253°	25.2'	N020°	50.7'
06	268°	25.2'	N020°	50.3'
07	283°	25.2'	N020°	49.8'
08	298°	25.1'	N020°	49.4'
09	313°	25.1'	N020°	48.9'
10	328°	25.0'	N020°	48.5'
11	343°	25.0'	N020°	48.0'
12	358°	25.0'	N020°	47.6'
13	013°	24.9'	N020°	47.1'
14	028°	24.9'	N020°	46.6'
15	043°	24.8'	N020°	46.2'
16	058°	24.8'	N020°	45.7'
17	073°	24.8'	N020°	45.3'
18	088°	24.7'	N020°	44.8'
19	103°	24.7'	N020°	44.3'
20	118°	24.6'	N020°	43.9'
21	133°	24.6'	N020°	43.4'
22	148°	24.6'	N020°	42.9'
23	163°	24.5'	N020°	42.5'
July 20				
00	178°	24.5'	N020°	42.0'
01	193°	24.5'	N020°	41.6'
02	208°	24.4'	N020°	41.1'
03	223°	24.4'	N020°	40.6'
04	238°	24.3'	N020°	40.2'
05	253°	24.3'	N020°	39.7'
06	268°	24.3'	N020°	39.2'
07	283°	24.2'	N020°	38.7'
08	298°	24.2'	N020°	38.3'
09	313°	24.2'	N020°	37.8'
10	328°	24.1'	N020°	37.3'
11	343°	24.1'	N020°	36.9'
12	358°	24.1'	N020°	36.4'
13	013°	24.0'	N020°	35.9'
14	028°	24.0'	N020°	35.4'
15	043°	24.0'	N020°	35.0'
16	058°	23.9'	N020°	34.5'
17	073°	23.9'	N020°	34.0'
18	088°	23.9'	N020°	33.5'
19	103°	23.8'	N020°	33.1'
20	118°	23.8'	N020°	32.6'
21	133°	23.8'	N020°	32.1'
22	148°	23.7'	N020°	31.6'
23	163°	23.7'	N020°	31.2'
July 21				
00	178°	23.7'	N020°	30.7'
01	193°	23.6'	N020°	30.2'
02	208°	23.6'	N020°	29.7'
03	223°	23.6'	N020°	29.2'
04	238°	23.5'	N020°	28.8'
05	253°	23.5'	N020°	28.3'
06	268°	23.5'	N020°	27.8'
07	283°	23.5'	N020°	27.3'
08	298°	23.4'	N020°	26.8'
09	313°	23.4'	N020°	26.3'
10	328°	23.4'	N020°	25.9'
11	343°	23.3'	N020°	25.4'
12	358°	23.3'	N020°	24.9'
13	013°	23.3'	N020°	24.4'
14	028°	23.2'	N020°	23.9'
15	043°	23.2'	N020°	23.4'
16	058°	23.2'	N020°	22.9'
17	073°	23.2'	N020°	22.4'
18	088°	23.1'	N020°	22.0'
19	103°	23.1'	N020°	21.5'
20	118°	23.1'	N020°	21.0'
21	133°	23.1'	N020°	20.5'
22	148°	23.0'	N020°	20.0'
23	163°	23.0'	N020°	19.5'
July 22				
00	178°	23.0'	N020°	19.0'
01	193°	23.0'	N020°	18.5'
02	208°	22.9'	N020°	18.0'
03	223°	22.9'	N020°	17.5'
04	238°	22.9'	N020°	17.0'
05	253°	22.9'	N020°	16.5'
06	268°	22.8'	N020°	16.0'
07	283°	22.8'	N020°	15.5'
08	298°	22.8'	N020°	15.0'
09	313°	22.8'	N020°	14.5'
10	328°	22.7'	N020°	14.0'
11	343°	22.7'	N020°	13.5'
12	358°	22.7'	N020°	13.0'
13	013°	22.7'	N020°	12.5'
14	028°	22.6'	N020°	12.0'
15	043°	22.6'	N020°	11.5'
16	058°	22.6'	N020°	11.0'
17	073°	22.6'	N020°	10.5'
18	088°	22.6'	N020°	10.0'
19	103°	22.5'	N020°	09.5'
20	118°	22.5'	N020°	09.0'
21	133°	22.5'	N020°	08.5'
22	148°	22.5'	N020°	08.0'
23	163°	22.5'	N020°	07.5'
July 23				
00	178°	22.4'	N020°	07.0'
01	193°	22.4'	N020°	06.5'
02	208°	22.4'	N020°	06.0'
03	223°	22.4'	N020°	05.5'
04	238°	22.4'	N020°	04.9'
05	253°	22.3'	N020°	04.4'
06	268°	22.3'	N020°	03.9'
07	283°	22.3'	N020°	03.4'
08	298°	22.3'	N020°	02.9'
09	313°	22.3'	N020°	02.4'
10	328°	22.3'	N020°	01.9'
11	343°	22.2'	N020°	01.4'
12	358°	22.2'	N020°	00.8'
13	013°	22.2'	N020°	00.3'
14	028°	22.2'	N019°	59.8'
15	043°	22.2'	N019°	59.3'
16	058°	22.2'	N019°	58.8'
17	073°	22.1'	N019°	58.3'
18	088°	22.1'	N019°	57.7'
19	103°	22.1'	N019°	57.2'
20	118°	22.1'	N019°	56.7'
21	133°	22.1'	N019°	56.2'
22	148°	22.1'	N019°	55.7'
23	163°	22.1'	N019°	55.1'
July 24				
00	178°	22.0'	N019°	54.6'
01	193°	22.0'	N019°	54.1'
02	208°	22.0'	N019°	53.6'
03	223°	22.0'	N019°	53.1'
04	238°	22.0'	N019°	52.5'
05	253°	22.0'	N019°	52.0'
06	268°	22.0'	N019°	51.5'
07	283°	22.0'	N019°	51.0'
08	298°	21.9'	N019°	50.4'
09	313°	21.9'	N019°	49.9'
10	328°	21.9'	N019°	49.4'
11	343°	21.9'	N019°	48.8'
12	358°	21.9'	N019°	48.3'
13	013°	21.9'	N019°	47.8'
14	028°	21.9'	N019°	47.3'
15	043°	21.9'	N019°	46.7'
16	058°	21.9'	N019°	46.2'
17	073°	21.8'	N019°	45.7'
18	088°	21.8'	N019°	45.1'
19	103°	21.8'	N019°	44.6'
20	118°	21.8'	N019°	44.1'
21	133°	21.8'	N019°	43.5'
22	148°	21.8'	N019°	43.0'
23	163°	21.8'	N019°	42.5'

Hr	GHA		DEC	
		July 25		
00	178°	21.8'	N019°	41.9'
01	193°	21.8'	N019°	41.4'
02	208°	21.8'	N019°	40.9'
03	223°	21.8'	N019°	40.3'
04	238°	21.8'	N019°	39.8'
05	253°	21.8'	N019°	39.2'
06	268°	21.8'	N019°	38.7'
07	283°	21.7'	N019°	38.2'
08	298°	21.7'	N019°	37.6'
09	313°	21.7'	N019°	37.1'
10	328°	21.7'	N019°	36.6'
11	343°	21.7'	N019°	36.0'
12	358°	21.7'	N019°	35.5'
13	013°	21.7'	N019°	34.9'
14	028°	21.7'	N019°	34.4'
15	043°	21.7'	N019°	33.8'
16	058°	21.7'	N019°	33.3'
17	073°	21.7'	N019°	32.7'
18	088°	21.7'	N019°	32.2'
19	103°	21.7'	N019°	31.7'
20	118°	21.7'	N019°	31.1'
21	133°	21.7'	N019°	30.6'
22	148°	21.7'	N019°	30.0'
23	163°	21.7'	N019°	29.5'
		July 26		
00	178°	21.7'	N019°	28.9'
01	193°	21.7'	N019°	28.4'
02	208°	21.7'	N019°	27.8'
03	223°	21.7'	N019°	27.3'
04	238°	21.7'	N019°	26.7'
05	253°	21.7'	N019°	26.2'
06	268°	21.7'	N019°	25.6'
07	283°	21.7'	N019°	25.1'
08	298°	21.7'	N019°	24.5'
09	313°	21.7'	N019°	24.0'
10	328°	21.7'	N019°	23.4'
11	343°	21.7'	N019°	22.8'
12	358°	21.7'	N019°	22.3'
13	013°	21.7'	N019°	21.7'
14	028°	21.7'	N019°	21.2'
15	043°	21.7'	N019°	20.6'
16	058°	21.7'	N019°	20.1'
17	073°	21.7'	N019°	19.5'
18	088°	21.7'	N019°	18.9'
19	103°	21.7'	N019°	18.4'
20	118°	21.7'	N019°	17.8'
21	133°	21.7'	N019°	17.3'
22	148°	21.7'	N019°	16.7'
23	163°	21.7'	N019°	16.1'
		July 27		
00	178°	21.7'	N019°	15.6'
01	193°	21.7'	N019°	15.0'
02	208°	21.7'	N019°	14.5'
03	223°	21.8'	N019°	13.9'
04	238°	21.8'	N019°	13.3'
05	253°	21.8'	N019°	12.8'

Hr	GHA		DEC	
06	268°	21.8'	N019°	12.2'
07	283°	21.8'	N019°	11.6'
08	298°	21.8'	N019°	11.1'
09	313°	21.8'	N019°	10.5'
10	328°	21.8'	N019°	09.9'
11	343°	21.8'	N019°	09.4'
12	358°	21.8'	N019°	08.8'
13	013°	21.8'	N019°	08.2'
14	028°	21.8'	N019°	07.7'
15	043°	21.8'	N019°	07.1'
16	058°	21.9'	N019°	06.5'
17	073°	21.9'	N019°	05.9'
18	088°	21.9'	N019°	05.4'
19	103°	21.9'	N019°	04.8'
20	118°	21.9'	N019°	04.2'
21	133°	21.9'	N019°	03.6'
22	148°	21.9'	N019°	03.1'
23	163°	21.9'	N019°	02.5'
		July 28		
00	178°	21.9'	N019°	01.9'
01	193°	21.9'	N019°	01.3'
02	208°	22.0'	N019°	00.8'
03	223°	22.0'	N019°	00.2'
04	238°	22.0'	N018°	59.6'
05	253°	22.0'	N018°	59.0'
06	268°	22.0'	N018°	58.5'
07	283°	22.0'	N018°	57.9'
08	298°	22.0'	N018°	57.3'
09	313°	22.0'	N018°	56.7'
10	328°	22.1'	N018°	56.1'
11	343°	22.1'	N018°	55.6'
12	358°	22.1'	N018°	55.0'
13	013°	22.1'	N018°	54.4'
14	028°	22.1'	N018°	53.8'
15	043°	22.1'	N018°	53.2'
16	058°	22.1'	N018°	52.6'
17	073°	22.2'	N018°	52.1'
18	088°	22.2'	N018°	51.5'
19	103°	22.2'	N018°	50.9'
20	118°	22.2'	N018°	50.3'
21	133°	22.2'	N018°	49.7'
22	148°	22.2'	N018°	49.1'
23	163°	22.3'	N018°	48.5'
		July 29		
00	178°	22.3'	N018°	48.0'
01	193°	22.3'	N018°	47.4'
02	208°	22.3'	N018°	46.8'
03	223°	22.3'	N018°	46.2'
04	238°	22.4'	N018°	45.6'
05	253°	22.4'	N018°	45.0'
06	268°	22.4'	N018°	44.4'
07	283°	22.4'	N018°	43.8'
08	298°	22.4'	N018°	43.2'
09	313°	22.5'	N018°	42.6'
10	328°	22.5'	N018°	42.0'
11	343°	22.5'	N018°	41.4'
12	358°	22.5'	N018°	40.9'

Hr	GHA		DEC	
13	013°	22.5'	N018°	40.3'
14	028°	22.6'	N018°	39.7'
15	043°	22.6'	N018°	39.1'
16	058°	22.6'	N018°	38.5'
17	073°	22.6'	N018°	37.9'
18	088°	22.6'	N018°	37.3'
19	103°	22.7'	N018°	36.7'
20	118°	22.7'	N018°	36.1'
21	133°	22.7'	N018°	35.5'
22	148°	22.7'	N018°	34.9'
23	163°	22.8'	N018°	34.3'
		July 30		
00	178°	22.8'	N018°	33.7'
01	193°	22.8'	N018°	33.1'
02	208°	22.8'	N018°	32.5'
03	223°	22.9'	N018°	31.9'
04	238°	22.9'	N018°	31.3'
05	253°	22.9'	N018°	30.7'
06	268°	22.9'	N018°	30.1'
07	283°	23.0'	N018°	29.5'
08	298°	23.0'	N018°	28.9'
09	313°	23.0'	N018°	28.2'
10	328°	23.0'	N018°	27.6'
11	343°	23.1'	N018°	27.0'
12	358°	23.1'	N018°	26.4'
13	013°	23.1'	N018°	25.8'
14	028°	23.1'	N018°	25.2'
15	043°	23.2'	N018°	24.6'
16	058°	23.2'	N018°	24.0'
17	073°	23.2'	N018°	23.4'
18	088°	23.3'	N018°	22.8'
19	103°	23.3'	N018°	22.2'
20	118°	23.3'	N018°	21.5'
21	133°	23.3'	N018°	20.9'
22	148°	23.4'	N018°	20.3'
23	163°	23.4'	N018°	19.7'
		July 31		
00	178°	23.4'	N018°	19.1'
01	193°	23.5'	N018°	18.5'
02	208°	23.5'	N018°	17.9'
03	223°	23.5'	N018°	17.3'
04	238°	23.6'	N018°	16.6'
05	253°	23.6'	N018°	16.0'
06	268°	23.6'	N018°	15.4'
07	283°	23.7'	N018°	14.8'
08	298°	23.7'	N018°	14.2'
09	313°	23.7'	N018°	13.5'
10	328°	23.7'	N018°	12.9'
11	343°	23.8'	N018°	12.3'
12	358°	23.8'	N018°	11.7'
13	013°	23.8'	N018°	11.1'
14	028°	23.9'	N018°	10.4'
15	043°	23.9'	N018°	09.8'
16	058°	24.0'	N018°	09.2'
17	073°	24.0'	N018°	08.6'
18	088°	24.0'	N018°	08.0'
19	103°	24.1'	N018°	07.3'

Hr	GHA		DEC	
20	118°	24.1'	N018°	06.7'
21	133°	24.1'	N018°	06.1'
22	148°	24.2'	N018°	05.5'
23	163°	24.2'	N018°	04.8'
August 1				
00	178°	24.2'	N018°	04.2'
01	193°	24.3'	N018°	03.6'
02	208°	24.3'	N018°	03.0'
03	223°	24.3'	N018°	02.3'
04	238°	24.4'	N018°	01.7'
05	253°	24.4'	N018°	01.1'
06	268°	24.5'	N018°	00.4'
07	283°	24.5'	N017°	59.8'
08	298°	24.5'	N017°	59.2'
09	313°	24.6'	N017°	58.6'
10	328°	24.6'	N017°	57.9'
11	343°	24.7'	N017°	57.3'
12	358°	24.7'	N017°	56.7'
13	013°	24.7'	N017°	56.0'
14	028°	24.8'	N017°	55.4'
15	043°	24.8'	N017°	54.8'
16	058°	24.9'	N017°	54.1'
17	073°	24.9'	N017°	53.5'
18	088°	24.9'	N017°	52.9'
19	103°	25.0'	N017°	52.2'
20	118°	25.0'	N017°	51.6'
21	133°	25.1'	N017°	50.9'
22	148°	25.1'	N017°	50.3'
23	163°	25.1'	N017°	49.7'
August 2				
00	178°	25.2'	N017°	49.0'
01	193°	25.2'	N017°	48.4'
02	208°	25.3'	N017°	47.8'
03	223°	25.3'	N017°	47.1'
04	238°	25.4'	N017°	46.5'
05	253°	25.4'	N017°	45.8'
06	268°	25.5'	N017°	45.2'
07	283°	25.5'	N017°	44.6'
08	298°	25.5'	N017°	43.9'
09	313°	25.6'	N017°	43.3'
10	328°	25.6'	N017°	42.6'
11	343°	25.7'	N017°	42.0'
12	358°	25.7'	N017°	41.3'
13	013°	25.8'	N017°	40.7'
14	028°	25.8'	N017°	40.0'
15	043°	25.9'	N017°	39.4'
16	058°	25.9'	N017°	38.8'
17	073°	26.0'	N017°	38.1'
18	088°	26.0'	N017°	37.5'
19	103°	26.1'	N017°	36.8'
20	118°	26.1'	N017°	36.2'
21	133°	26.2'	N017°	35.5'
22	148°	26.2'	N017°	34.9'
23	163°	26.2'	N017°	34.2'
August 3				
00	178°	26.3'	N017°	33.6'
01	193°	26.3'	N017°	32.9'

Hr	GHA		DEC	
02	208°	26.4'	N017°	32.3'
03	223°	26.4'	N017°	31.6'
04	238°	26.5'	N017°	31.0'
05	253°	26.5'	N017°	30.3'
06	268°	26.6'	N017°	29.7'
07	283°	26.6'	N017°	29.0'
08	298°	26.7'	N017°	28.3'
09	313°	26.8'	N017°	27.7'
10	328°	26.8'	N017°	27.0'
11	343°	26.9'	N017°	26.4'
12	358°	26.9'	N017°	25.7'
13	013°	27.0'	N017°	25.1'
14	028°	27.0'	N017°	24.4'
15	043°	27.1'	N017°	23.8'
16	058°	27.1'	N017°	23.1'
17	073°	27.2'	N017°	22.4'
18	088°	27.2'	N017°	21.8'
19	103°	27.3'	N017°	21.1'
20	118°	27.3'	N017°	20.5'
21	133°	27.4'	N017°	19.8'
22	148°	27.4'	N017°	19.1'
23	163°	27.5'	N017°	18.5'
August 4				
00	178°	27.6'	N017°	17.8'
01	193°	27.6'	N017°	17.2'
02	208°	27.7'	N017°	16.5'
03	223°	27.7'	N017°	15.8'
04	238°	27.8'	N017°	15.2'
05	253°	27.8'	N017°	14.5'
06	268°	27.9'	N017°	13.8'
07	283°	28.0'	N017°	13.2'
08	298°	28.0'	N017°	12.5'
09	313°	28.1'	N017°	11.8'
10	328°	28.1'	N017°	11.2'
11	343°	28.2'	N017°	10.5'
12	358°	28.2'	N017°	09.8'
13	013°	28.3'	N017°	09.2'
14	028°	28.4'	N017°	08.5'
15	043°	28.4'	N017°	07.8'
16	058°	28.5'	N017°	07.2'
17	073°	28.5'	N017°	06.5'
18	088°	28.6'	N017°	05.8'
19	103°	28.7'	N017°	05.1'
20	118°	28.7'	N017°	04.5'
21	133°	28.8'	N017°	03.8'
22	148°	28.8'	N017°	03.1'
23	163°	28.9'	N017°	02.5'
August 5				
00	178°	29.0'	N017°	01.8'
01	193°	29.0'	N017°	01.1'
02	208°	29.1'	N017°	00.4'
03	223°	29.2'	N016°	59.8'
04	238°	29.2'	N016°	59.1'
05	253°	29.3'	N016°	58.4'
06	268°	29.3'	N016°	57.7'
07	283°	29.4'	N016°	57.1'
08	298°	29.5'	N016°	56.4'

Hr	GHA		DEC	
09	313°	29.5'	N016°	55.7'
10	328°	29.6'	N016°	55.0'
11	343°	29.7'	N016°	54.3'
12	358°	29.7'	N016°	53.7'
13	013°	29.8'	N016°	53.0'
14	028°	29.9'	N016°	52.3'
15	043°	29.9'	N016°	51.6'
16	058°	30.0'	N016°	50.9'
17	073°	30.1'	N016°	50.3'
18	088°	30.1'	N016°	49.6'
19	103°	30.2'	N016°	48.9'
20	118°	30.3'	N016°	48.2'
21	133°	30.3'	N016°	47.5'
22	148°	30.4'	N016°	46.8'
23	163°	30.5'	N016°	46.2'
August 6				
00	178°	30.5'	N016°	45.5'
01	193°	30.6'	N016°	44.8'
02	208°	30.7'	N016°	44.1'
03	223°	30.7'	N016°	43.4'
04	238°	30.8'	N016°	42.7'
05	253°	30.9'	N016°	42.0'
06	268°	30.9'	N016°	41.4'
07	283°	31.0'	N016°	40.7'
08	298°	31.1'	N016°	40.0'
09	313°	31.2'	N016°	39.3'
10	328°	31.2'	N016°	38.6'
11	343°	31.3'	N016°	37.9'
12	358°	31.4'	N016°	37.2'
13	013°	31.4'	N016°	36.5'
14	028°	31.5'	N016°	35.8'
15	043°	31.6'	N016°	35.1'
16	058°	31.7'	N016°	34.5'
17	073°	31.7'	N016°	33.8'
18	088°	31.8'	N016°	33.1'
19	103°	31.9'	N016°	32.4'
20	118°	31.9'	N016°	31.7'
21	133°	32.0'	N016°	31.0'
22	148°	32.1'	N016°	30.3'
23	163°	32.2'	N016°	29.6'
August 7				
00	178°	32.2'	N016°	28.9'
01	193°	32.3'	N016°	28.2'
02	208°	32.4'	N016°	27.5'
03	223°	32.5'	N016°	26.8'
04	238°	32.5'	N016°	26.1'
05	253°	32.6'	N016°	25.4'
06	268°	32.7'	N016°	24.7'
07	283°	32.8'	N016°	24.0'
08	298°	32.8'	N016°	23.3'
09	313°	32.9'	N016°	22.6'
10	328°	33.0'	N016°	21.9'
11	343°	33.1'	N016°	21.2'
12	358°	33.1'	N016°	20.5'
13	013°	33.2'	N016°	19.8'
14	028°	33.3'	N016°	19.1'
15	043°	33.4'	N016°	18.4'

Hr	GHA		DEC		Hr	GHA		DEC		Hr	GHA		DEC	
16	058°	33.5'	N016°	17.7'	23	163°	38.2'	N015°	38.3'	05	253°	43.5'	N014°	58.4'
17	073°	33.5'	N016°	17.0'	August 10					06	268°	43.6'	N014°	57.6'
18	088°	33.6'	N016°	16.3'	00	178°	38.2'	N015°	37.6'	07	283°	43.7'	N014°	56.9'
19	103°	33.7'	N016°	15.6'	01	193°	38.3'	N015°	36.9'	08	298°	43.8'	N014°	56.1'
20	118°	33.8'	N016°	14.9'	02	208°	38.4'	N015°	36.1'	09	313°	43.9'	N014°	55.4'
21	133°	33.9'	N016°	14.2'	03	223°	38.5'	N015°	35.4'	10	328°	44.0'	N014°	54.6'
22	148°	33.9'	N016°	13.5'	04	238°	38.6'	N015°	34.7'	11	343°	44.1'	N014°	53.9'
23	163°	34.0'	N016°	12.8'	05	253°	38.7'	N015°	33.9'	12	358°	44.2'	N014°	53.1'
August 8					06	268°	38.8'	N015°	33.2'	13	013°	44.4'	N014°	52.4'
00	178°	34.1'	N016°	12.1'	07	283°	38.9'	N015°	32.5'	14	028°	44.5'	N014°	51.6'
01	193°	34.2'	N016°	11.3'	08	298°	39.0'	N015°	31.8'	15	043°	44.6'	N014°	50.9'
02	208°	34.3'	N016°	10.6'	09	313°	39.1'	N015°	31.0'	16	058°	44.7'	N014°	50.1'
03	223°	34.3'	N016°	09.9'	10	328°	39.2'	N015°	30.3'	17	073°	44.8'	N014°	49.3'
04	238°	34.4'	N016°	09.2'	11	343°	39.3'	N015°	29.6'	18	088°	44.9'	N014°	48.6'
05	253°	34.5'	N016°	08.5'	12	358°	39.4'	N015°	28.8'	19	103°	45.0'	N014°	47.8'
06	268°	34.6'	N016°	07.8'	13	013°	39.5'	N015°	28.1'	20	118°	45.1'	N014°	47.1'
07	283°	34.7'	N016°	07.1'	14	028°	39.6'	N015°	27.4'	21	133°	45.2'	N014°	46.3'
08	298°	34.7'	N016°	06.4'	15	043°	39.7'	N015°	26.6'	22	148°	45.3'	N014°	45.6'
09	313°	34.8'	N016°	05.7'	16	058°	39.8'	N015°	25.9'	23	163°	45.4'	N014°	44.8'
10	328°	34.9'	N016°	05.0'	17	073°	39.9'	N015°	25.1'	August 13				
11	343°	35.0'	N016°	04.2'	18	088°	40.0'	N015°	24.4'	00	178°	45.6'	N014°	44.0'
12	358°	35.1'	N016°	03.5'	19	103°	40.1'	N015°	23.7'	01	193°	45.7'	N014°	43.3'
13	013°	35.2'	N016°	02.8'	20	118°	40.2'	N015°	22.9'	02	208°	45.8'	N014°	42.5'
14	028°	35.2'	N016°	02.1'	21	133°	40.2'	N015°	22.2'	03	223°	45.9'	N014°	41.8'
15	043°	35.3'	N016°	01.4'	22	148°	40.3'	N015°	21.5'	04	238°	46.0'	N014°	41.0'
16	058°	35.4'	N016°	00.7'	23	163°	40.4'	N015°	20.7'	05	253°	46.1'	N014°	40.2'
17	073°	35.5'	N015°	60.0'	August 11					06	268°	46.2'	N014°	39.5'
18	088°	35.6'	N015°	59.3'	00	178°	40.5'	N015°	20.0'	07	283°	46.3'	N014°	38.7'
19	103°	35.7'	N015°	58.5'	01	193°	40.6'	N015°	19.2'	08	298°	46.4'	N014°	38.0'
20	118°	35.8'	N015°	57.8'	02	208°	40.7'	N015°	18.5'	09	313°	46.6'	N014°	37.2'
21	133°	35.8'	N015°	57.1'	03	223°	40.8'	N015°	17.8'	10	328°	46.7'	N014°	36.4'
22	148°	35.9'	N015°	56.4'	04	238°	40.9'	N015°	17.0'	11	343°	46.8'	N014°	35.7'
23	163°	36.0'	N015°	55.7'	05	253°	41.0'	N015°	16.3'	12	358°	46.9'	N014°	34.9'
August 9					06	268°	41.1'	N015°	15.5'	13	013°	47.0'	N014°	34.1'
00	178°	36.1'	N015°	55.0'	07	283°	41.2'	N015°	14.8'	14	028°	47.1'	N014°	33.4'
01	193°	36.2'	N015°	54.2'	08	298°	41.3'	N015°	14.1'	15	043°	47.2'	N014°	32.6'
02	208°	36.3'	N015°	53.5'	09	313°	41.4'	N015°	13.3'	16	058°	47.3'	N014°	31.8'
03	223°	36.4'	N015°	52.8'	10	328°	41.5'	N015°	12.6'	17	073°	47.5'	N014°	31.1'
04	238°	36.4'	N015°	52.1'	11	343°	41.6'	N015°	11.8'	18	088°	47.6'	N014°	30.3'
05	253°	36.5'	N015°	51.4'	12	358°	41.7'	N015°	11.1'	19	103°	47.7'	N014°	29.5'
06	268°	36.6'	N015°	50.6'	13	013°	41.8'	N015°	10.3'	20	118°	47.8'	N014°	28.8'
07	283°	36.7'	N015°	49.9'	14	028°	41.9'	N015°	09.6'	21	133°	47.9'	N014°	28.0'
08	298°	36.8'	N015°	49.2'	15	043°	42.0'	N015°	08.9'	22	148°	48.0'	N014°	27.2'
09	313°	36.9'	N015°	48.5'	16	058°	42.2'	N015°	08.1'	23	163°	48.2'	N014°	26.5'
10	328°	37.0'	N015°	47.7'	17	073°	42.3'	N015°	07.4'	August 14				
11	343°	37.1'	N015°	47.0'	18	088°	42.4'	N015°	06.6'	00	178°	48.3'	N014°	25.7'
12	358°	37.2'	N015°	46.3'	19	103°	42.5'	N015°	05.9'	01	193°	48.4'	N014°	24.9'
13	013°	37.2'	N015°	45.6'	20	118°	42.6'	N015°	05.1'	02	208°	48.5'	N014°	24.2'
14	028°	37.3'	N015°	44.9'	21	133°	42.7'	N015°	04.4'	03	223°	48.6'	N014°	23.4'
15	043°	37.4'	N015°	44.1'	22	148°	42.8'	N015°	03.6'	04	238°	48.7'	N014°	22.6'
16	058°	37.5'	N015°	43.4'	23	163°	42.9'	N015°	02.9'	05	253°	48.9'	N014°	21.9'
17	073°	37.6'	N015°	42.7'	August 12					06	268°	49.0'	N014°	21.1'
18	088°	37.7'	N015°	42.0'	00	178°	43.0'	N015°	02.1'	07	283°	49.1'	N014°	20.3'
19	103°	37.8'	N015°	41.2'	01	193°	43.1'	N015°	01.4'	08	298°	49.2'	N014°	19.6'
20	118°	37.9'	N015°	40.5'	02	208°	43.2'	N015°	00.6'	09	313°	49.3'	N014°	18.8'
21	133°	38.0'	N015°	39.8'	03	223°	43.3'	N014°	59.9'	10	328°	49.4'	N014°	18.0'
22	148°	38.1'	N015°	39.0'	04	238°	43.4'	N014°	59.1'	11	343°	49.6'	N014°	17.2'

Hr	GHA		DEC	
12	358°	49.7'	N014°	16.5'
13	013°	49.8'	N014°	15.7'
14	028°	49.9'	N014°	14.9'
15	043°	50.0'	N014°	14.1'
16	058°	50.2'	N014°	13.4'
17	073°	50.3'	N014°	12.6'
18	088°	50.4'	N014°	11.8'
19	103°	50.5'	N014°	11.0'
20	118°	50.6'	N014°	10.3'
21	133°	50.8'	N014°	09.5'
22	148°	50.9'	N014°	08.7'
23	163°	51.0'	N014°	07.9'
August 15				
00	178°	51.1'	N014°	07.2'
01	193°	51.2'	N014°	06.4'
02	208°	51.4'	N014°	05.6'
03	223°	51.5'	N014°	04.8'
04	238°	51.6'	N014°	04.0'
05	253°	51.7'	N014°	03.3'
06	268°	51.9'	N014°	02.5'
07	283°	52.0'	N014°	01.7'
08	298°	52.1'	N014°	00.9'
09	313°	52.2'	N014°	00.1'
10	328°	52.3'	N013°	59.4'
11	343°	52.5'	N013°	58.6'
12	358°	52.6'	N013°	57.8'
13	013°	52.7'	N013°	57.0'
14	028°	52.8'	N013°	56.2'
15	043°	53.0'	N013°	55.4'
16	058°	53.1'	N013°	54.7'
17	073°	53.2'	N013°	53.9'
18	088°	53.3'	N013°	53.1'
19	103°	53.5'	N013°	52.3'
20	118°	53.6'	N013°	51.5'
21	133°	53.7'	N013°	50.7'
22	148°	53.8'	N013°	49.9'
23	163°	54.0'	N013°	49.2'
August 16				
00	178°	54.1'	N013°	48.4'
01	193°	54.2'	N013°	47.6'
02	208°	54.4'	N013°	46.8'
03	223°	54.5'	N013°	46.0'
04	238°	54.6'	N013°	45.2'
05	253°	54.7'	N013°	44.4'
06	268°	54.9'	N013°	43.6'
07	283°	55.0'	N013°	42.9'
08	298°	55.1'	N013°	42.1'
09	313°	55.3'	N013°	41.3'
10	328°	55.4'	N013°	40.5'
11	343°	55.5'	N013°	39.7'
12	358°	55.6'	N013°	38.9'
13	013°	55.8'	N013°	38.1'
14	028°	55.9'	N013°	37.3'
15	043°	56.0'	N013°	36.5'
16	058°	56.2'	N013°	35.7'
17	073°	56.3'	N013°	34.9'
18	088°	56.4'	N013°	34.1'

Hr	GHA		DEC	
19	103°	56.6'	N013°	33.3'
20	118°	56.7'	N013°	32.6'
21	133°	56.8'	N013°	31.8'
22	148°	57.0'	N013°	31.0'
23	163°	57.1'	N013°	30.2'
August 17				
00	178°	57.2'	N013°	29.4'
01	193°	57.4'	N013°	28.6'
02	208°	57.5'	N013°	27.8'
03	223°	57.6'	N013°	27.0'
04	238°	57.8'	N013°	26.2'
05	253°	57.9'	N013°	25.4'
06	268°	58.0'	N013°	24.6'
07	283°	58.2'	N013°	23.8'
08	298°	58.3'	N013°	23.0'
09	313°	58.4'	N013°	22.2'
10	328°	58.6'	N013°	21.4'
11	343°	58.7'	N013°	20.6'
12	358°	58.8'	N013°	19.8'
13	013°	59.0'	N013°	19.0'
14	028°	59.1'	N013°	18.2'
15	043°	59.2'	N013°	17.4'
16	058°	59.4'	N013°	16.6'
17	073°	59.5'	N013°	15.8'
18	088°	59.6'	N013°	15.0'
19	103°	59.8'	N013°	14.2'
20	118°	59.9'	N013°	13.4'
21	134°	00.0'	N013°	12.6'
22	149°	00.2'	N013°	11.8'
23	164°	00.3'	N013°	11.0'
August 18				
00	179°	00.5'	N013°	10.2'
01	194°	00.6'	N013°	09.4'
02	209°	00.7'	N013°	08.5'
03	224°	00.9'	N013°	07.7'
04	239°	01.0'	N013°	06.9'
05	254°	01.2'	N013°	06.1'
06	269°	01.3'	N013°	05.3'
07	284°	01.4'	N013°	04.5'
08	299°	01.6'	N013°	03.7'
09	314°	01.7'	N013°	02.9'
10	329°	01.9'	N013°	02.1'
11	344°	02.0'	N013°	01.3'
12	359°	02.1'	N013°	00.5'
13	014°	02.3'	N012°	59.7'
14	029°	02.4'	N012°	58.9'
15	044°	02.6'	N012°	58.0'
16	059°	02.7'	N012°	57.2'
17	074°	02.8'	N012°	56.4'
18	089°	03.0'	N012°	55.6'
19	104°	03.1'	N012°	54.8'
20	119°	03.3'	N012°	54.0'
21	134°	03.4'	N012°	53.2'
22	149°	03.5'	N012°	52.4'
23	164°	03.7'	N012°	51.6'
August 19				
00	179°	03.8'	N012°	50.7'

Hr	GHA		DEC	
01	194°	04.0'	N012°	49.9'
02	209°	04.1'	N012°	49.1'
03	224°	04.3'	N012°	48.3'
04	239°	04.4'	N012°	47.5'
05	254°	04.5'	N012°	46.7'
06	269°	04.7'	N012°	45.9'
07	284°	04.8'	N012°	45.0'
08	299°	05.0'	N012°	44.2'
09	314°	05.1'	N012°	43.4'
10	329°	05.3'	N012°	42.6'
11	344°	05.4'	N012°	41.8'
12	359°	05.6'	N012°	40.9'
13	014°	05.7'	N012°	40.1'
14	029°	05.9'	N012°	39.3'
15	044°	06.0'	N012°	38.5'
16	059°	06.1'	N012°	37.7'
17	074°	06.3'	N012°	36.9'
18	089°	06.4'	N012°	36.0'
19	104°	06.6'	N012°	35.2'
20	119°	06.7'	N012°	34.4'
21	134°	06.9'	N012°	33.6'
22	149°	07.0'	N012°	32.8'
23	164°	07.2'	N012°	31.9'
August 20				
00	179°	07.3'	N012°	31.1'
01	194°	07.5'	N012°	30.3'
02	209°	07.6'	N012°	29.5'
03	224°	07.8'	N012°	28.6'
04	239°	07.9'	N012°	27.8'
05	254°	08.1'	N012°	27.0'
06	269°	08.2'	N012°	26.2'
07	284°	08.4'	N012°	25.4'
08	299°	08.5'	N012°	24.5'
09	314°	08.7'	N012°	23.7'
10	329°	08.8'	N012°	22.9'
11	344°	09.0'	N012°	22.1'
12	359°	09.1'	N012°	21.2'
13	014°	09.3'	N012°	20.4'
14	029°	09.4'	N012°	19.6'
15	044°	09.6'	N012°	18.7'
16	059°	09.7'	N012°	17.9'
17	074°	09.9'	N012°	17.1'
18	089°	10.0'	N012°	16.3'
19	104°	10.2'	N012°	15.4'
20	119°	10.3'	N012°	14.6'
21	134°	10.5'	N012°	13.8'
22	149°	10.6'	N012°	12.9'
23	164°	10.8'	N012°	12.1'
August 21				
00	179°	10.9'	N012°	11.3'
01	194°	11.1'	N012°	10.5'
02	209°	11.2'	N012°	09.6'
03	224°	11.4'	N012°	08.8'
04	239°	11.5'	N012°	08.0'
05	254°	11.7'	N012°	07.1'
06	269°	11.9'	N012°	06.3'
07	284°	12.0'	N012°	05.5'

Hr	GHA		DEC	
08	299°	12.2'	N012°	04.6'
09	314°	12.3'	N012°	03.8'
10	329°	12.5'	N012°	03.0'
11	344°	12.6'	N012°	02.1'
12	359°	12.8'	N012°	01.3'
13	014°	12.9'	N012°	00.5'
14	029°	13.1'	N011°	59.6'
15	044°	13.3'	N011°	58.8'
16	059°	13.4'	N011°	58.0'
17	074°	13.6'	N011°	57.1'
18	089°	13.7'	N011°	56.3'
19	104°	13.9'	N011°	55.5'
20	119°	14.0'	N011°	54.6'
21	134°	14.2'	N011°	53.8'
22	149°	14.3'	N011°	52.9'
23	164°	14.5'	N011°	52.1'
August 22				
00	179°	14.7'	N011°	51.3'
01	194°	14.8'	N011°	50.4'
02	209°	15.0'	N011°	49.6'
03	224°	15.1'	N011°	48.8'
04	239°	15.3'	N011°	47.9'
05	254°	15.5'	N011°	47.1'
06	269°	15.6'	N011°	46.2'
07	284°	15.8'	N011°	45.4'
08	299°	15.9'	N011°	44.6'
09	314°	16.1'	N011°	43.7'
10	329°	16.3'	N011°	42.9'
11	344°	16.4'	N011°	42.0'
12	359°	16.6'	N011°	41.2'
13	014°	16.7'	N011°	40.4'
14	029°	16.9'	N011°	39.5'
15	044°	17.1'	N011°	38.7'
16	059°	17.2'	N011°	37.8'
17	074°	17.4'	N011°	37.0'
18	089°	17.5'	N011°	36.1'
19	104°	17.7'	N011°	35.3'
20	119°	17.9'	N011°	34.4'
21	134°	18.0'	N011°	33.6'
22	149°	18.2'	N011°	32.8'
23	164°	18.3'	N011°	31.9'
August 23				
00	179°	18.5'	N011°	31.1'
01	194°	18.7'	N011°	30.2'
02	209°	18.8'	N011°	29.4'
03	224°	19.0'	N011°	28.5'
04	239°	19.2'	N011°	27.7'
05	254°	19.3'	N011°	26.8'
06	269°	19.5'	N011°	26.0'
07	284°	19.6'	N011°	25.1'
08	299°	19.8'	N011°	24.3'
09	314°	20.0'	N011°	23.4'
10	329°	20.1'	N011°	22.6'
11	344°	20.3'	N011°	21.7'
12	359°	20.5'	N011°	20.9'
13	014°	20.6'	N011°	20.0'
14	029°	20.8'	N011°	19.2'

Hr	GHA		DEC	
15	044°	21.0'	N011°	18.3'
16	059°	21.1'	N011°	17.5'
17	074°	21.3'	N011°	16.6'
18	089°	21.5'	N011°	15.8'
19	104°	21.6'	N011°	14.9'
20	119°	21.8'	N011°	14.1'
21	134°	22.0'	N011°	13.2'
22	149°	22.1'	N011°	12.4'
23	164°	22.3'	N011°	11.5'
August 24				
00	179°	22.5'	N011°	10.7'
01	194°	22.6'	N011°	09.8'
02	209°	22.8'	N011°	09.0'
03	224°	23.0'	N011°	08.1'
04	239°	23.1'	N011°	07.3'
05	254°	23.3'	N011°	06.4'
06	269°	23.5'	N011°	05.6'
07	284°	23.6'	N011°	04.7'
08	299°	23.8'	N011°	03.8'
09	314°	24.0'	N011°	03.0'
10	329°	24.1'	N011°	02.1'
11	344°	24.3'	N011°	01.3'
12	359°	24.5'	N011°	00.4'
13	014°	24.6'	N010°	59.6'
14	029°	24.8'	N010°	58.7'
15	044°	25.0'	N010°	57.9'
16	059°	25.2'	N010°	57.0'
17	074°	25.3'	N010°	56.1'
18	089°	25.5'	N010°	55.3'
19	104°	25.7'	N010°	54.4'
20	119°	25.8'	N010°	53.6'
21	134°	26.0'	N010°	52.7'
22	149°	26.2'	N010°	51.8'
23	164°	26.3'	N010°	51.0'
August 25				
00	179°	26.5'	N010°	50.1'
01	194°	26.7'	N010°	49.3'
02	209°	26.9'	N010°	48.4'
03	224°	27.0'	N010°	47.5'
04	239°	27.2'	N010°	46.7'
05	254°	27.4'	N010°	45.8'
06	269°	27.5'	N010°	45.0'
07	284°	27.7'	N010°	44.1'
08	299°	27.9'	N010°	43.2'
09	314°	28.1'	N010°	42.4'
10	329°	28.2'	N010°	41.5'
11	344°	28.4'	N010°	40.6'
12	359°	28.6'	N010°	39.8'
13	014°	28.8'	N010°	38.9'
14	029°	28.9'	N010°	38.0'
15	044°	29.1'	N010°	37.2'
16	059°	29.3'	N010°	36.3'
17	074°	29.5'	N010°	35.5'
18	089°	29.6'	N010°	34.6'
19	104°	29.8'	N010°	33.7'
20	119°	30.0'	N010°	32.9'
21	134°	30.2'	N010°	32.0'

Hr	GHA		DEC	
22	149°	30.3'	N010°	31.1'
23	164°	30.5'	N010°	30.3'
August 26				
00	179°	30.7'	N010°	29.4'
01	194°	30.9'	N010°	28.5'
02	209°	31.0'	N010°	27.7'
03	224°	31.2'	N010°	26.8'
04	239°	31.4'	N010°	25.9'
05	254°	31.6'	N010°	25.0'
06	269°	31.7'	N010°	24.2'
07	284°	31.9'	N010°	23.3'
08	299°	32.1'	N010°	22.4'
09	314°	32.3'	N010°	21.6'
10	329°	32.4'	N010°	20.7'
11	344°	32.6'	N010°	19.8'
12	359°	32.8'	N010°	19.0'
13	014°	33.0'	N010°	18.1'
14	029°	33.2'	N010°	17.2'
15	044°	33.3'	N010°	16.3'
16	059°	33.5'	N010°	15.5'
17	074°	33.7'	N010°	14.6'
18	089°	33.9'	N010°	13.7'
19	104°	34.0'	N010°	12.9'
20	119°	34.2'	N010°	12.0'
21	134°	34.4'	N010°	11.1'
22	149°	34.6'	N010°	10.2'
23	164°	34.8'	N010°	09.4'
August 27				
00	179°	34.9'	N010°	08.5'
01	194°	35.1'	N010°	07.6'
02	209°	35.3'	N010°	06.7'
03	224°	35.5'	N010°	05.9'
04	239°	35.7'	N010°	05.0'
05	254°	35.8'	N010°	04.1'
06	269°	36.0'	N010°	03.2'
07	284°	36.2'	N010°	02.4'
08	299°	36.4'	N010°	01.5'
09	314°	36.6'	N010°	00.6'
10	329°	36.7'	N009°	59.7'
11	344°	36.9'	N009°	58.9'
12	359°	37.1'	N009°	58.0'
13	014°	37.3'	N009°	57.1'
14	029°	37.5'	N009°	56.2'
15	044°	37.7'	N009°	55.3'
16	059°	37.8'	N009°	54.5'
17	074°	38.0'	N009°	53.6'
18	089°	38.2'	N009°	52.7'
19	104°	38.4'	N009°	51.8'
20	119°	38.6'	N009°	50.9'
21	134°	38.7'	N009°	50.1'
22	149°	38.9'	N009°	49.2'
23	164°	39.1'	N009°	48.3'
August 28				
00	179°	39.3'	N009°	47.4'
01	194°	39.5'	N009°	46.5'
02	209°	39.7'	N009°	45.7'
03	224°	39.8'	N009°	44.8'

Hr	GHA		DEC	
04	239°	40.0'	N009°	43.9'
05	254°	40.2'	N009°	43.0'
06	269°	40.4'	N009°	42.1'
07	284°	40.6'	N009°	41.3'
08	299°	40.8'	N009°	40.4'
09	314°	41.0'	N009°	39.5'
10	329°	41.1'	N009°	38.6'
11	344°	41.3'	N009°	37.7'
12	359°	41.5'	N009°	36.8'
13	014°	41.7'	N009°	36.0'
14	029°	41.9'	N009°	35.1'
15	044°	42.1'	N009°	34.2'
16	059°	42.3'	N009°	33.3'
17	074°	42.4'	N009°	32.4'
18	089°	42.6'	N009°	31.5'
19	104°	42.8'	N009°	30.6'
20	119°	43.0'	N009°	29.8'
21	134°	43.2'	N009°	28.9'
22	149°	43.4'	N009°	28.0'
23	164°	43.6'	N009°	27.1'
August 29				
00	179°	43.7'	N009°	26.2'
01	194°	43.9'	N009°	25.3'
02	209°	44.1'	N009°	24.4'
03	224°	44.3'	N009°	23.6'
04	239°	44.5'	N009°	22.7'
05	254°	44.7'	N009°	21.8'
06	269°	44.9'	N009°	20.9'
07	284°	45.1'	N009°	20.0'
08	299°	45.3'	N009°	19.1'
09	314°	45.4'	N009°	18.2'
10	329°	45.6'	N009°	17.3'
11	344°	45.8'	N009°	16.4'
12	359°	46.0'	N009°	15.5'
13	014°	46.2'	N009°	14.7'
14	029°	46.4'	N009°	13.8'
15	044°	46.6'	N009°	12.9'
16	059°	46.8'	N009°	12.0'
17	074°	47.0'	N009°	11.1'
18	089°	47.1'	N009°	10.2'
19	104°	47.3'	N009°	09.3'
20	119°	47.5'	N009°	08.4'
21	134°	47.7'	N009°	07.5'
22	149°	47.9'	N009°	06.6'
23	164°	48.1'	N009°	05.7'
August 30				
00	179°	48.3'	N009°	04.8'
01	194°	48.5'	N009°	04.0'
02	209°	48.7'	N009°	03.1'
03	224°	48.9'	N009°	02.2'
04	239°	49.0'	N009°	01.3'
05	254°	49.2'	N009°	00.4'
06	269°	49.4'	N008°	59.5'
07	284°	49.6'	N008°	58.6'
08	299°	49.8'	N008°	57.7'
09	314°	50.0'	N008°	56.8'
10	329°	50.2'	N008°	55.9'
11	344°	50.4'	N008°	55.0'
12	359°	50.6'	N008°	54.1'
13	014°	50.8'	N008°	53.2'
14	029°	51.0'	N008°	52.3'
15	044°	51.2'	N008°	51.4'
16	059°	51.4'	N008°	50.5'
17	074°	51.5'	N008°	49.6'
18	089°	51.7'	N008°	48.7'
19	104°	51.9'	N008°	47.8'
20	119°	52.1'	N008°	46.9'
21	134°	52.3'	N008°	46.0'
22	149°	52.5'	N008°	45.1'
23	164°	52.7'	N008°	44.2'
August 31				
00	179°	52.9'	N008°	43.3'
01	194°	53.1'	N008°	42.4'
02	209°	53.3'	N008°	41.5'
03	224°	53.5'	N008°	40.6'
04	239°	53.7'	N008°	39.7'
05	254°	53.9'	N008°	38.8'
06	269°	54.1'	N008°	37.9'
07	284°	54.3'	N008°	37.0'
08	299°	54.5'	N008°	36.1'
09	314°	54.7'	N008°	35.2'
10	329°	54.9'	N008°	34.3'
11	344°	55.1'	N008°	33.4'
12	359°	55.2'	N008°	32.5'
13	014°	55.4'	N008°	31.6'
14	029°	55.6'	N008°	30.7'
15	044°	55.8'	N008°	29.8'
16	059°	56.0'	N008°	28.9'
17	074°	56.2'	N008°	28.0'
18	089°	56.4'	N008°	27.1'
19	104°	56.6'	N008°	26.2'
20	119°	56.8'	N008°	25.3'
21	134°	57.0'	N008°	24.4'
22	149°	57.2'	N008°	23.5'
23	164°	57.4'	N008°	22.6'
September 1				
00	179°	57.6'	N008°	21.7'
01	194°	57.8'	N008°	20.8'
02	209°	58.0'	N008°	19.9'
03	224°	58.2'	N008°	19.0'
04	239°	58.4'	N008°	18.1'
05	254°	58.6'	N008°	17.2'
06	269°	58.8'	N008°	16.3'
07	284°	59.0'	N008°	15.3'
08	299°	59.2'	N008°	14.4'
09	314°	59.4'	N008°	13.5'
10	329°	59.6'	N008°	12.6'
11	344°	59.8'	N008°	11.7'
12	359°	60.0'	N008°	10.8'
13	015°	00.2'	N008°	09.9'
14	030°	00.4'	N008°	09.0'
15	045°	00.6'	N008°	08.1'
16	060°	00.8'	N008°	07.2'
17	075°	01.0'	N008°	06.3'
18	090°	01.2'	N008°	05.4'
19	105°	01.4'	N008°	04.5'
20	120°	01.6'	N008°	03.5'
21	135°	01.8'	N008°	02.6'
22	150°	02.0'	N008°	01.7'
23	165°	02.2'	N008°	00.8'
September 2				
00	180°	02.4'	N007°	59.9'
01	195°	02.6'	N007°	59.0'
02	210°	02.8'	N007°	58.1'
03	225°	03.0'	N007°	57.2'
04	240°	03.2'	N007°	56.3'
05	255°	03.4'	N007°	55.3'
06	270°	03.6'	N007°	54.4'
07	285°	03.8'	N007°	53.5'
08	300°	04.0'	N007°	52.6'
09	315°	04.2'	N007°	51.7'
10	330°	04.4'	N007°	50.8'
11	345°	04.6'	N007°	49.9'
12	000°	04.8'	N007°	49.0'
13	015°	05.0'	N007°	48.0'
14	030°	05.2'	N007°	47.1'
15	045°	05.4'	N007°	46.2'
16	060°	05.6'	N007°	45.3'
17	075°	05.8'	N007°	44.4'
18	090°	06.0'	N007°	43.5'
19	105°	06.2'	N007°	42.6'
20	120°	06.4'	N007°	41.7'
21	135°	06.6'	N007°	40.7'
22	150°	06.8'	N007°	39.8'
23	165°	07.0'	N007°	38.9'
September 3				
00	180°	07.2'	N007°	38.0'
01	195°	07.4'	N007°	37.1'
02	210°	07.6'	N007°	36.2'
03	225°	07.8'	N007°	35.2'
04	240°	08.0'	N007°	34.3'
05	255°	08.2'	N007°	33.4'
06	270°	08.5'	N007°	32.5'
07	285°	08.7'	N007°	31.6'
08	300°	08.9'	N007°	30.7'
09	315°	09.1'	N007°	29.7'
10	330°	09.3'	N007°	28.8'
11	345°	09.5'	N007°	27.9'
12	000°	09.7'	N007°	27.0'
13	015°	09.9'	N007°	26.1'
14	030°	10.1'	N007°	25.2'
15	045°	10.3'	N007°	24.2'
16	060°	10.5'	N007°	23.3'
17	075°	10.7'	N007°	22.4'
18	090°	10.9'	N007°	21.5'
19	105°	11.1'	N007°	20.6'
20	120°	11.3'	N007°	19.6'
21	135°	11.5'	N007°	18.7'
22	150°	11.7'	N007°	17.8'
23	165°	11.9'	N007°	16.9'

Hr	GHA		DEC	
		September 4		
00	180°	12.1'	N007°	16.0'
01	195°	12.4'	N007°	15.0'
02	210°	12.6'	N007°	14.1'
03	225°	12.8'	N007°	13.2'
04	240°	13.0'	N007°	12.3'
05	255°	13.2'	N007°	11.3'
06	270°	13.4'	N007°	10.4'
07	285°	13.6'	N007°	09.5'
08	300°	13.8'	N007°	08.6'
09	315°	14.0'	N007°	07.7'
10	330°	14.2'	N007°	06.7'
11	345°	14.4'	N007°	05.8'
12	000°	14.6'	N007°	04.9'
13	015°	14.8'	N007°	04.0'
14	030°	15.0'	N007°	03.0'
15	045°	15.2'	N007°	02.1'
16	060°	15.5'	N007°	01.2'
17	075°	15.7'	N007°	00.3'
18	090°	15.9'	N006°	59.3'
19	105°	16.1'	N006°	58.4'
20	120°	16.3'	N006°	57.5'
21	135°	16.5'	N006°	56.6'
22	150°	16.7'	N006°	55.7'
23	165°	16.9'	N006°	54.7'
		September 5		
00	180°	17.1'	N006°	53.8'
01	195°	17.3'	N006°	52.9'
02	210°	17.5'	N006°	51.9'
03	225°	17.7'	N006°	51.0'
04	240°	18.0'	N006°	50.1'
05	255°	18.2'	N006°	49.2'
06	270°	18.4'	N006°	48.2'
07	285°	18.6'	N006°	47.3'
08	300°	18.8'	N006°	46.4'
09	315°	19.0'	N006°	45.5'
10	330°	19.2'	N006°	44.5'
11	345°	19.4'	N006°	43.6'
12	000°	19.6'	N006°	42.7'
13	015°	19.8'	N006°	41.8'
14	030°	20.1'	N006°	40.8'
15	045°	20.3'	N006°	39.9'
16	060°	20.5'	N006°	39.0'
17	075°	20.7'	N006°	38.0'
18	090°	20.9'	N006°	37.1'
19	105°	21.1'	N006°	36.2'
20	120°	21.3'	N006°	35.3'
21	135°	21.5'	N006°	34.3'
22	150°	21.7'	N006°	33.4'
23	165°	21.9'	N006°	32.5'
		September 6		
00	180°	22.2'	N006°	31.5'
01	195°	22.4'	N006°	30.6'
02	210°	22.6'	N006°	29.7'
03	225°	22.8'	N006°	28.7'
04	240°	23.0'	N006°	27.8'
05	255°	23.2'	N006°	26.9'
06	270°	23.4'	N006°	26.0'
07	285°	23.6'	N006°	25.0'
08	300°	23.8'	N006°	24.1'
09	315°	24.1'	N006°	23.2'
10	330°	24.3'	N006°	22.2'
11	345°	24.5'	N006°	21.3'
12	000°	24.7'	N006°	20.4'
13	015°	24.9'	N006°	19.4'
14	030°	25.1'	N006°	18.5'
15	045°	25.3'	N006°	17.6'
16	060°	25.5'	N006°	16.6'
17	075°	25.8'	N006°	15.7'
18	090°	26.0'	N006°	14.8'
19	105°	26.2'	N006°	13.8'
20	120°	26.4'	N006°	12.9'
21	135°	26.6'	N006°	12.0'
22	150°	26.8'	N006°	11.0'
23	165°	27.0'	N006°	10.1'
		September 7		
00	180°	27.2'	N006°	09.2'
01	195°	27.5'	N006°	08.2'
02	210°	27.7'	N006°	07.3'
03	225°	27.9'	N006°	06.4'
04	240°	28.1'	N006°	05.4'
05	255°	28.3'	N006°	04.5'
06	270°	28.5'	N006°	03.6'
07	285°	28.7'	N006°	02.6'
08	300°	29.0'	N006°	01.7'
09	315°	29.2'	N006°	00.7'
10	330°	29.4'	N005°	59.8'
11	345°	29.6'	N005°	58.9'
12	000°	29.8'	N005°	57.9'
13	015°	30.0'	N005°	57.0'
14	030°	30.2'	N005°	56.1'
15	045°	30.5'	N005°	55.1'
16	060°	30.7'	N005°	54.2'
17	075°	30.9'	N005°	53.3'
18	090°	31.1'	N005°	52.3'
19	105°	31.3'	N005°	51.4'
20	120°	31.5'	N005°	50.4'
21	135°	31.7'	N005°	49.5'
22	150°	32.0'	N005°	48.6'
23	165°	32.2'	N005°	47.6'
		September 8		
00	180°	32.4'	N005°	46.7'
01	195°	32.6'	N005°	45.7'
02	210°	32.8'	N005°	44.8'
03	225°	33.0'	N005°	43.9'
04	240°	33.2'	N005°	42.9'
05	255°	33.5'	N005°	42.0'
06	270°	33.7'	N005°	41.1'
07	285°	33.9'	N005°	40.1'
08	300°	34.1'	N005°	39.2'
09	315°	34.3'	N005°	38.2'
10	330°	34.5'	N005°	37.3'
11	345°	34.8'	N005°	36.4'
12	000°	35.0'	N005°	35.4'
13	015°	35.2'	N005°	34.5'
14	030°	35.4'	N005°	33.5'
15	045°	35.6'	N005°	32.6'
16	060°	35.8'	N005°	31.6'
17	075°	36.1'	N005°	30.7'
18	090°	36.3'	N005°	29.8'
19	105°	36.5'	N005°	28.8'
20	120°	36.7'	N005°	27.9'
21	135°	36.9'	N005°	26.9'
22	150°	37.1'	N005°	26.0'
23	165°	37.3'	N005°	25.1'
		September 9		
00	180°	37.6'	N005°	24.1'
01	195°	37.8'	N005°	23.2'
02	210°	38.0'	N005°	22.2'
03	225°	38.2'	N005°	21.3'
04	240°	38.4'	N005°	20.3'
05	255°	38.7'	N005°	19.4'
06	270°	38.9'	N005°	18.5'
07	285°	39.1'	N005°	17.5'
08	300°	39.3'	N005°	16.6'
09	315°	39.5'	N005°	15.6'
10	330°	39.7'	N005°	14.7'
11	345°	40.0'	N005°	13.7'
12	000°	40.2'	N005°	12.8'
13	015°	40.4'	N005°	11.8'
14	030°	40.6'	N005°	10.9'
15	045°	40.8'	N005°	10.0'
16	060°	41.0'	N005°	09.0'
17	075°	41.3'	N005°	08.1'
18	090°	41.5'	N005°	07.1'
19	105°	41.7'	N005°	06.2'
20	120°	41.9'	N005°	05.2'
21	135°	42.1'	N005°	04.3'
22	150°	42.4'	N005°	03.3'
23	165°	42.6'	N005°	02.4'
		September 10		
00	180°	42.8'	N005°	01.5'
01	195°	43.0'	N005°	00.5'
02	210°	43.2'	N004°	59.6'
03	225°	43.4'	N004°	58.6'
04	240°	43.7'	N004°	57.7'
05	255°	43.9'	N004°	56.7'
06	270°	44.1'	N004°	55.8'
07	285°	44.3'	N004°	54.8'
08	300°	44.5'	N004°	53.9'
09	315°	44.8'	N004°	52.9'
10	330°	45.0'	N004°	52.0'
11	345°	45.2'	N004°	51.0'
12	000°	45.4'	N004°	50.1'
13	015°	45.6'	N004°	49.1'
14	030°	45.9'	N004°	48.2'
15	045°	46.1'	N004°	47.2'
16	060°	46.3'	N004°	46.3'
17	075°	46.5'	N004°	45.3'
18	090°	46.7'	N004°	44.4'
19	105°	46.9'	N004°	43.5'

Hr	GHA		DEC	
20	120°	47.2'	N004°	42.5'
21	135°	47.4'	N004°	41.6'
22	150°	47.6'	N004°	40.6'
23	165°	47.8'	N004°	39.7'
September 11				
00	180°	48.0'	N004°	38.7'
01	195°	48.3'	N004°	37.8'
02	210°	48.5'	N004°	36.8'
03	225°	48.7'	N004°	35.9'
04	240°	48.9'	N004°	34.9'
05	255°	49.1'	N004°	34.0'
06	270°	49.4'	N004°	33.0'
07	285°	49.6'	N004°	32.1'
08	300°	49.8'	N004°	31.1'
09	315°	50.0'	N004°	30.2'
10	330°	50.2'	N004°	29.2'
11	345°	50.5'	N004°	28.3'
12	000°	50.7'	N004°	27.3'
13	015°	50.9'	N004°	26.3'
14	030°	51.1'	N004°	25.4'
15	045°	51.3'	N004°	24.4'
16	060°	51.6'	N004°	23.5'
17	075°	51.8'	N004°	22.5'
18	090°	52.0'	N004°	21.6'
19	105°	52.2'	N004°	20.6'
20	120°	52.4'	N004°	19.7'
21	135°	52.7'	N004°	18.7'
22	150°	52.9'	N004°	17.8'
23	165°	53.1'	N004°	16.8'
September 12				
00	180°	53.3'	N004°	15.9'
01	195°	53.6'	N004°	14.9'
02	210°	53.8'	N004°	14.0'
03	225°	54.0'	N004°	13.0'
04	240°	54.2'	N004°	12.1'
05	255°	54.4'	N004°	11.1'
06	270°	54.7'	N004°	10.2'
07	285°	54.9'	N004°	09.2'
08	300°	55.1'	N004°	08.3'
09	315°	55.3'	N004°	07.3'
10	330°	55.5'	N004°	06.3'
11	345°	55.8'	N004°	05.4'
12	000°	56.0'	N004°	04.4'
13	015°	56.2'	N004°	03.5'
14	030°	56.4'	N004°	02.5'
15	045°	56.7'	N004°	01.6'
16	060°	56.9'	N004°	00.6'
17	075°	57.1'	N003°	59.7'
18	090°	57.3'	N003°	58.7'
19	105°	57.5'	N003°	57.8'
20	120°	57.8'	N003°	56.8'
21	135°	58.0'	N003°	55.8'
22	150°	58.2'	N003°	54.9'
23	165°	58.4'	N003°	53.9'
September 13				
00	180°	58.6'	N003°	53.0'
01	195°	58.9'	N003°	52.0'

Hr	GHA		DEC	
02	210°	59.1'	N003°	51.1'
03	225°	59.3'	N003°	50.1'
04	240°	59.5'	N003°	49.2'
05	255°	59.8'	N003°	48.2'
06	270°	60.0'	N003°	47.2'
07	286°	00.2'	N003°	46.3'
08	301°	00.4'	N003°	45.3'
09	316°	00.6'	N003°	44.4'
10	331°	00.9'	N003°	43.4'
11	346°	01.1'	N003°	42.5'
12	001°	01.3'	N003°	41.5'
13	016°	01.5'	N003°	40.5'
14	031°	01.8'	N003°	39.6'
15	046°	02.0'	N003°	38.6'
16	061°	02.2'	N003°	37.7'
17	076°	02.4'	N003°	36.7'
18	091°	02.6'	N003°	35.8'
19	106°	02.9'	N003°	34.8'
20	121°	03.1'	N003°	33.8'
21	136°	03.3'	N003°	32.9'
22	151°	03.5'	N003°	31.9'
23	166°	03.8'	N003°	31.0'
September 14				
00	181°	04.0'	N003°	30.0'
01	196°	04.2'	N003°	29.0'
02	211°	04.4'	N003°	28.1'
03	226°	04.6'	N003°	27.1'
04	241°	04.9'	N003°	26.2'
05	256°	05.1'	N003°	25.2'
06	271°	05.3'	N003°	24.3'
07	286°	05.5'	N003°	23.3'
08	301°	05.8'	N003°	22.3'
09	316°	06.0'	N003°	21.4'
10	331°	06.2'	N003°	20.4'
11	346°	06.4'	N003°	19.5'
12	001°	06.7'	N003°	18.5'
13	016°	06.9'	N003°	17.5'
14	031°	07.1'	N003°	16.6'
15	046°	07.3'	N003°	15.6'
16	061°	07.5'	N003°	14.7'
17	076°	07.8'	N003°	13.7'
18	091°	08.0'	N003°	12.7'
19	106°	08.2'	N003°	11.8'
20	121°	08.4'	N003°	10.8'
21	136°	08.7'	N003°	09.9'
22	151°	08.9'	N003°	08.9'
23	166°	09.1'	N003°	07.9'
September 15				
00	181°	09.3'	N003°	07.0'
01	196°	09.5'	N003°	06.0'
02	211°	09.8'	N003°	05.0'
03	226°	10.0'	N003°	04.1'
04	241°	10.2'	N003°	03.1'
05	256°	10.4'	N003°	02.2'
06	271°	10.7'	N003°	01.2'
07	286°	10.9'	N003°	00.2'
08	301°	11.1'	N002°	59.3'

Hr	GHA		DEC	
09	316°	11.3'	N002°	58.3'
10	331°	11.6'	N002°	57.4'
11	346°	11.8'	N002°	56.4'
12	001°	12.0'	N002°	55.4'
13	016°	12.2'	N002°	54.5'
14	031°	12.5'	N002°	53.5'
15	046°	12.7'	N002°	52.5'
16	061°	12.9'	N002°	51.6'
17	076°	13.1'	N002°	50.6'
18	091°	13.3'	N002°	49.7'
19	106°	13.6'	N002°	48.7'
20	121°	13.8'	N002°	47.7'
21	136°	14.0'	N002°	46.8'
22	151°	14.2'	N002°	45.8'
23	166°	14.5'	N002°	44.8'
September 16				
00	181°	14.7'	N002°	43.9'
01	196°	14.9'	N002°	42.9'
02	211°	15.1'	N002°	42.0'
03	226°	15.4'	N002°	41.0'
04	241°	15.6'	N002°	40.0'
05	256°	15.8'	N002°	39.1'
06	271°	16.0'	N002°	38.1'
07	286°	16.2'	N002°	37.1'
08	301°	16.5'	N002°	36.2'
09	316°	16.7'	N002°	35.2'
10	331°	16.9'	N002°	34.2'
11	346°	17.1'	N002°	33.3'
12	001°	17.4'	N002°	32.3'
13	016°	17.6'	N002°	31.3'
14	031°	17.8'	N002°	30.4'
15	046°	18.0'	N002°	29.4'
16	061°	18.3'	N002°	28.5'
17	076°	18.5'	N002°	27.5'
18	091°	18.7'	N002°	26.5'
19	106°	18.9'	N002°	25.6'
20	121°	19.2'	N002°	24.6'
21	136°	19.4'	N002°	23.6'
22	151°	19.6'	N002°	22.7'
23	166°	19.8'	N002°	21.7'
September 17				
00	181°	20.1'	N002°	20.7'
01	196°	20.3'	N002°	19.8'
02	211°	20.5'	N002°	18.8'
03	226°	20.7'	N002°	17.8'
04	241°	20.9'	N002°	16.9'
05	256°	21.2'	N002°	15.9'
06	271°	21.4'	N002°	14.9'
07	286°	21.6'	N002°	14.0'
08	301°	21.8'	N002°	13.0'
09	316°	22.1'	N002°	12.0'
10	331°	22.3'	N002°	11.1'
11	346°	22.5'	N002°	10.1'
12	001°	22.7'	N002°	09.1'
13	016°	23.0'	N002°	08.2'
14	031°	23.2'	N002°	07.2'
15	046°	23.4'	N002°	06.2'

Hr	GHA		DEC	
16	061°	23.6'	N002°	05.3'
17	076°	23.9'	N002°	04.3'
18	091°	24.1'	N002°	03.3'
19	106°	24.3'	N002°	02.4'
20	121°	24.5'	N002°	01.4'
21	136°	24.7'	N002°	00.4'
22	151°	25.0'	N001°	59.5'
23	166°	25.2'	N001°	58.5'
September 18				
00	181°	25.4'	N001°	57.5'
01	196°	25.6'	N001°	56.6'
02	211°	25.9'	N001°	55.6'
03	226°	26.1'	N001°	54.6'
04	241°	26.3'	N001°	53.7'
05	256°	26.5'	N001°	52.7'
06	271°	26.8'	N001°	51.7'
07	286°	27.0'	N001°	50.8'
08	301°	27.2'	N001°	49.8'
09	316°	27.4'	N001°	48.8'
10	331°	27.7'	N001°	47.9'
11	346°	27.9'	N001°	46.9'
12	001°	28.1'	N001°	45.9'
13	016°	28.3'	N001°	45.0'
14	031°	28.5'	N001°	44.0'
15	046°	28.8'	N001°	43.0'
16	061°	29.0'	N001°	42.1'
17	076°	29.2'	N001°	41.1'
18	091°	29.4'	N001°	40.1'
19	106°	29.7'	N001°	39.2'
20	121°	29.9'	N001°	38.2'
21	136°	30.1'	N001°	37.2'
22	151°	30.3'	N001°	36.2'
23	166°	30.6'	N001°	35.3'
September 19				
00	181°	30.8'	N001°	34.3'
01	196°	31.0'	N001°	33.3'
02	211°	31.2'	N001°	32.4'
03	226°	31.4'	N001°	31.4'
04	241°	31.7'	N001°	30.4'
05	256°	31.9'	N001°	29.5'
06	271°	32.1'	N001°	28.5'
07	286°	32.3'	N001°	27.5'
08	301°	32.6'	N001°	26.6'
09	316°	32.8'	N001°	25.6'
10	331°	33.0'	N001°	24.6'
11	346°	33.2'	N001°	23.6'
12	001°	33.5'	N001°	22.7'
13	016°	33.7'	N001°	21.7'
14	031°	33.9'	N001°	20.7'
15	046°	34.1'	N001°	19.8'
16	061°	34.3'	N001°	18.8'
17	076°	34.6'	N001°	17.8'
18	091°	34.8'	N001°	16.9'
19	106°	35.0'	N001°	15.9'
20	121°	35.2'	N001°	14.9'
21	136°	35.5'	N001°	14.0'
22	151°	35.7'	N001°	13.0'

Hr	GHA		DEC	
23	166°	35.9'	N001°	12.0'
September 20				
00	181°	36.1'	N001°	11.0'
01	196°	36.4'	N001°	10.1'
02	211°	36.6'	N001°	09.1'
03	226°	36.8'	N001°	08.1'
04	241°	37.0'	N001°	07.2'
05	256°	37.2'	N001°	06.2'
06	271°	37.5'	N001°	05.2'
07	286°	37.7'	N001°	04.2'
08	301°	37.9'	N001°	03.3'
09	316°	38.1'	N001°	02.3'
10	331°	38.4'	N001°	01.3'
11	346°	38.6'	N001°	00.4'
12	001°	38.8'	N000°	59.4'
13	016°	39.0'	N000°	58.4'
14	031°	39.2'	N000°	57.5'
15	046°	39.5'	N000°	56.5'
16	061°	39.7'	N000°	55.5'
17	076°	39.9'	N000°	54.5'
18	091°	40.1'	N000°	53.6'
19	106°	40.4'	N000°	52.6'
20	121°	40.6'	N000°	51.6'
21	136°	40.8'	N000°	50.7'
22	151°	41.0'	N000°	49.7'
23	166°	41.2'	N000°	48.7'
September 21				
00	181°	41.5'	N000°	47.7'
01	196°	41.7'	N000°	46.8'
02	211°	41.9'	N000°	45.8'
03	226°	42.1'	N000°	44.8'
04	241°	42.4'	N000°	43.9'
05	256°	42.6'	N000°	42.9'
06	271°	42.8'	N000°	41.9'
07	286°	43.0'	N000°	40.9'
08	301°	43.2'	N000°	40.0'
09	316°	43.5'	N000°	39.0'
10	331°	43.7'	N000°	38.0'
11	346°	43.9'	N000°	37.1'
12	001°	44.1'	N000°	36.1'
13	016°	44.3'	N000°	35.1'
14	031°	44.6'	N000°	34.1'
15	046°	44.8'	N000°	33.2'
16	061°	45.0'	N000°	32.2'
17	076°	45.2'	N000°	31.2'
18	091°	45.5'	N000°	30.3'
19	106°	45.7'	N000°	29.3'
20	121°	45.9'	N000°	28.3'
21	136°	46.1'	N000°	27.3'
22	151°	46.3'	N000°	26.4'
23	166°	46.6'	N000°	25.4'
September 22				
00	181°	46.8'	N000°	24.4'
01	196°	47.0'	N000°	23.4'
02	211°	47.2'	N000°	22.5'
03	226°	47.4'	N000°	21.5'
04	241°	47.7'	N000°	20.5'

Hr	GHA		DEC	
05	256°	47.9'	N000°	19.6'
06	271°	48.1'	N000°	18.6'
07	286°	48.3'	N000°	17.6'
08	301°	48.6'	N000°	16.6'
09	316°	48.8'	N000°	15.7'
10	331°	49.0'	N000°	14.7'
11	346°	49.2'	N000°	13.7'
12	001°	49.4'	N000°	12.7'
13	016°	49.7'	N000°	11.8'
14	031°	49.9'	N000°	10.8'
15	046°	50.1'	N000°	09.8'
16	061°	50.3'	N000°	08.9'
17	076°	50.5'	N000°	07.9'
18	091°	50.8'	N000°	06.9'
19	106°	51.0'	N000°	05.9'
20	121°	51.2'	N000°	05.0'
21	136°	51.4'	N000°	04.0'
22	151°	51.6'	N000°	03.0'
23	166°	51.9'	N000°	02.0'
September 23				
00	181°	52.1'	N000°	01.1'
01	196°	52.3'	N000°	00.1'
02	211°	52.5'	S000°	00.9'
03	226°	52.7'	S000°	01.8'
04	241°	53.0'	S000°	02.8'
05	256°	53.2'	S000°	03.8'
06	271°	53.4'	S000°	04.8'
07	286°	53.6'	S000°	05.7'
08	301°	53.8'	S000°	06.7'
09	316°	54.1'	S000°	07.7'
10	331°	54.3'	S000°	08.7'
11	346°	54.5'	S000°	09.6'
12	001°	54.7'	S000°	10.6'
13	016°	54.9'	S000°	11.6'
14	031°	55.2'	S000°	12.5'
15	046°	55.4'	S000°	13.5'
16	061°	55.6'	S000°	14.5'
17	076°	55.8'	S000°	15.5'
18	091°	56.0'	S000°	16.4'
19	106°	56.2'	S000°	17.4'
20	121°	56.5'	S000°	18.4'
21	136°	56.7'	S000°	19.4'
22	151°	56.9'	S000°	20.3'
23	166°	57.1'	S000°	21.3'
September 24				
00	181°	57.3'	S000°	22.3'
01	196°	57.6'	S000°	23.3'
02	211°	57.8'	S000°	24.2'
03	226°	58.0'	S000°	25.2'
04	241°	58.2'	S000°	26.2'
05	256°	58.4'	S000°	27.1'
06	271°	58.6'	S000°	28.1'
07	286°	58.9'	S000°	29.1'
08	301°	59.1'	S000°	30.1'
09	316°	59.3'	S000°	31.0'
10	331°	59.5'	S000°	32.0'
11	346°	59.7'	S000°	33.0'

Hr	GHA	DEC
12	001° 60.0'	S000° 34.0'
13	017° 00.2'	S000° 34.9'
14	032° 00.4'	S000° 35.9'
15	047° 00.6'	S000° 36.9'
16	062° 00.8'	S000° 37.9'
17	077° 01.0'	S000° 38.8'
18	092° 01.3'	S000° 39.8'
19	107° 01.5'	S000° 40.8'
20	122° 01.7'	S000° 41.7'
21	137° 01.9'	S000° 42.7'
22	152° 02.1'	S000° 43.7'
23	167° 02.4'	S000° 44.7'
September 25		
00	182° 02.6'	S000° 45.6'
01	197° 02.8'	S000° 46.6'
02	212° 03.0'	S000° 47.6'
03	227° 03.2'	S000° 48.6'
04	242° 03.4'	S000° 49.5'
05	257° 03.7'	S000° 50.5'
06	272° 03.9'	S000° 51.5'
07	287° 04.1'	S000° 52.5'
08	302° 04.3'	S000° 53.4'
09	317° 04.5'	S000° 54.4'
10	332° 04.7'	S000° 55.4'
11	347° 05.0'	S000° 56.4'
12	002° 05.2'	S000° 57.3'
13	017° 05.4'	S000° 58.3'
14	032° 05.6'	S000° 59.3'
15	047° 05.8'	S001° 00.2'
16	062° 06.0'	S001° 01.2'
17	077° 06.2'	S001° 02.2'
18	092° 06.5'	S001° 03.2'
19	107° 06.7'	S001° 04.1'
20	122° 06.9'	S001° 05.1'
21	137° 07.1'	S001° 06.1'
22	152° 07.3'	S001° 07.1'
23	167° 07.5'	S001° 08.0'
September 26		
00	182° 07.8'	S001° 09.0'
01	197° 08.0'	S001° 10.0'
02	212° 08.2'	S001° 11.0'
03	227° 08.4'	S001° 11.9'
04	242° 08.6'	S001° 12.9'
05	257° 08.8'	S001° 13.9'
06	272° 09.0'	S001° 14.8'
07	287° 09.3'	S001° 15.8'
08	302° 09.5'	S001° 16.8'
09	317° 09.7'	S001° 17.8'
10	332° 09.9'	S001° 18.7'
11	347° 10.1'	S001° 19.7'
12	002° 10.3'	S001° 20.7'
13	017° 10.5'	S001° 21.7'
14	032° 10.8'	S001° 22.6'
15	047° 11.0'	S001° 23.6'
16	062° 11.2'	S001° 24.6'
17	077° 11.4'	S001° 25.6'
18	092° 11.6'	S001° 26.5'
19	107° 11.8'	S001° 27.5'
20	122° 12.0'	S001° 28.5'
21	137° 12.3'	S001° 29.5'
22	152° 12.5'	S001° 30.4'
23	167° 12.7'	S001° 31.4'
September 27		
00	182° 12.9'	S001° 32.4'
01	197° 13.1'	S001° 33.3'
02	212° 13.3'	S001° 34.3'
03	227° 13.5'	S001° 35.3'
04	242° 13.8'	S001° 36.3'
05	257° 14.0'	S001° 37.2'
06	272° 14.2'	S001° 38.2'
07	287° 14.4'	S001° 39.2'
08	302° 14.6'	S001° 40.2'
09	317° 14.8'	S001° 41.1'
10	332° 15.0'	S001° 42.1'
11	347° 15.2'	S001° 43.1'
12	002° 15.5'	S001° 44.0'
13	017° 15.7'	S001° 45.0'
14	032° 15.9'	S001° 46.0'
15	047° 16.1'	S001° 47.0'
16	062° 16.3'	S001° 47.9'
17	077° 16.5'	S001° 48.9'
18	092° 16.7'	S001° 49.9'
19	107° 16.9'	S001° 50.9'
20	122° 17.1'	S001° 51.8'
21	137° 17.4'	S001° 52.8'
22	152° 17.6'	S001° 53.8'
23	167° 17.8'	S001° 54.7'
September 28		
00	182° 18.0'	S001° 55.7'
01	197° 18.2'	S001° 56.7'
02	212° 18.4'	S001° 57.7'
03	227° 18.6'	S001° 58.6'
04	242° 18.8'	S001° 59.6'
05	257° 19.0'	S002° 00.6'
06	272° 19.3'	S002° 01.6'
07	287° 19.5'	S002° 02.5'
08	302° 19.7'	S002° 03.5'
09	317° 19.9'	S002° 04.5'
10	332° 20.1'	S002° 05.4'
11	347° 20.3'	S002° 06.4'
12	002° 20.5'	S002° 07.4'
13	017° 20.7'	S002° 08.4'
14	032° 20.9'	S002° 09.3'
15	047° 21.1'	S002° 10.3'
16	062° 21.4'	S002° 11.3'
17	077° 21.6'	S002° 12.3'
18	092° 21.8'	S002° 13.2'
19	107° 22.0'	S002° 14.2'
20	122° 22.2'	S002° 15.2'
21	137° 22.4'	S002° 16.1'
22	152° 22.6'	S002° 17.1'
23	167° 22.8'	S002° 18.1'
September 29		
00	182° 23.0'	S002° 19.1'
01	197° 23.2'	S002° 20.0'
02	212° 23.4'	S002° 21.0'
03	227° 23.7'	S002° 22.0'
04	242° 23.9'	S002° 22.9'
05	257° 24.1'	S002° 23.9'
06	272° 24.3'	S002° 24.9'
07	287° 24.5'	S002° 25.9'
08	302° 24.7'	S002° 26.8'
09	317° 24.9'	S002° 27.8'
10	332° 25.1'	S002° 28.8'
11	347° 25.3'	S002° 29.7'
12	002° 25.5'	S002° 30.7'
13	017° 25.7'	S002° 31.7'
14	032° 25.9'	S002° 32.7'
15	047° 26.1'	S002° 33.6'
16	062° 26.4'	S002° 34.6'
17	077° 26.6'	S002° 35.6'
18	092° 26.8'	S002° 36.5'
19	107° 27.0'	S002° 37.5'
20	122° 27.2'	S002° 38.5'
21	137° 27.4'	S002° 39.5'
22	152° 27.6'	S002° 40.4'
23	167° 27.8'	S002° 41.4'
September 30		
00	182° 28.0'	S002° 42.4'
01	197° 28.2'	S002° 43.3'
02	212° 28.4'	S002° 44.3'
03	227° 28.6'	S002° 45.3'
04	242° 28.8'	S002° 46.3'
05	257° 29.0'	S002° 47.2'
06	272° 29.2'	S002° 48.2'
07	287° 29.4'	S002° 49.2'
08	302° 29.7'	S002° 50.1'
09	317° 29.9'	S002° 51.1'
10	332° 30.1'	S002° 52.1'
11	347° 30.3'	S002° 53.1'
12	002° 30.5'	S002° 54.0'
13	017° 30.7'	S002° 55.0'
14	032° 30.9'	S002° 56.0'
15	047° 31.1'	S002° 56.9'
16	062° 31.3'	S002° 57.9'
17	077° 31.5'	S002° 58.9'
18	092° 31.7'	S002° 59.8'
19	107° 31.9'	S003° 00.8'
20	122° 32.1'	S003° 01.8'
21	137° 32.3'	S003° 02.8'
22	152° 32.5'	S003° 03.7'
23	167° 32.7'	S003° 04.7'
October 1		
00	182° 32.9'	S003° 05.7'
01	197° 33.1'	S003° 06.6'
02	212° 33.3'	S003° 07.6'
03	227° 33.5'	S003° 08.6'
04	242° 33.7'	S003° 09.5'
05	257° 33.9'	S003° 10.5'
06	272° 34.1'	S003° 11.5'
07	287° 34.3'	S003° 12.4'

Hr	GHA		DEC	
08	302°	34.5'	S003°	13.4'
09	317°	34.7'	S003°	14.4'
10	332°	34.9'	S003°	15.4'
11	347°	35.1'	S003°	16.3'
12	002°	35.3'	S003°	17.3'
13	017°	35.5'	S003°	18.3'
14	032°	35.7'	S003°	19.2'
15	047°	36.0'	S003°	20.2'
16	062°	36.2'	S003°	21.2'
17	077°	36.4'	S003°	22.1'
18	092°	36.6'	S003°	23.1'
19	107°	36.8'	S003°	24.1'
20	122°	37.0'	S003°	25.0'
21	137°	37.2'	S003°	26.0'
22	152°	37.4'	S003°	27.0'
23	167°	37.6'	S003°	27.9'
October 2				
00	182°	37.8'	S003°	28.9'
01	197°	38.0'	S003°	29.9'
02	212°	38.2'	S003°	30.9'
03	227°	38.4'	S003°	31.8'
04	242°	38.6'	S003°	32.8'
05	257°	38.8'	S003°	33.8'
06	272°	39.0'	S003°	34.7'
07	287°	39.2'	S003°	35.7'
08	302°	39.4'	S003°	36.7'
09	317°	39.6'	S003°	37.6'
10	332°	39.8'	S003°	38.6'
11	347°	40.0'	S003°	39.6'
12	002°	40.1'	S003°	40.5'
13	017°	40.3'	S003°	41.5'
14	032°	40.5'	S003°	42.5'
15	047°	40.7'	S003°	43.4'
16	062°	40.9'	S003°	44.4'
17	077°	41.1'	S003°	45.4'
18	092°	41.3'	S003°	46.3'
19	107°	41.5'	S003°	47.3'
20	122°	41.7'	S003°	48.3'
21	137°	41.9'	S003°	49.2'
22	152°	42.1'	S003°	50.2'
23	167°	42.3'	S003°	51.2'
October 3				
00	182°	42.5'	S003°	52.1'
01	197°	42.7'	S003°	53.1'
02	212°	42.9'	S003°	54.1'
03	227°	43.1'	S003°	55.0'
04	242°	43.3'	S003°	56.0'
05	257°	43.5'	S003°	57.0'
06	272°	43.7'	S003°	57.9'
07	287°	43.9'	S003°	58.9'
08	302°	44.1'	S003°	59.9'
09	317°	44.3'	S004°	00.8'
10	332°	44.5'	S004°	01.8'
11	347°	44.7'	S004°	02.8'
12	002°	44.9'	S004°	03.7'
13	017°	45.1'	S004°	04.7'
14	032°	45.3'	S004°	05.7'

Hr	GHA		DEC	
15	047°	45.5'	S004°	06.6'
16	062°	45.7'	S004°	07.6'
17	077°	45.8'	S004°	08.6'
18	092°	46.0'	S004°	09.5'
19	107°	46.2'	S004°	10.5'
20	122°	46.4'	S004°	11.4'
21	137°	46.6'	S004°	12.4'
22	152°	46.8'	S004°	13.4'
23	167°	47.0'	S004°	14.3'
October 4				
00	182°	47.2'	S004°	15.3'
01	197°	47.4'	S004°	16.3'
02	212°	47.6'	S004°	17.2'
03	227°	47.8'	S004°	18.2'
04	242°	48.0'	S004°	19.2'
05	257°	48.2'	S004°	20.1'
06	272°	48.4'	S004°	21.1'
07	287°	48.6'	S004°	22.1'
08	302°	48.7'	S004°	23.0'
09	317°	48.9'	S004°	24.0'
10	332°	49.1'	S004°	24.9'
11	347°	49.3'	S004°	25.9'
12	002°	49.5'	S004°	26.9'
13	017°	49.7'	S004°	27.8'
14	032°	49.9'	S004°	28.8'
15	047°	50.1'	S004°	29.8'
16	062°	50.3'	S004°	30.7'
17	077°	50.5'	S004°	31.7'
18	092°	50.7'	S004°	32.7'
19	107°	50.9'	S004°	33.6'
20	122°	51.0'	S004°	34.6'
21	137°	51.2'	S004°	35.5'
22	152°	51.4'	S004°	36.5'
23	167°	51.6'	S004°	37.5'
October 5				
00	182°	51.8'	S004°	38.4'
01	197°	52.0'	S004°	39.4'
02	212°	52.2'	S004°	40.4'
03	227°	52.4'	S004°	41.3'
04	242°	52.6'	S004°	42.3'
05	257°	52.8'	S004°	43.2'
06	272°	52.9'	S004°	44.2'
07	287°	53.1'	S004°	45.2'
08	302°	53.3'	S004°	46.1'
09	317°	53.5'	S004°	47.1'
10	332°	53.7'	S004°	48.0'
11	347°	53.9'	S004°	49.0'
12	002°	54.1'	S004°	50.0'
13	017°	54.3'	S004°	50.9'
14	032°	54.4'	S004°	51.9'
15	047°	54.6'	S004°	52.8'
16	062°	54.8'	S004°	53.8'
17	077°	55.0'	S004°	54.8'
18	092°	55.2'	S004°	55.7'
19	107°	55.4'	S004°	56.7'
20	122°	55.6'	S004°	57.7'
21	137°	55.8'	S004°	58.6'

Hr	GHA		DEC	
22	152°	55.9'	S004°	59.6'
23	167°	56.1'	S005°	00.5'
October 6				
00	182°	56.3'	S005°	01.5'
01	197°	56.5'	S005°	02.5'
02	212°	56.7'	S005°	03.4'
03	227°	56.9'	S005°	04.4'
04	242°	57.1'	S005°	05.3'
05	257°	57.2'	S005°	06.3'
06	272°	57.4'	S005°	07.2'
07	287°	57.6'	S005°	08.2'
08	302°	57.8'	S005°	09.2'
09	317°	58.0'	S005°	10.1'
10	332°	58.2'	S005°	11.1'
11	347°	58.3'	S005°	12.0'
12	002°	58.5'	S005°	13.0'
13	017°	58.7'	S005°	14.0'
14	032°	58.9'	S005°	14.9'
15	047°	59.1'	S005°	15.9'
16	062°	59.3'	S005°	16.8'
17	077°	59.4'	S005°	17.8'
18	092°	59.6'	S005°	18.7'
19	107°	59.8'	S005°	19.7'
20	122°	60.0'	S005°	20.7'
21	138°	00.2'	S005°	21.6'
22	153°	00.4'	S005°	22.6'
23	168°	00.5'	S005°	23.5'
October 7				
00	183°	00.7'	S005°	24.5'
01	198°	00.9'	S005°	25.5'
02	213°	01.1'	S005°	26.4'
03	228°	01.3'	S005°	27.4'
04	243°	01.4'	S005°	28.3'
05	258°	01.6'	S005°	29.3'
06	273°	01.8'	S005°	30.2'
07	288°	02.0'	S005°	31.2'
08	303°	02.2'	S005°	32.1'
09	318°	02.4'	S005°	33.1'
10	333°	02.5'	S005°	34.1'
11	348°	02.7'	S005°	35.0'
12	003°	02.9'	S005°	36.0'
13	018°	03.1'	S005°	36.9'
14	033°	03.2'	S005°	37.9'
15	048°	03.4'	S005°	38.8'
16	063°	03.6'	S005°	39.8'
17	078°	03.8'	S005°	40.7'
18	093°	04.0'	S005°	41.7'
19	108°	04.1'	S005°	42.7'
20	123°	04.3'	S005°	43.6'
21	138°	04.5'	S005°	44.6'
22	153°	04.7'	S005°	45.5'
23	168°	04.9'	S005°	46.5'
October 8				
00	183°	05.0'	S005°	47.4'
01	198°	05.2'	S005°	48.4'
02	213°	05.4'	S005°	49.3'
03	228°	05.6'	S005°	50.3'

Sun Almanac

Hr	GHA		DEC		Hr	GHA		DEC		Hr	GHA		DEC	
04	243°	05.7'	S005°	51.2'	11	348°	15.2'	S006°	43.5'	18	093°	24.0'	S007°	35.2'
05	258°	05.9'	S005°	52.2'	12	003°	15.3'	S006°	44.4'	19	108°	24.1'	S007°	36.2'
06	273°	06.1'	S005°	53.1'	13	018°	15.5'	S006°	45.4'	20	123°	24.3'	S007°	37.1'
07	288°	06.3'	S005°	54.1'	14	033°	15.7'	S006°	46.3'	21	138°	24.4'	S007°	38.0'
08	303°	06.4'	S005°	55.1'	15	048°	15.8'	S006°	47.3'	22	153°	24.6'	S007°	39.0'
09	318°	06.6'	S005°	56.0'	16	063°	16.0'	S006°	48.2'	23	168°	24.7'	S007°	39.9'
10	333°	06.8'	S005°	57.0'	17	078°	16.2'	S006°	49.1'		October 13			
11	348°	07.0'	S005°	57.9'	18	093°	16.3'	S006°	50.1'	00	183°	24.9'	S007°	40.8'
12	003°	07.1'	S005°	58.9'	19	108°	16.5'	S006°	51.0'	01	198°	25.1'	S007°	41.8'
13	018°	07.3'	S005°	59.8'	20	123°	16.7'	S006°	52.0'	02	213°	25.2'	S007°	42.7'
14	033°	07.5'	S006°	00.8'	21	138°	16.8'	S006°	52.9'	03	228°	25.4'	S007°	43.7'
15	048°	07.7'	S006°	01.7'	22	153°	17.0'	S006°	53.9'	04	243°	25.5'	S007°	44.6'
16	063°	07.8'	S006°	02.7'	23	168°	17.1'	S006°	54.8'	05	258°	25.7'	S007°	45.5'
17	078°	08.0'	S006°	03.6'		October 11				06	273°	25.8'	S007°	46.5'
18	093°	08.2'	S006°	04.6'	00	183°	17.3'	S006°	55.8'	07	288°	26.0'	S007°	47.4'
19	108°	08.4'	S006°	05.5'	01	198°	17.5'	S006°	56.7'	08	303°	26.1'	S007°	48.3'
20	123°	08.5'	S006°	06.5'	02	213°	17.6'	S006°	57.6'	09	318°	26.3'	S007°	49.3'
21	138°	08.7'	S006°	07.4'	03	228°	17.8'	S006°	58.6'	10	333°	26.4'	S007°	50.2'
22	153°	08.9'	S006°	08.4'	04	243°	18.0'	S006°	59.5'	11	348°	26.6'	S007°	51.1'
23	168°	09.1'	S006°	09.3'	05	258°	18.1'	S007°	00.5'	12	003°	26.7'	S007°	52.1'
	October 9				06	273°	18.3'	S007°	01.4'	13	018°	26.9'	S007°	53.0'
00	183°	09.2'	S006°	10.3'	07	288°	18.4'	S007°	02.4'	14	033°	27.0'	S007°	53.9'
01	198°	09.4'	S006°	11.2'	08	303°	18.6'	S007°	03.3'	15	048°	27.2'	S007°	54.9'
02	213°	09.6'	S006°	12.2'	09	318°	18.8'	S007°	04.2'	16	063°	27.3'	S007°	55.8'
03	228°	09.8'	S006°	13.1'	10	333°	18.9'	S007°	05.2'	17	078°	27.5'	S007°	56.7'
04	243°	09.9'	S006°	14.1'	11	348°	19.1'	S007°	06.1'	18	093°	27.6'	S007°	57.7'
05	258°	10.1'	S006°	15.0'	12	003°	19.3'	S007°	07.1'	19	108°	27.8'	S007°	58.6'
06	273°	10.3'	S006°	16.0'	13	018°	19.4'	S007°	08.0'	20	123°	27.9'	S007°	59.5'
07	288°	10.4'	S006°	16.9'	14	033°	19.6'	S007°	08.9'	21	138°	28.1'	S008°	00.4'
08	303°	10.6'	S006°	17.9'	15	048°	19.7'	S007°	09.9'	22	153°	28.2'	S008°	01.4'
09	318°	10.8'	S006°	18.8'	16	063°	19.9'	S007°	10.8'	23	168°	28.4'	S008°	02.3'
10	333°	11.0'	S006°	19.8'	17	078°	20.1'	S007°	11.8'		October 14			
11	348°	11.1'	S006°	20.7'	18	093°	20.2'	S007°	12.7'	00	183°	28.5'	S008°	03.2'
12	003°	11.3'	S006°	21.7'	19	108°	20.4'	S007°	13.7'	01	198°	28.7'	S008°	04.2'
13	018°	11.5'	S006°	22.6'	20	123°	20.5'	S007°	14.6'	02	213°	28.8'	S008°	05.1'
14	033°	11.6'	S006°	23.6'	21	138°	20.7'	S007°	15.5'	03	228°	28.9'	S008°	06.0'
15	048°	11.8'	S006°	24.5'	22	153°	20.9'	S007°	16.5'	04	243°	29.1'	S008°	07.0'
16	063°	12.0'	S006°	25.5'	23	168°	21.0'	S007°	17.4'	05	258°	29.2'	S008°	07.9'
17	078°	12.1'	S006°	26.4'		October 12				06	273°	29.4'	S008°	08.8'
18	093°	12.3'	S006°	27.4'	00	183°	21.2'	S007°	18.4'	07	288°	29.5'	S008°	09.8'
19	108°	12.5'	S006°	28.3'	01	198°	21.3'	S007°	19.3'	08	303°	29.7'	S008°	10.7'
20	123°	12.7'	S006°	29.3'	02	213°	21.5'	S007°	20.2'	09	318°	29.8'	S008°	11.6'
21	138°	12.8'	S006°	30.2'	03	228°	21.6'	S007°	21.2'	10	333°	30.0'	S008°	12.5'
22	153°	13.0'	S006°	31.2'	04	243°	21.8'	S007°	22.1'	11	348°	30.1'	S008°	13.5'
23	168°	13.2'	S006°	32.1'	05	258°	22.0'	S007°	23.0'	12	003°	30.3'	S008°	14.4'
	October 10				06	273°	22.1'	S007°	24.0'	13	018°	30.4'	S008°	15.3'
00	183°	13.3'	S006°	33.1'	07	288°	22.3'	S007°	24.9'	14	033°	30.5'	S008°	16.3'
01	198°	13.5'	S006°	34.0'	08	303°	22.4'	S007°	25.9'	15	048°	30.7'	S008°	17.2'
02	213°	13.7'	S006°	35.0'	09	318°	22.6'	S007°	26.8'	16	063°	30.8'	S008°	18.1'
03	228°	13.8'	S006°	35.9'	10	333°	22.7'	S007°	27.7'	17	078°	31.0'	S008°	19.0'
04	243°	14.0'	S006°	36.9'	11	348°	22.9'	S007°	28.7'	18	093°	31.1'	S008°	20.0'
05	258°	14.2'	S006°	37.8'	12	003°	23.1'	S007°	29.6'	19	108°	31.3'	S008°	20.9'
06	273°	14.3'	S006°	38.7'	13	018°	23.2'	S007°	30.6'	20	123°	31.4'	S008°	21.8'
07	288°	14.5'	S006°	39.7'	14	033°	23.4'	S007°	31.5'	21	138°	31.6'	S008°	22.7'
08	303°	14.7'	S006°	40.6'	15	048°	23.5'	S007°	32.4'	22	153°	31.7'	S008°	23.7'
09	318°	14.8'	S006°	41.6'	16	063°	23.7'	S007°	33.4'	23	168°	31.8'	S008°	24.6'
10	333°	15.0'	S006°	42.5'	17	078°	23.8'	S007°	34.3'					

Hr	GHA		DEC		Hr	GHA		DEC		Hr	GHA		DEC	
	October 15				06	273°	39.3'	S009°	15.2'	13	018°	45.9'	S010°	05.1'
00	183°	32.0'	S008°	25.5'	07	288°	39.4'	S009°	16.1'	14	033°	46.0'	S010°	06.0'
01	198°	32.1'	S008°	26.4'	08	303°	39.5'	S009°	17.0'	15	048°	46.2'	S010°	06.9'
02	213°	32.3'	S008°	27.4'	09	318°	39.7'	S009°	18.0'	16	063°	46.3'	S010°	07.8'
03	228°	32.4'	S008°	28.3'	10	333°	39.8'	S009°	18.9'	17	078°	46.4'	S010°	08.7'
04	243°	32.5'	S008°	29.2'	11	348°	39.9'	S009°	19.8'	18	093°	46.5'	S010°	09.6'
05	258°	32.7'	S008°	30.1'	12	003°	40.0'	S009°	20.7'	19	108°	46.6'	S010°	10.5'
06	273°	32.8'	S008°	31.1'	13	018°	40.2'	S009°	21.6'	20	123°	46.7'	S010°	11.4'
07	288°	33.0'	S008°	32.0'	14	033°	40.3'	S009°	22.5'	21	138°	46.8'	S010°	12.3'
08	303°	33.1'	S008°	32.9'	15	048°	40.4'	S009°	23.4'	22	153°	46.9'	S010°	13.2'
09	318°	33.2'	S008°	33.8'	16	063°	40.5'	S009°	24.3'	23	168°	47.1'	S010°	14.1'
10	333°	33.4'	S008°	34.8'	17	078°	40.7'	S009°	25.3'		October 20			
11	348°	33.5'	S008°	35.7'	18	093°	40.8'	S009°	26.2'	00	183°	47.2'	S010°	15.0'
12	003°	33.7'	S008°	36.6'	19	108°	40.9'	S009°	27.1'	01	198°	47.3'	S010°	15.9'
13	018°	33.8'	S008°	37.5'	20	123°	41.0'	S009°	28.0'	02	213°	47.4'	S010°	16.8'
14	033°	33.9'	S008°	38.5'	21	138°	41.2'	S009°	28.9'	03	228°	47.5'	S010°	17.7'
15	048°	34.1'	S008°	39.4'	22	153°	41.3'	S009°	29.8'	04	243°	47.6'	S010°	18.6'
16	063°	34.2'	S008°	40.3'	23	168°	41.4'	S009°	30.7'	05	258°	47.7'	S010°	19.5'
17	078°	34.4'	S008°	41.2'		October 18				06	273°	47.8'	S010°	20.4'
18	093°	34.5'	S008°	42.2'	00	183°	41.5'	S009°	31.6'	07	288°	47.9'	S010°	21.3'
19	108°	34.6'	S008°	43.1'	01	198°	41.7'	S009°	32.5'	08	303°	48.0'	S010°	22.2'
20	123°	34.8'	S008°	44.0'	02	213°	41.8'	S009°	33.4'	09	318°	48.1'	S010°	23.1'
21	138°	34.9'	S008°	44.9'	03	228°	41.9'	S009°	34.4'	10	333°	48.3'	S010°	24.0'
22	153°	35.0'	S008°	45.8'	04	243°	42.0'	S009°	35.3'	11	348°	48.4'	S010°	24.9'
23	168°	35.2'	S008°	46.8'	05	258°	42.2'	S009°	36.2'	12	003°	48.5'	S010°	25.8'
	October 16				06	273°	42.3'	S009°	37.1'	13	018°	48.6'	S010°	26.7'
00	183°	35.3'	S008°	47.7'	07	288°	42.4'	S009°	38.0'	14	033°	48.7'	S010°	27.6'
01	198°	35.4'	S008°	48.6'	08	303°	42.5'	S009°	38.9'	15	048°	48.8'	S010°	28.5'
02	213°	35.6'	S008°	49.5'	09	318°	42.6'	S009°	39.8'	16	063°	48.9'	S010°	29.4'
03	228°	35.7'	S008°	50.4'	10	333°	42.8'	S009°	40.7'	17	078°	49.0'	S010°	30.2'
04	243°	35.8'	S008°	51.4'	11	348°	42.9'	S009°	41.6'	18	093°	49.1'	S010°	31.1'
05	258°	36.0'	S008°	52.3'	12	003°	43.0'	S009°	42.5'	19	108°	49.2'	S010°	32.0'
06	273°	36.1'	S008°	53.2'	13	018°	43.1'	S009°	43.4'	20	123°	49.3'	S010°	32.9'
07	288°	36.3'	S008°	54.1'	14	033°	43.2'	S009°	44.3'	21	138°	49.4'	S010°	33.8'
08	303°	36.4'	S008°	55.0'	15	048°	43.4'	S009°	45.2'	22	153°	49.5'	S010°	34.7'
09	318°	36.5'	S008°	56.0'	16	063°	43.5'	S009°	46.2'	23	168°	49.6'	S010°	35.6'
10	333°	36.7'	S008°	56.9'	17	078°	43.6'	S009°	47.1'		October 21			
11	348°	36.8'	S008°	57.8'	18	093°	43.7'	S009°	48.0'	00	183°	49.7'	S010°	36.5'
12	003°	36.9'	S008°	58.7'	19	108°	43.8'	S009°	48.9'	01	198°	49.8'	S010°	37.4'
13	018°	37.1'	S008°	59.6'	20	123°	44.0'	S009°	49.8'	02	213°	49.9'	S010°	38.3'
14	033°	37.2'	S009°	00.6'	21	138°	44.1'	S009°	50.7'	03	228°	50.0'	S010°	39.2'
15	048°	37.3'	S009°	01.5'	22	153°	44.2'	S009°	51.6'	04	243°	50.2'	S010°	40.1'
16	063°	37.5'	S009°	02.4'	23	168°	44.3'	S009°	52.5'	05	258°	50.3'	S010°	40.9'
17	078°	37.6'	S009°	03.3'		October 19				06	273°	50.4'	S010°	41.8'
18	093°	37.7'	S009°	04.2'	00	183°	44.4'	S009°	53.4'	07	288°	50.5'	S010°	42.7'
19	108°	37.8'	S009°	05.1'	01	198°	44.5'	S009°	54.3'	08	303°	50.6'	S010°	43.6'
20	123°	38.0'	S009°	06.1'	02	213°	44.7'	S009°	55.2'	09	318°	50.7'	S010°	44.5'
21	138°	38.1'	S009°	07.0'	03	228°	44.8'	S009°	56.1'	10	333°	50.8'	S010°	45.4'
22	153°	38.2'	S009°	07.9'	04	243°	44.9'	S009°	57.0'	11	348°	50.9'	S010°	46.3'
23	168°	38.4'	S009°	08.8'	05	258°	45.0'	S009°	57.9'	12	003°	51.0'	S010°	47.2'
	October 17				06	273°	45.1'	S009°	58.8'	13	018°	51.1'	S010°	48.1'
00	183°	38.5'	S009°	09.7'	07	288°	45.2'	S009°	59.7'	14	033°	51.2'	S010°	48.9'
01	198°	38.6'	S009°	10.6'	08	303°	45.4'	S010°	00.6'	15	048°	51.3'	S010°	49.8'
02	213°	38.8'	S009°	11.6'	09	318°	45.5'	S010°	01.5'	16	063°	51.4'	S010°	50.7'
03	228°	38.9'	S009°	12.5'	10	333°	45.6'	S010°	02.4'	17	078°	51.5'	S010°	51.6'
04	243°	39.0'	S009°	13.4'	11	348°	45.7'	S010°	03.3'	18	093°	51.6'	S010°	52.5'
05	258°	39.1'	S009°	14.3'	12	003°	45.8'	S010°	04.2'	19	108°	51.7'	S010°	53.4'

Hr	GHA		DEC	
20	123°	51.8'	S010°	54.3'
21	138°	51.9'	S010°	55.2'
22	153°	52.0'	S010°	56.0'
23	168°	52.1'	S010°	56.9'
October 22				
00	183°	52.1'	S010°	57.8'
01	198°	52.2'	S010°	58.7'
02	213°	52.3'	S010°	59.6'
03	228°	52.4'	S011°	00.5'
04	243°	52.5'	S011°	01.3'
05	258°	52.6'	S011°	02.2'
06	273°	52.7'	S011°	03.1'
07	288°	52.8'	S011°	04.0'
08	303°	52.9'	S011°	04.9'
09	318°	53.0'	S011°	05.8'
10	333°	53.1'	S011°	06.6'
11	348°	53.2'	S011°	07.5'
12	003°	53.3'	S011°	08.4'
13	018°	53.4'	S011°	09.3'
14	033°	53.5'	S011°	10.2'
15	048°	53.6'	S011°	11.1'
16	063°	53.7'	S011°	11.9'
17	078°	53.8'	S011°	12.8'
18	093°	53.8'	S011°	13.7'
19	108°	53.9'	S011°	14.6'
20	123°	54.0'	S011°	15.5'
21	138°	54.1'	S011°	16.3'
22	153°	54.2'	S011°	17.2'
23	168°	54.3'	S011°	18.1'
October 23				
00	183°	54.4'	S011°	19.0'
01	198°	54.5'	S011°	19.8'
02	213°	54.6'	S011°	20.7'
03	228°	54.7'	S011°	21.6'
04	243°	54.7'	S011°	22.5'
05	258°	54.8'	S011°	23.4'
06	273°	54.9'	S011°	24.2'
07	288°	55.0'	S011°	25.1'
08	303°	55.1'	S011°	26.0'
09	318°	55.2'	S011°	26.9'
10	333°	55.3'	S011°	27.7'
11	348°	55.4'	S011°	28.6'
12	003°	55.4'	S011°	29.5'
13	018°	55.5'	S011°	30.4'
14	033°	55.6'	S011°	31.2'
15	048°	55.7'	S011°	32.1'
16	063°	55.8'	S011°	33.0'
17	078°	55.9'	S011°	33.8'
18	093°	56.0'	S011°	34.7'
19	108°	56.0'	S011°	35.6'
20	123°	56.1'	S011°	36.5'
21	138°	56.2'	S011°	37.3'
22	153°	56.3'	S011°	38.2'
23	168°	56.4'	S011°	39.1'
October 24				
00	183°	56.5'	S011°	40.0'
01	198°	56.5'	S011°	40.8'

Hr	GHA		DEC	
02	213°	56.6'	S011°	41.7'
03	228°	56.7'	S011°	42.6'
04	243°	56.8'	S011°	43.4'
05	258°	56.9'	S011°	44.3'
06	273°	57.0'	S011°	45.2'
07	288°	57.0'	S011°	46.0'
08	303°	57.1'	S011°	46.9'
09	318°	57.2'	S011°	47.8'
10	333°	57.3'	S011°	48.6'
11	348°	57.4'	S011°	49.5'
12	003°	57.4'	S011°	50.4'
13	018°	57.5'	S011°	51.2'
14	033°	57.6'	S011°	52.1'
15	048°	57.7'	S011°	53.0'
16	063°	57.7'	S011°	53.8'
17	078°	57.8'	S011°	54.7'
18	093°	57.9'	S011°	55.6'
19	108°	58.0'	S011°	56.4'
20	123°	58.1'	S011°	57.3'
21	138°	58.1'	S011°	58.2'
22	153°	58.2'	S011°	59.0'
23	168°	58.3'	S011°	59.9'
October 25				
00	183°	58.4'	S012°	00.8'
01	198°	58.4'	S012°	01.6'
02	213°	58.5'	S012°	02.5'
03	228°	58.6'	S012°	03.3'
04	243°	58.7'	S012°	04.2'
05	258°	58.7'	S012°	05.1'
06	273°	58.8'	S012°	05.9'
07	288°	58.9'	S012°	06.8'
08	303°	59.0'	S012°	07.7'
09	318°	59.0'	S012°	08.5'
10	333°	59.1'	S012°	09.4'
11	348°	59.2'	S012°	10.2'
12	003°	59.2'	S012°	11.1'
13	018°	59.3'	S012°	12.0'
14	033°	59.4'	S012°	12.8'
15	048°	59.5'	S012°	13.7'
16	063°	59.5'	S012°	14.5'
17	078°	59.6'	S012°	15.4'
18	093°	59.7'	S012°	16.2'
19	108°	59.7'	S012°	17.1'
20	123°	59.8'	S012°	18.0'
21	138°	59.9'	S012°	18.8'
22	153°	59.9'	S012°	19.7'
23	169°	00.0'	S012°	20.5'
October 26				
00	184°	00.1'	S012°	21.4'
01	199°	00.1'	S012°	22.2'
02	214°	00.2'	S012°	23.1'
03	229°	00.3'	S012°	23.9'
04	244°	00.3'	S012°	24.8'
05	259°	00.4'	S012°	25.7'
06	274°	00.5'	S012°	26.5'
07	289°	00.5'	S012°	27.4'
08	304°	00.6'	S012°	28.2'

Hr	GHA		DEC	
09	319°	00.7'	S012°	29.1'
10	334°	00.7'	S012°	29.9'
11	349°	00.8'	S012°	30.8'
12	004°	00.9'	S012°	31.6'
13	019°	00.9'	S012°	32.5'
14	034°	01.0'	S012°	33.3'
15	049°	01.1'	S012°	34.2'
16	064°	01.1'	S012°	35.0'
17	079°	01.2'	S012°	35.9'
18	094°	01.2'	S012°	36.7'
19	109°	01.3'	S012°	37.6'
20	124°	01.4'	S012°	38.4'
21	139°	01.4'	S012°	39.3'
22	154°	01.5'	S012°	40.1'
23	169°	01.6'	S012°	41.0'
October 27				
00	184°	01.6'	S012°	41.8'
01	199°	01.7'	S012°	42.7'
02	214°	01.7'	S012°	43.5'
03	229°	01.8'	S012°	44.4'
04	244°	01.9'	S012°	45.2'
05	259°	01.9'	S012°	46.0'
06	274°	02.0'	S012°	46.9'
07	289°	02.0'	S012°	47.7'
08	304°	02.1'	S012°	48.6'
09	319°	02.1'	S012°	49.4'
10	334°	02.2'	S012°	50.3'
11	349°	02.3'	S012°	51.1'
12	004°	02.3'	S012°	52.0'
13	019°	02.4'	S012°	52.8'
14	034°	02.4'	S012°	53.6'
15	049°	02.5'	S012°	54.5'
16	064°	02.5'	S012°	55.3'
17	079°	02.6'	S012°	56.2'
18	094°	02.6'	S012°	57.0'
19	109°	02.7'	S012°	57.9'
20	124°	02.8'	S012°	58.7'
21	139°	02.8'	S012°	59.5'
22	154°	02.9'	S013°	00.4'
23	169°	02.9'	S013°	01.2'
October 28				
00	184°	03.0'	S013°	02.1'
01	199°	03.0'	S013°	02.9'
02	214°	03.1'	S013°	03.7'
03	229°	03.1'	S013°	04.6'
04	244°	03.2'	S013°	05.4'
05	259°	03.2'	S013°	06.2'
06	274°	03.3'	S013°	07.1'
07	289°	03.3'	S013°	07.9'
08	304°	03.4'	S013°	08.8'
09	319°	03.4'	S013°	09.6'
10	334°	03.5'	S013°	10.4'
11	349°	03.5'	S013°	11.3'
12	004°	03.6'	S013°	12.1'
13	019°	03.6'	S013°	12.9'
14	034°	03.7'	S013°	13.8'
15	049°	03.7'	S013°	14.6'

Hr	GHA		DEC	
16	064°	03.8'	S013°	15.4'
17	079°	03.8'	S013°	16.3'
18	094°	03.9'	S013°	17.1'
19	109°	03.9'	S013°	17.9'
20	124°	03.9'	S013°	18.8'
21	139°	04.0'	S013°	19.6'
22	154°	04.0'	S013°	20.4'
23	169°	04.1'	S013°	21.3'
October 29				
00	184°	04.1'	S013°	22.1'
01	199°	04.2'	S013°	22.9'
02	214°	04.2'	S013°	23.7'
03	229°	04.3'	S013°	24.6'
04	244°	04.3'	S013°	25.4'
05	259°	04.3'	S013°	26.2'
06	274°	04.4'	S013°	27.1'
07	289°	04.4'	S013°	27.9'
08	304°	04.5'	S013°	28.7'
09	319°	04.5'	S013°	29.5'
10	334°	04.6'	S013°	30.4'
11	349°	04.6'	S013°	31.2'
12	004°	04.6'	S013°	32.0'
13	019°	04.7'	S013°	32.9'
14	034°	04.7'	S013°	33.7'
15	049°	04.8'	S013°	34.5'
16	064°	04.8'	S013°	35.3'
17	079°	04.8'	S013°	36.2'
18	094°	04.9'	S013°	37.0'
19	109°	04.9'	S013°	37.8'
20	124°	04.9'	S013°	38.6'
21	139°	05.0'	S013°	39.4'
22	154°	05.0'	S013°	40.3'
23	169°	05.1'	S013°	41.1'
October 30				
00	184°	05.1'	S013°	41.9'
01	199°	05.1'	S013°	42.7'
02	214°	05.2'	S013°	43.6'
03	229°	05.2'	S013°	44.4'
04	244°	05.2'	S013°	45.2'
05	259°	05.3'	S013°	46.0'
06	274°	05.3'	S013°	46.8'
07	289°	05.3'	S013°	47.7'
08	304°	05.4'	S013°	48.5'
09	319°	05.4'	S013°	49.3'
10	334°	05.4'	S013°	50.1'
11	349°	05.5'	S013°	50.9'
12	004°	05.5'	S013°	51.7'
13	019°	05.5'	S013°	52.6'
14	034°	05.6'	S013°	53.4'
15	049°	05.6'	S013°	54.2'
16	064°	05.6'	S013°	55.0'
17	079°	05.7'	S013°	55.8'
18	094°	05.7'	S013°	56.6'
19	109°	05.7'	S013°	57.5'
20	124°	05.8'	S013°	58.3'
21	139°	05.8'	S013°	59.1'
22	154°	05.8'	S013°	59.9'
23	169°	05.8'	S014°	00.7'
October 31				
00	184°	05.9'	S014°	01.5'
01	199°	05.9'	S014°	02.3'
02	214°	05.9'	S014°	03.1'
03	229°	06.0'	S014°	04.0'
04	244°	06.0'	S014°	04.8'
05	259°	06.0'	S014°	05.6'
06	274°	06.0'	S014°	06.4'
07	289°	06.1'	S014°	07.2'
08	304°	06.1'	S014°	08.0'
09	319°	06.1'	S014°	08.8'
10	334°	06.1'	S014°	09.6'
11	349°	06.2'	S014°	10.4'
12	004°	06.2'	S014°	11.2'
13	019°	06.2'	S014°	12.0'
14	034°	06.2'	S014°	12.9'
15	049°	06.3'	S014°	13.7'
16	064°	06.3'	S014°	14.5'
17	079°	06.3'	S014°	15.3'
18	094°	06.3'	S014°	16.1'
19	109°	06.4'	S014°	16.9'
20	124°	06.4'	S014°	17.7'
21	139°	06.4'	S014°	18.5'
22	154°	06.4'	S014°	19.3'
23	169°	06.4'	S014°	20.1'
November 1				
00	184°	06.5'	S014°	20.9'
01	199°	06.5'	S014°	21.7'
02	214°	06.5'	S014°	22.5'
03	229°	06.5'	S014°	23.3'
04	244°	06.5'	S014°	24.1'
05	259°	06.6'	S014°	24.9'
06	274°	06.6'	S014°	25.7'
07	289°	06.6'	S014°	26.5'
08	304°	06.6'	S014°	27.3'
09	319°	06.6'	S014°	28.1'
10	334°	06.6'	S014°	28.9'
11	349°	06.7'	S014°	29.7'
12	004°	06.7'	S014°	30.5'
13	019°	06.7'	S014°	31.3'
14	034°	06.7'	S014°	32.1'
15	049°	06.7'	S014°	32.9'
16	064°	06.7'	S014°	33.7'
17	079°	06.7'	S014°	34.5'
18	094°	06.8'	S014°	35.3'
19	109°	06.8'	S014°	36.1'
20	124°	06.8'	S014°	36.9'
21	139°	06.8'	S014°	37.7'
22	154°	06.8'	S014°	38.5'
23	169°	06.8'	S014°	39.3'
November 2				
00	184°	06.8'	S014°	40.1'
01	199°	06.9'	S014°	40.9'
02	214°	06.9'	S014°	41.6'
03	229°	06.9'	S014°	42.4'
04	244°	06.9'	S014°	43.2'
05	259°	06.9'	S014°	44.0'
06	274°	06.9'	S014°	44.8'
07	289°	06.9'	S014°	45.6'
08	304°	06.9'	S014°	46.4'
09	319°	06.9'	S014°	47.2'
10	334°	06.9'	S014°	48.0'
11	349°	06.9'	S014°	48.8'
12	004°	07.0'	S014°	49.5'
13	019°	07.0'	S014°	50.3'
14	034°	07.0'	S014°	51.1'
15	049°	07.0'	S014°	51.9'
16	064°	07.0'	S014°	52.7'
17	079°	07.0'	S014°	53.5'
18	094°	07.0'	S014°	54.3'
19	109°	07.0'	S014°	55.1'
20	124°	07.0'	S014°	55.8'
21	139°	07.0'	S014°	56.6'
22	154°	07.0'	S014°	57.4'
23	169°	07.0'	S014°	58.2'
November 3				
00	184°	07.0'	S014°	59.0'
01	199°	07.0'	S014°	59.8'
02	214°	07.0'	S015°	00.5'
03	229°	07.0'	S015°	01.3'
04	244°	07.0'	S015°	02.1'
05	259°	07.0'	S015°	02.9'
06	274°	07.0'	S015°	03.7'
07	289°	07.0'	S015°	04.4'
08	304°	07.0'	S015°	05.2'
09	319°	07.0'	S015°	06.0'
10	334°	07.0'	S015°	06.8'
11	349°	07.0'	S015°	07.6'
12	004°	07.0'	S015°	08.3'
13	019°	07.0'	S015°	09.1'
14	034°	07.0'	S015°	09.9'
15	049°	07.0'	S015°	10.7'
16	064°	07.0'	S015°	11.5'
17	079°	07.0'	S015°	12.2'
18	094°	07.0'	S015°	13.0'
19	109°	07.0'	S015°	13.8'
20	124°	07.0'	S015°	14.6'
21	139°	07.0'	S015°	15.3'
22	154°	07.0'	S015°	16.1'
23	169°	07.0'	S015°	16.9'
November 4				
00	184°	07.0'	S015°	17.6'
01	199°	07.0'	S015°	18.4'
02	214°	07.0'	S015°	19.2'
03	229°	07.0'	S015°	20.0'
04	244°	07.0'	S015°	20.7'
05	259°	07.0'	S015°	21.5'
06	274°	07.0'	S015°	22.3'
07	289°	07.0'	S015°	23.0'
08	304°	06.9'	S015°	23.8'
09	319°	06.9'	S015°	24.6'
10	334°	06.9'	S015°	25.4'
11	349°	06.9'	S015°	26.1'

Hr	GHA		DEC	
12	004°	06.9'	S015°	26.9'
13	019°	06.9'	S015°	27.7'
14	034°	06.9'	S015°	28.4'
15	049°	06.9'	S015°	29.2'
16	064°	06.9'	S015°	30.0'
17	079°	06.9'	S015°	30.7'
18	094°	06.8'	S015°	31.5'
19	109°	06.8'	S015°	32.3'
20	124°	06.8'	S015°	33.0'
21	139°	06.8'	S015°	33.8'
22	154°	06.8'	S015°	34.5'
23	169°	06.8'	S015°	35.3'
November 5				
00	184°	06.8'	S015°	36.1'
01	199°	06.8'	S015°	36.8'
02	214°	06.7'	S015°	37.6'
03	229°	06.7'	S015°	38.4'
04	244°	06.7'	S015°	39.1'
05	259°	06.7'	S015°	39.9'
06	274°	06.7'	S015°	40.6'
07	289°	06.7'	S015°	41.4'
08	304°	06.6'	S015°	42.2'
09	319°	06.6'	S015°	42.9'
10	334°	06.6'	S015°	43.7'
11	349°	06.6'	S015°	44.4'
12	004°	06.6'	S015°	45.2'
13	019°	06.6'	S015°	45.9'
14	034°	06.5'	S015°	46.7'
15	049°	06.5'	S015°	47.5'
16	064°	06.5'	S015°	48.2'
17	079°	06.5'	S015°	49.0'
18	094°	06.5'	S015°	49.7'
19	109°	06.4'	S015°	50.5'
20	124°	06.4'	S015°	51.2'
21	139°	06.4'	S015°	52.0'
22	154°	06.4'	S015°	52.7'
23	169°	06.4'	S015°	53.5'
November 6				
00	184°	06.3'	S015°	54.2'
01	199°	06.3'	S015°	55.0'
02	214°	06.3'	S015°	55.7'
03	229°	06.3'	S015°	56.5'
04	244°	06.2'	S015°	57.2'
05	259°	06.2'	S015°	58.0'
06	274°	06.2'	S015°	58.7'
07	289°	06.2'	S015°	59.5'
08	304°	06.1'	S016°	00.2'
09	319°	06.1'	S016°	01.0'
10	334°	06.1'	S016°	01.7'
11	349°	06.1'	S016°	02.5'
12	004°	06.0'	S016°	03.2'
13	019°	06.0'	S016°	04.0'
14	034°	06.0'	S016°	04.7'
15	049°	06.0'	S016°	05.5'
16	064°	05.9'	S016°	06.2'
17	079°	05.9'	S016°	06.9'
18	094°	05.9'	S016°	07.7'

Hr	GHA		DEC	
19	109°	05.8'	S016°	08.4'
20	124°	05.8'	S016°	09.2'
21	139°	05.8'	S016°	09.9'
22	154°	05.8'	S016°	10.7'
23	169°	05.7'	S016°	11.4'
November 7				
00	184°	05.7'	S016°	12.1'
01	199°	05.7'	S016°	12.9'
02	214°	05.6'	S016°	13.6'
03	229°	05.6'	S016°	14.4'
04	244°	05.6'	S016°	15.1'
05	259°	05.5'	S016°	15.8'
06	274°	05.5'	S016°	16.6'
07	289°	05.5'	S016°	17.3'
08	304°	05.4'	S016°	18.0'
09	319°	05.4'	S016°	18.8'
10	334°	05.4'	S016°	19.5'
11	349°	05.3'	S016°	20.3'
12	004°	05.3'	S016°	21.0'
13	019°	05.3'	S016°	21.7'
14	034°	05.2'	S016°	22.5'
15	049°	05.2'	S016°	23.2'
16	064°	05.1'	S016°	23.9'
17	079°	05.1'	S016°	24.7'
18	094°	05.1'	S016°	25.4'
19	109°	05.0'	S016°	26.1'
20	124°	05.0'	S016°	26.8'
21	139°	05.0'	S016°	27.6'
22	154°	04.9'	S016°	28.3'
23	169°	04.9'	S016°	29.0'
November 8				
00	184°	04.8'	S016°	29.8'
01	199°	04.8'	S016°	30.5'
02	214°	04.8'	S016°	31.2'
03	229°	04.7'	S016°	32.0'
04	244°	04.7'	S016°	32.7'
05	259°	04.6'	S016°	33.4'
06	274°	04.6'	S016°	34.1'
07	289°	04.6'	S016°	34.9'
08	304°	04.5'	S016°	35.6'
09	319°	04.5'	S016°	36.3'
10	334°	04.4'	S016°	37.0'
11	349°	04.4'	S016°	37.8'
12	004°	04.3'	S016°	38.5'
13	019°	04.3'	S016°	39.2'
14	034°	04.2'	S016°	39.9'
15	049°	04.2'	S016°	40.6'
16	064°	04.2'	S016°	41.4'
17	079°	04.1'	S016°	42.1'
18	094°	04.1'	S016°	42.8'
19	109°	04.0'	S016°	43.5'
20	124°	04.0'	S016°	44.3'
21	139°	03.9'	S016°	45.0'
22	154°	03.9'	S016°	45.7'
23	169°	03.8'	S016°	46.4'
November 9				
00	184°	03.8'	S016°	47.1'

Hr	GHA		DEC	
01	199°	03.7'	S016°	47.8'
02	214°	03.7'	S016°	48.6'
03	229°	03.6'	S016°	49.3'
04	244°	03.6'	S016°	50.0'
05	259°	03.5'	S016°	50.7'
06	274°	03.5'	S016°	51.4'
07	289°	03.4'	S016°	52.1'
08	304°	03.4'	S016°	52.8'
09	319°	03.3'	S016°	53.6'
10	334°	03.3'	S016°	54.3'
11	349°	03.2'	S016°	55.0'
12	004°	03.2'	S016°	55.7'
13	019°	03.1'	S016°	56.4'
14	034°	03.1'	S016°	57.1'
15	049°	03.0'	S016°	57.8'
16	064°	03.0'	S016°	58.5'
17	079°	02.9'	S016°	59.2'
18	094°	02.8'	S016°	60.0'
19	109°	02.8'	S017°	00.7'
20	124°	02.7'	S017°	01.4'
21	139°	02.7'	S017°	02.1'
22	154°	02.6'	S017°	02.8'
23	169°	02.6'	S017°	03.5'
November 10				
00	184°	02.5'	S017°	04.2'
01	199°	02.4'	S017°	04.9'
02	214°	02.4'	S017°	05.6'
03	229°	02.3'	S017°	06.3'
04	244°	02.3'	S017°	07.0'
05	259°	02.2'	S017°	07.7'
06	274°	02.2'	S017°	08.4'
07	289°	02.1'	S017°	09.1'
08	304°	02.0'	S017°	09.8'
09	319°	02.0'	S017°	10.5'
10	334°	01.9'	S017°	11.2'
11	349°	01.9'	S017°	11.9'
12	004°	01.8'	S017°	12.6'
13	019°	01.7'	S017°	13.3'
14	034°	01.7'	S017°	14.0'
15	049°	01.6'	S017°	14.7'
16	064°	01.5'	S017°	15.4'
17	079°	01.5'	S017°	16.1'
18	094°	01.4'	S017°	16.8'
19	109°	01.3'	S017°	17.5'
20	124°	01.3'	S017°	18.2'
21	139°	01.2'	S017°	18.9'
22	154°	01.2'	S017°	19.6'
23	169°	01.1'	S017°	20.3'
November 11				
00	184°	01.0'	S017°	21.0'
01	199°	01.0'	S017°	21.7'
02	214°	00.9'	S017°	22.4'
03	229°	00.8'	S017°	23.0'
04	244°	00.8'	S017°	23.7'
05	259°	00.7'	S017°	24.4'
06	274°	00.6'	S017°	25.1'
07	289°	00.5'	S017°	25.8'

Hr	GHA		DEC	
08	304°	00.5'	S017°	26.5'
09	319°	00.4'	S017°	27.2'
10	334°	00.3'	S017°	27.9'
11	349°	00.3'	S017°	28.6'
12	004°	00.2'	S017°	29.2'
13	019°	00.1'	S017°	29.9'
14	034°	00.1'	S017°	30.6'
15	048°	60.0'	S017°	31.3'
16	063°	59.9'	S017°	32.0'
17	078°	59.8'	S017°	32.7'
18	093°	59.8'	S017°	33.4'
19	108°	59.7'	S017°	34.0'
20	123°	59.6'	S017°	34.7'
21	138°	59.5'	S017°	35.4'
22	153°	59.5'	S017°	36.1'
23	168°	59.4'	S017°	36.8'
November 12				
00	183°	59.3'	S017°	37.5'
01	198°	59.2'	S017°	38.1'
02	213°	59.2'	S017°	38.8'
03	228°	59.1'	S017°	39.5'
04	243°	59.0'	S017°	40.2'
05	258°	58.9'	S017°	40.8'
06	273°	58.9'	S017°	41.5'
07	288°	58.8'	S017°	42.2'
08	303°	58.7'	S017°	42.9'
09	318°	58.6'	S017°	43.6'
10	333°	58.6'	S017°	44.2'
11	348°	58.5'	S017°	44.9'
12	003°	58.4'	S017°	45.6'
13	018°	58.3'	S017°	46.3'
14	033°	58.2'	S017°	46.9'
15	048°	58.2'	S017°	47.6'
16	063°	58.1'	S017°	48.3'
17	078°	58.0'	S017°	48.9'
18	093°	57.9'	S017°	49.6'
19	108°	57.8'	S017°	50.3'
20	123°	57.7'	S017°	51.0'
21	138°	57.7'	S017°	51.6'
22	153°	57.6'	S017°	52.3'
23	168°	57.5'	S017°	53.0'
November 13				
00	183°	57.4'	S017°	53.6'
01	198°	57.3'	S017°	54.3'
02	213°	57.2'	S017°	55.0'
03	228°	57.2'	S017°	55.6'
04	243°	57.1'	S017°	56.3'
05	258°	57.0'	S017°	57.0'
06	273°	56.9'	S017°	57.6'
07	288°	56.8'	S017°	58.3'
08	303°	56.7'	S017°	59.0'
09	318°	56.6'	S017°	59.6'
10	333°	56.6'	S018°	00.3'
11	348°	56.5'	S018°	00.9'
12	003°	56.4'	S018°	01.6'
13	018°	56.3'	S018°	02.3'
14	033°	56.2'	S018°	02.9'

Hr	GHA		DEC	
15	048°	56.1'	S018°	03.6'
16	063°	56.0'	S018°	04.2'
17	078°	55.9'	S018°	04.9'
18	093°	55.8'	S018°	05.6'
19	108°	55.7'	S018°	06.2'
20	123°	55.7'	S018°	06.9'
21	138°	55.6'	S018°	07.5'
22	153°	55.5'	S018°	08.2'
23	168°	55.4'	S018°	08.8'
November 14				
00	183°	55.3'	S018°	09.5'
01	198°	55.2'	S018°	10.1'
02	213°	55.1'	S018°	10.8'
03	228°	55.0'	S018°	11.5'
04	243°	54.9'	S018°	12.1'
05	258°	54.8'	S018°	12.8'
06	273°	54.7'	S018°	13.4'
07	288°	54.6'	S018°	14.1'
08	303°	54.5'	S018°	14.7'
09	318°	54.4'	S018°	15.4'
10	333°	54.3'	S018°	16.0'
11	348°	54.2'	S018°	16.7'
12	003°	54.1'	S018°	17.3'
13	018°	54.0'	S018°	18.0'
14	033°	54.0'	S018°	18.6'
15	048°	53.9'	S018°	19.3'
16	063°	53.8'	S018°	19.9'
17	078°	53.7'	S018°	20.5'
18	093°	53.6'	S018°	21.2'
19	108°	53.5'	S018°	21.8'
20	123°	53.4'	S018°	22.5'
21	138°	53.3'	S018°	23.1'
22	153°	53.2'	S018°	23.8'
23	168°	53.1'	S018°	24.4'
November 15				
00	183°	53.0'	S018°	25.0'
01	198°	52.8'	S018°	25.7'
02	213°	52.7'	S018°	26.3'
03	228°	52.6'	S018°	27.0'
04	243°	52.5'	S018°	27.6'
05	258°	52.4'	S018°	28.2'
06	273°	52.3'	S018°	28.9'
07	288°	52.2'	S018°	29.5'
08	303°	52.1'	S018°	30.2'
09	318°	52.0'	S018°	30.8'
10	333°	51.9'	S018°	31.4'
11	348°	51.8'	S018°	32.1'
12	003°	51.7'	S018°	32.7'
13	018°	51.6'	S018°	33.3'
14	033°	51.5'	S018°	34.0'
15	048°	51.4'	S018°	34.6'
16	063°	51.3'	S018°	35.2'
17	078°	51.2'	S018°	35.9'
18	093°	51.1'	S018°	36.5'
19	108°	51.0'	S018°	37.1'
20	123°	50.8'	S018°	37.8'
21	138°	50.7'	S018°	38.4'

Hr	GHA		DEC	
22	153°	50.6'	S018°	39.0'
23	168°	50.5'	S018°	39.6'
November 16				
00	183°	50.4'	S018°	40.3'
01	198°	50.3'	S018°	40.9'
02	213°	50.2'	S018°	41.5'
03	228°	50.1'	S018°	42.1'
04	243°	50.0'	S018°	42.8'
05	258°	49.8'	S018°	43.4'
06	273°	49.7'	S018°	44.0'
07	288°	49.6'	S018°	44.6'
08	303°	49.5'	S018°	45.3'
09	318°	49.4'	S018°	45.9'
10	333°	49.3'	S018°	46.5'
11	348°	49.2'	S018°	47.1'
12	003°	49.1'	S018°	47.8'
13	018°	48.9'	S018°	48.4'
14	033°	48.8'	S018°	49.0'
15	048°	48.7'	S018°	49.6'
16	063°	48.6'	S018°	50.2'
17	078°	48.5'	S018°	50.9'
18	093°	48.4'	S018°	51.5'
19	108°	48.2'	S018°	52.1'
20	123°	48.1'	S018°	52.7'
21	138°	48.0'	S018°	53.3'
22	153°	47.9'	S018°	53.9'
23	168°	47.8'	S018°	54.6'
November 17				
00	183°	47.6'	S018°	55.2'
01	198°	47.5'	S018°	55.8'
02	213°	47.4'	S018°	56.4'
03	228°	47.3'	S018°	57.0'
04	243°	47.2'	S018°	57.6'
05	258°	47.1'	S018°	58.2'
06	273°	46.9'	S018°	58.8'
07	288°	46.8'	S018°	59.4'
08	303°	46.7'	S019°	00.1'
09	318°	46.6'	S019°	00.7'
10	333°	46.4'	S019°	01.3'
11	348°	46.3'	S019°	01.9'
12	003°	46.2'	S019°	02.5'
13	018°	46.1'	S019°	03.1'
14	033°	45.9'	S019°	03.7'
15	048°	45.8'	S019°	04.3'
16	063°	45.7'	S019°	04.9'
17	078°	45.6'	S019°	05.5'
18	093°	45.4'	S019°	06.1'
19	108°	45.3'	S019°	06.7'
20	123°	45.2'	S019°	07.3'
21	138°	45.1'	S019°	07.9'
22	153°	44.9'	S019°	08.5'
23	168°	44.8'	S019°	09.1'
November 18				
00	183°	44.7'	S019°	09.7'
01	198°	44.6'	S019°	10.3'
02	213°	44.4'	S019°	10.9'
03	228°	44.3'	S019°	11.5'

Hr	GHA		DEC	
04	243°	44.2'	S019°	12.1'
05	258°	44.0'	S019°	12.7'
06	273°	43.9'	S019°	13.3'
07	288°	43.8'	S019°	13.9'
08	303°	43.6'	S019°	14.5'
09	318°	43.5'	S019°	15.1'
10	333°	43.4'	S019°	15.7'
11	348°	43.3'	S019°	16.3'
12	003°	43.1'	S019°	16.9'
13	018°	43.0'	S019°	17.5'
14	033°	42.9'	S019°	18.1'
15	048°	42.7'	S019°	18.6'
16	063°	42.6'	S019°	19.2'
17	078°	42.5'	S019°	19.8'
18	093°	42.3'	S019°	20.4'
19	108°	42.2'	S019°	21.0'
20	123°	42.1'	S019°	21.6'
21	138°	41.9'	S019°	22.2'
22	153°	41.8'	S019°	22.8'
23	168°	41.6'	S019°	23.4'
November 19				
00	183°	41.5'	S019°	23.9'
01	198°	41.4'	S019°	24.5'
02	213°	41.2'	S019°	25.1'
03	228°	41.1'	S019°	25.7'
04	243°	41.0'	S019°	26.3'
05	258°	40.8'	S019°	26.9'
06	273°	40.7'	S019°	27.4'
07	288°	40.5'	S019°	28.0'
08	303°	40.4'	S019°	28.6'
09	318°	40.3'	S019°	29.2'
10	333°	40.1'	S019°	29.8'
11	348°	40.0'	S019°	30.3'
12	003°	39.8'	S019°	30.9'
13	018°	39.7'	S019°	31.5'
14	033°	39.6'	S019°	32.1'
15	048°	39.4'	S019°	32.6'
16	063°	39.3'	S019°	33.2'
17	078°	39.1'	S019°	33.8'
18	093°	39.0'	S019°	34.4'
19	108°	38.8'	S019°	34.9'
20	123°	38.7'	S019°	35.5'
21	138°	38.6'	S019°	36.1'
22	153°	38.4'	S019°	36.7'
23	168°	38.3'	S019°	37.2'
November 20				
00	183°	38.1'	S019°	37.8'
01	198°	38.0'	S019°	38.4'
02	213°	37.8'	S019°	38.9'
03	228°	37.7'	S019°	39.5'
04	243°	37.5'	S019°	40.1'
05	258°	37.4'	S019°	40.7'
06	273°	37.3'	S019°	41.2'
07	288°	37.1'	S019°	41.8'
08	303°	37.0'	S019°	42.3'
09	318°	36.8'	S019°	42.9'
10	333°	36.7'	S019°	43.5'

Hr	GHA		DEC	
11	348°	36.5'	S019°	44.0'
12	003°	36.4'	S019°	44.6'
13	018°	36.2'	S019°	45.2'
14	033°	36.1'	S019°	45.7'
15	048°	35.9'	S019°	46.3'
16	063°	35.8'	S019°	46.9'
17	078°	35.6'	S019°	47.4'
18	093°	35.5'	S019°	48.0'
19	108°	35.3'	S019°	48.5'
20	123°	35.2'	S019°	49.1'
21	138°	35.0'	S019°	49.6'
22	153°	34.9'	S019°	50.2'
23	168°	34.7'	S019°	50.8'
November 21				
00	183°	34.5'	S019°	51.3'
01	198°	34.4'	S019°	51.9'
02	213°	34.2'	S019°	52.4'
03	228°	34.1'	S019°	53.0'
04	243°	33.9'	S019°	53.5'
05	258°	33.8'	S019°	54.1'
06	273°	33.6'	S019°	54.6'
07	288°	33.5'	S019°	55.2'
08	303°	33.3'	S019°	55.7'
09	318°	33.1'	S019°	56.3'
10	333°	33.0'	S019°	56.8'
11	348°	32.8'	S019°	57.4'
12	003°	32.7'	S019°	57.9'
13	018°	32.5'	S019°	58.5'
14	033°	32.4'	S019°	59.0'
15	048°	32.2'	S019°	59.6'
16	063°	32.0'	S020°	00.1'
17	078°	31.9'	S020°	00.7'
18	093°	31.7'	S020°	01.2'
19	108°	31.6'	S020°	01.8'
20	123°	31.4'	S020°	02.3'
21	138°	31.2'	S020°	02.8'
22	153°	31.1'	S020°	03.4'
23	168°	30.9'	S020°	03.9'
November 22				
00	183°	30.8'	S020°	04.5'
01	198°	30.6'	S020°	05.0'
02	213°	30.4'	S020°	05.5'
03	228°	30.3'	S020°	06.1'
04	243°	30.1'	S020°	06.6'
05	258°	29.9'	S020°	07.2'
06	273°	29.8'	S020°	07.7'
07	288°	29.6'	S020°	08.2'
08	303°	29.5'	S020°	08.8'
09	318°	29.3'	S020°	09.3'
10	333°	29.1'	S020°	09.8'
11	348°	29.0'	S020°	10.4'
12	003°	28.8'	S020°	10.9'
13	018°	28.6'	S020°	11.4'
14	033°	28.5'	S020°	12.0'
15	048°	28.3'	S020°	12.5'
16	063°	28.1'	S020°	13.0'
17	078°	28.0'	S020°	13.6'

Hr	GHA		DEC	
18	093°	27.8'	S020°	14.1'
19	108°	27.6'	S020°	14.6'
20	123°	27.5'	S020°	15.1'
21	138°	27.3'	S020°	15.7'
22	153°	27.1'	S020°	16.2'
23	168°	26.9'	S020°	16.7'
November 23				
00	183°	26.8'	S020°	17.3'
01	198°	26.6'	S020°	17.8'
02	213°	26.4'	S020°	18.3'
03	228°	26.3'	S020°	18.8'
04	243°	26.1'	S020°	19.3'
05	258°	25.9'	S020°	19.9'
06	273°	25.7'	S020°	20.4'
07	288°	25.6'	S020°	20.9'
08	303°	25.4'	S020°	21.4'
09	318°	25.2'	S020°	21.9'
10	333°	25.1'	S020°	22.5'
11	348°	24.9'	S020°	23.0'
12	003°	24.7'	S020°	23.5'
13	018°	24.5'	S020°	24.0'
14	033°	24.4'	S020°	24.5'
15	048°	24.2'	S020°	25.1'
16	063°	24.0'	S020°	25.6'
17	078°	23.8'	S020°	26.1'
18	093°	23.7'	S020°	26.6'
19	108°	23.5'	S020°	27.1'
20	123°	23.3'	S020°	27.6'
21	138°	23.1'	S020°	28.1'
22	153°	22.9'	S020°	28.6'
23	168°	22.8'	S020°	29.2'
November 24				
00	183°	22.6'	S020°	29.7'
01	198°	22.4'	S020°	30.2'
02	213°	22.2'	S020°	30.7'
03	228°	22.1'	S020°	31.2'
04	243°	21.9'	S020°	31.7'
05	258°	21.7'	S020°	32.2'
06	273°	21.5'	S020°	32.7'
07	288°	21.3'	S020°	33.2'
08	303°	21.2'	S020°	33.7'
09	318°	21.0'	S020°	34.2'
10	333°	20.8'	S020°	34.7'
11	348°	20.6'	S020°	35.2'
12	003°	20.4'	S020°	35.7'
13	018°	20.2'	S020°	36.2'
14	033°	20.1'	S020°	36.7'
15	048°	19.9'	S020°	37.2'
16	063°	19.7'	S020°	37.7'
17	078°	19.5'	S020°	38.2'
18	093°	19.3'	S020°	38.7'
19	108°	19.1'	S020°	39.2'
20	123°	19.0'	S020°	39.7'
21	138°	18.8'	S020°	40.2'
22	153°	18.6'	S020°	40.7'
23	168°	18.4'	S020°	41.2'

Hr	GHA		DEC	
	November 25			
00	183°	18.2'	S020°	41.7'
01	198°	18.0'	S020°	42.2'
02	213°	17.8'	S020°	42.7'
03	228°	17.7'	S020°	43.2'
04	243°	17.5'	S020°	43.7'
05	258°	17.3'	S020°	44.1'
06	273°	17.1'	S020°	44.6'
07	288°	16.9'	S020°	45.1'
08	303°	16.7'	S020°	45.6'
09	318°	16.5'	S020°	46.1'
10	333°	16.3'	S020°	46.6'
11	348°	16.2'	S020°	47.1'
12	003°	16.0'	S020°	47.6'
13	018°	15.8'	S020°	48.0'
14	033°	15.6'	S020°	48.5'
15	048°	15.4'	S020°	49.0'
16	063°	15.2'	S020°	49.5'
17	078°	15.0'	S020°	50.0'
18	093°	14.8'	S020°	50.5'
19	108°	14.6'	S020°	50.9'
20	123°	14.4'	S020°	51.4'
21	138°	14.2'	S020°	51.9'
22	153°	14.0'	S020°	52.4'
23	168°	13.8'	S020°	52.9'
	November 26			
00	183°	13.7'	S020°	53.3'
01	198°	13.5'	S020°	53.8'
02	213°	13.3'	S020°	54.3'
03	228°	13.1'	S020°	54.8'
04	243°	12.9'	S020°	55.2'
05	258°	12.7'	S020°	55.7'
06	273°	12.5'	S020°	56.2'
07	288°	12.3'	S020°	56.7'
08	303°	12.1'	S020°	57.1'
09	318°	11.9'	S020°	57.6'
10	333°	11.7'	S020°	58.1'
11	348°	11.5'	S020°	58.5'
12	003°	11.3'	S020°	59.0'
13	018°	11.1'	S020°	59.5'
14	033°	10.9'	S020°	60.0'
15	048°	10.7'	S021°	00.4'
16	063°	10.5'	S021°	00.9'
17	078°	10.3'	S021°	01.4'
18	093°	10.1'	S021°	01.8'
19	108°	09.9'	S021°	02.3'
20	123°	09.7'	S021°	02.7'
21	138°	09.5'	S021°	03.2'
22	153°	09.3'	S021°	03.7'
23	168°	09.1'	S021°	04.1'
	November 27			
00	183°	08.9'	S021°	04.6'
01	198°	08.7'	S021°	05.1'
02	213°	08.5'	S021°	05.5'
03	228°	08.3'	S021°	06.0'
04	243°	08.1'	S021°	06.4'
05	258°	07.9'	S021°	06.9'
06	273°	07.7'	S021°	07.3'
07	288°	07.5'	S021°	07.8'
08	303°	07.3'	S021°	08.3'
09	318°	07.1'	S021°	08.7'
10	333°	06.9'	S021°	09.2'
11	348°	06.7'	S021°	09.6'
12	003°	06.5'	S021°	10.1'
13	018°	06.3'	S021°	10.5'
14	033°	06.1'	S021°	11.0'
15	048°	05.8'	S021°	11.4'
16	063°	05.6'	S021°	11.9'
17	078°	05.4'	S021°	12.3'
18	093°	05.2'	S021°	12.8'
19	108°	05.0'	S021°	13.2'
20	123°	04.8'	S021°	13.7'
21	138°	04.6'	S021°	14.1'
22	153°	04.4'	S021°	14.6'
23	168°	04.2'	S021°	15.0'
	November 28			
00	183°	04.0'	S021°	15.5'
01	198°	03.8'	S021°	15.9'
02	213°	03.6'	S021°	16.3'
03	228°	03.3'	S021°	16.8'
04	243°	03.1'	S021°	17.2'
05	258°	02.9'	S021°	17.7'
06	273°	02.7'	S021°	18.1'
07	288°	02.5'	S021°	18.5'
08	303°	02.3'	S021°	19.0'
09	318°	02.1'	S021°	19.4'
10	333°	01.9'	S021°	19.9'
11	348°	01.7'	S021°	20.3'
12	003°	01.4'	S021°	20.7'
13	018°	01.2'	S021°	21.2'
14	033°	01.0'	S021°	21.6'
15	048°	00.8'	S021°	22.0'
16	063°	00.6'	S021°	22.5'
17	078°	00.4'	S021°	22.9'
18	093°	00.2'	S021°	23.3'
19	107°	59.9'	S021°	23.8'
20	122°	59.7'	S021°	24.2'
21	137°	59.5'	S021°	24.6'
22	152°	59.3'	S021°	25.1'
23	167°	59.1'	S021°	25.5'
	November 29			
00	182°	58.9'	S021°	25.9'
01	197°	58.6'	S021°	26.3'
02	212°	58.4'	S021°	26.8'
03	227°	58.2'	S021°	27.2'
04	242°	58.0'	S021°	27.6'
05	257°	57.8'	S021°	28.0'
06	272°	57.6'	S021°	28.5'
07	287°	57.3'	S021°	28.9'
08	302°	57.1'	S021°	29.3'
09	317°	56.9'	S021°	29.7'
10	332°	56.7'	S021°	30.2'
11	347°	56.5'	S021°	30.6'
12	002°	56.2'	S021°	31.0'
13	017°	56.0'	S021°	31.4'
14	032°	55.8'	S021°	31.8'
15	047°	55.6'	S021°	32.2'
16	062°	55.4'	S021°	32.7'
17	077°	55.1'	S021°	33.1'
18	092°	54.9'	S021°	33.5'
19	107°	54.7'	S021°	33.9'
20	122°	54.5'	S021°	34.3'
21	137°	54.3'	S021°	34.7'
22	152°	54.0'	S021°	35.1'
23	167°	53.8'	S021°	35.6'
	November 30			
00	182°	53.6'	S021°	36.0'
01	197°	53.4'	S021°	36.4'
02	212°	53.1'	S021°	36.8'
03	227°	52.9'	S021°	37.2'
04	242°	52.7'	S021°	37.6'
05	257°	52.5'	S021°	38.0'
06	272°	52.2'	S021°	38.4'
07	287°	52.0'	S021°	38.8'
08	302°	51.8'	S021°	39.2'
09	317°	51.6'	S021°	39.6'
10	332°	51.3'	S021°	40.0'
11	347°	51.1'	S021°	40.4'
12	002°	50.9'	S021°	40.8'
13	017°	50.7'	S021°	41.2'
14	032°	50.4'	S021°	41.6'
15	047°	50.2'	S021°	42.0'
16	062°	50.0'	S021°	42.4'
17	077°	49.7'	S021°	42.8'
18	092°	49.5'	S021°	43.2'
19	107°	49.3'	S021°	43.6'
20	122°	49.1'	S021°	44.0'
21	137°	48.8'	S021°	44.4'
22	152°	48.6'	S021°	44.8'
23	167°	48.4'	S021°	45.2'
	December 1			
00	182°	48.1'	S021°	45.6'
01	197°	47.9'	S021°	46.0'
02	212°	47.7'	S021°	46.4'
03	227°	47.4'	S021°	46.8'
04	242°	47.2'	S021°	47.2'
05	257°	47.0'	S021°	47.6'
06	272°	46.7'	S021°	48.0'
07	287°	46.5'	S021°	48.3'
08	302°	46.3'	S021°	48.7'
09	317°	46.0'	S021°	49.1'
10	332°	45.8'	S021°	49.5'
11	347°	45.6'	S021°	49.9'
12	002°	45.3'	S021°	50.3'
13	017°	45.1'	S021°	50.7'
14	032°	44.9'	S021°	51.0'
15	047°	44.6'	S021°	51.4'
16	062°	44.4'	S021°	51.8'
17	077°	44.2'	S021°	52.2'
18	092°	43.9'	S021°	52.6'
19	107°	43.7'	S021°	53.0'

Sun Almanac

Hr	GHA		DEC	
20	122°	43.5'	S021°	53.3'
21	137°	43.2'	S021°	53.7'
22	152°	43.0'	S021°	54.1'
23	167°	42.8'	S021°	54.5'
December 2				
00	182°	42.5'	S021°	54.8'
01	197°	42.3'	S021°	55.2'
02	212°	42.0'	S021°	55.6'
03	227°	41.8'	S021°	56.0'
04	242°	41.6'	S021°	56.3'
05	257°	41.3'	S021°	56.7'
06	272°	41.1'	S021°	57.1'
07	287°	40.9'	S021°	57.5'
08	302°	40.6'	S021°	57.8'
09	317°	40.4'	S021°	58.2'
10	332°	40.1'	S021°	58.6'
11	347°	39.9'	S021°	58.9'
12	002°	39.7'	S021°	59.3'
13	017°	39.4'	S021°	59.7'
14	032°	39.2'	S022°	00.0'
15	047°	38.9'	S022°	00.4'
16	062°	38.7'	S022°	00.8'
17	077°	38.4'	S022°	01.1'
18	092°	38.2'	S022°	01.5'
19	107°	38.0'	S022°	01.8'
20	122°	37.7'	S022°	02.2'
21	137°	37.5'	S022°	02.6'
22	152°	37.2'	S022°	02.9'
23	167°	37.0'	S022°	03.3'
December 3				
00	182°	36.7'	S022°	03.6'
01	197°	36.5'	S022°	04.0'
02	212°	36.3'	S022°	04.4'
03	227°	36.0'	S022°	04.7'
04	242°	35.8'	S022°	05.1'
05	257°	35.5'	S022°	05.4'
06	272°	35.3'	S022°	05.8'
07	287°	35.0'	S022°	06.1'
08	302°	34.8'	S022°	06.5'
09	317°	34.5'	S022°	06.8'
10	332°	34.3'	S022°	07.2'
11	347°	34.1'	S022°	07.5'
12	002°	33.8'	S022°	07.9'
13	017°	33.6'	S022°	08.2'
14	032°	33.3'	S022°	08.6'
15	047°	33.1'	S022°	08.9'
16	062°	32.8'	S022°	09.3'
17	077°	32.6'	S022°	09.6'
18	092°	32.3'	S022°	10.0'
19	107°	32.1'	S022°	10.3'
20	122°	31.8'	S022°	10.7'
21	137°	31.6'	S022°	11.0'
22	152°	31.3'	S022°	11.3'
23	167°	31.1'	S022°	11.7'
December 4				
00	182°	30.8'	S022°	12.0'
01	197°	30.6'	S022°	12.4'

Hr	GHA		DEC	
02	212°	30.3'	S022°	12.7'
03	227°	30.1'	S022°	13.0'
04	242°	29.8'	S022°	13.4'
05	257°	29.6'	S022°	13.7'
06	272°	29.3'	S022°	14.1'
07	287°	29.1'	S022°	14.4'
08	302°	28.8'	S022°	14.7'
09	317°	28.6'	S022°	15.1'
10	332°	28.3'	S022°	15.4'
11	347°	28.1'	S022°	15.7'
12	002°	27.8'	S022°	16.1'
13	017°	27.6'	S022°	16.4'
14	032°	27.3'	S022°	16.7'
15	047°	27.0'	S022°	17.0'
16	062°	26.8'	S022°	17.4'
17	077°	26.5'	S022°	17.7'
18	092°	26.3'	S022°	18.0'
19	107°	26.0'	S022°	18.4'
20	122°	25.8'	S022°	18.7'
21	137°	25.5'	S022°	19.0'
22	152°	25.3'	S022°	19.3'
23	167°	25.0'	S022°	19.7'
December 5				
00	182°	24.8'	S022°	20.0'
01	197°	24.5'	S022°	20.3'
02	212°	24.2'	S022°	20.6'
03	227°	24.0'	S022°	20.9'
04	242°	23.7'	S022°	21.3'
05	257°	23.5'	S022°	21.6'
06	272°	23.2'	S022°	21.9'
07	287°	23.0'	S022°	22.2'
08	302°	22.7'	S022°	22.5'
09	317°	22.4'	S022°	22.9'
10	332°	22.2'	S022°	23.2'
11	347°	21.9'	S022°	23.5'
12	002°	21.7'	S022°	23.8'
13	017°	21.4'	S022°	24.1'
14	032°	21.2'	S022°	24.4'
15	047°	20.9'	S022°	24.7'
16	062°	20.6'	S022°	25.0'
17	077°	20.4'	S022°	25.4'
18	092°	20.1'	S022°	25.7'
19	107°	19.9'	S022°	26.0'
20	122°	19.6'	S022°	26.3'
21	137°	19.3'	S022°	26.6'
22	152°	19.1'	S022°	26.9'
23	167°	18.8'	S022°	27.2'
December 6				
00	182°	18.5'	S022°	27.5'
01	197°	18.3'	S022°	27.8'
02	212°	18.0'	S022°	28.1'
03	227°	17.8'	S022°	28.4'
04	242°	17.5'	S022°	28.7'
05	257°	17.2'	S022°	29.0'
06	272°	17.0'	S022°	29.3'
07	287°	16.7'	S022°	29.6'
08	302°	16.4'	S022°	29.9'

Hr	GHA		DEC	
09	317°	16.2'	S022°	30.2'
10	332°	15.9'	S022°	30.5'
11	347°	15.7'	S022°	30.8'
12	002°	15.4'	S022°	31.1'
13	017°	15.1'	S022°	31.4'
14	032°	14.9'	S022°	31.7'
15	047°	14.6'	S022°	32.0'
16	062°	14.3'	S022°	32.3'
17	077°	14.1'	S022°	32.6'
18	092°	13.8'	S022°	32.9'
19	107°	13.5'	S022°	33.1'
20	122°	13.3'	S022°	33.4'
21	137°	13.0'	S022°	33.7'
22	152°	12.7'	S022°	34.0'
23	167°	12.5'	S022°	34.3'
December 7				
00	182°	12.2'	S022°	34.6'
01	197°	11.9'	S022°	34.9'
02	212°	11.7'	S022°	35.2'
03	227°	11.4'	S022°	35.4'
04	242°	11.1'	S022°	35.7'
05	257°	10.9'	S022°	36.0'
06	272°	10.6'	S022°	36.3'
07	287°	10.3'	S022°	36.6'
08	302°	10.1'	S022°	36.8'
09	317°	09.8'	S022°	37.1'
10	332°	09.5'	S022°	37.4'
11	347°	09.3'	S022°	37.7'
12	002°	09.0'	S022°	38.0'
13	017°	08.7'	S022°	38.2'
14	032°	08.4'	S022°	38.5'
15	047°	08.2'	S022°	38.8'
16	062°	07.9'	S022°	39.1'
17	077°	07.6'	S022°	39.3'
18	092°	07.4'	S022°	39.6'
19	107°	07.1'	S022°	39.9'
20	122°	06.8'	S022°	40.1'
21	137°	06.5'	S022°	40.4'
22	152°	06.3'	S022°	40.7'
23	167°	06.0'	S022°	41.0'
December 8				
00	182°	05.7'	S022°	41.2'
01	197°	05.5'	S022°	41.5'
02	212°	05.2'	S022°	41.8'
03	227°	04.9'	S022°	42.0'
04	242°	04.6'	S022°	42.3'
05	257°	04.4'	S022°	42.6'
06	272°	04.1'	S022°	42.8'
07	287°	03.8'	S022°	43.1'
08	302°	03.5'	S022°	43.3'
09	317°	03.3'	S022°	43.6'
10	332°	03.0'	S022°	43.9'
11	347°	02.7'	S022°	44.1'
12	002°	02.5'	S022°	44.4'
13	017°	02.2'	S022°	44.6'
14	032°	01.9'	S022°	44.9'
15	047°	01.6'	S022°	45.1'

Sun Almanac

Hr	GHA		DEC	
16	062°	01.4'	S022°	45.4'
17	077°	01.1'	S022°	45.7'
18	092°	00.8'	S022°	45.9'
19	107°	00.5'	S022°	46.2'
20	122°	00.2'	S022°	46.4'
21	136°	60.0'	S022°	46.7'
22	151°	59.7'	S022°	46.9'
23	166°	59.4'	S022°	47.2'
December 9				
00	181°	59.1'	S022°	47.4'
01	196°	58.9'	S022°	47.7'
02	211°	58.6'	S022°	47.9'
03	226°	58.3'	S022°	48.2'
04	241°	58.0'	S022°	48.4'
05	256°	57.8'	S022°	48.7'
06	271°	57.5'	S022°	48.9'
07	286°	57.2'	S022°	49.1'
08	301°	56.9'	S022°	49.4'
09	316°	56.6'	S022°	49.6'
10	331°	56.4'	S022°	49.9'
11	346°	56.1'	S022°	50.1'
12	001°	55.8'	S022°	50.3'
13	016°	55.5'	S022°	50.6'
14	031°	55.2'	S022°	50.8'
15	046°	55.0'	S022°	51.1'
16	061°	54.7'	S022°	51.3'
17	076°	54.4'	S022°	51.5'
18	091°	54.1'	S022°	51.8'
19	106°	53.8'	S022°	52.0'
20	121°	53.6'	S022°	52.2'
21	136°	53.3'	S022°	52.5'
22	151°	53.0'	S022°	52.7'
23	166°	52.7'	S022°	52.9'
December 10				
00	181°	52.4'	S022°	53.2'
01	196°	52.2'	S022°	53.4'
02	211°	51.9'	S022°	53.6'
03	226°	51.6'	S022°	53.9'
04	241°	51.3'	S022°	54.1'
05	256°	51.0'	S022°	54.3'
06	271°	50.7'	S022°	54.5'
07	286°	50.5'	S022°	54.8'
08	301°	50.2'	S022°	55.0'
09	316°	49.9'	S022°	55.2'
10	331°	49.6'	S022°	55.4'
11	346°	49.3'	S022°	55.7'
12	001°	49.0'	S022°	55.9'
13	016°	48.8'	S022°	56.1'
14	031°	48.5'	S022°	56.3'
15	046°	48.2'	S022°	56.5'
16	061°	47.9'	S022°	56.7'
17	076°	47.6'	S022°	57.0'
18	091°	47.3'	S022°	57.2'
19	106°	47.1'	S022°	57.4'
20	121°	46.8'	S022°	57.6'
21	136°	46.5'	S022°	57.8'
22	151°	46.2'	S022°	58.0'
23	166°	45.9'	S022°	58.3'
December 11				
00	181°	45.6'	S022°	58.5'
01	196°	45.3'	S022°	58.7'
02	211°	45.1'	S022°	58.9'
03	226°	44.8'	S022°	59.1'
04	241°	44.5'	S022°	59.3'
05	256°	44.2'	S022°	59.5'
06	271°	43.9'	S022°	59.7'
07	286°	43.6'	S022°	59.9'
08	301°	43.3'	S023°	00.1'
09	316°	43.1'	S023°	00.3'
10	331°	42.8'	S023°	00.5'
11	346°	42.5'	S023°	00.7'
12	001°	42.2'	S023°	00.9'
13	016°	41.9'	S023°	01.1'
14	031°	41.6'	S023°	01.3'
15	046°	41.3'	S023°	01.5'
16	061°	41.0'	S023°	01.7'
17	076°	40.7'	S023°	01.9'
18	091°	40.5'	S023°	02.1'
19	106°	40.2'	S023°	02.3'
20	121°	39.9'	S023°	02.5'
21	136°	39.6'	S023°	02.7'
22	151°	39.3'	S023°	02.9'
23	166°	39.0'	S023°	03.1'
December 12				
00	181°	38.7'	S023°	03.3'
01	196°	38.4'	S023°	03.5'
02	211°	38.1'	S023°	03.7'
03	226°	37.9'	S023°	03.9'
04	241°	37.6'	S023°	04.1'
05	256°	37.3'	S023°	04.3'
06	271°	37.0'	S023°	04.4'
07	286°	36.7'	S023°	04.6'
08	301°	36.4'	S023°	04.8'
09	316°	36.1'	S023°	05.0'
10	331°	35.8'	S023°	05.2'
11	346°	35.5'	S023°	05.4'
12	001°	35.2'	S023°	05.6'
13	016°	34.9'	S023°	05.7'
14	031°	34.6'	S023°	05.9'
15	046°	34.4'	S023°	06.1'
16	061°	34.1'	S023°	06.3'
17	076°	33.8'	S023°	06.5'
18	091°	33.5'	S023°	06.6'
19	106°	33.2'	S023°	06.8'
20	121°	32.9'	S023°	07.0'
21	136°	32.6'	S023°	07.2'
22	151°	32.3'	S023°	07.3'
23	166°	32.0'	S023°	07.5'
December 13				
00	181°	31.7'	S023°	07.7'
01	196°	31.4'	S023°	07.9'
02	211°	31.1'	S023°	08.0'
03	226°	30.8'	S023°	08.2'
04	241°	30.5'	S023°	08.4'
05	256°	30.3'	S023°	08.5'
06	271°	30.0'	S023°	08.7'
07	286°	29.7'	S023°	08.9'
08	301°	29.4'	S023°	09.1'
09	316°	29.1'	S023°	09.2'
10	331°	28.8'	S023°	09.4'
11	346°	28.5'	S023°	09.6'
12	001°	28.2'	S023°	09.7'
13	016°	27.9'	S023°	09.9'
14	031°	27.6'	S023°	10.0'
15	046°	27.3'	S023°	10.2'
16	061°	27.0'	S023°	10.4'
17	076°	26.7'	S023°	10.5'
18	091°	26.4'	S023°	10.7'
19	106°	26.1'	S023°	10.8'
20	121°	25.8'	S023°	11.0'
21	136°	25.5'	S023°	11.2'
22	151°	25.2'	S023°	11.3'
23	166°	24.9'	S023°	11.5'
December 14				
00	181°	24.6'	S023°	11.6'
01	196°	24.3'	S023°	11.8'
02	211°	24.0'	S023°	11.9'
03	226°	23.8'	S023°	12.1'
04	241°	23.5'	S023°	12.2'
05	256°	23.2'	S023°	12.4'
06	271°	22.9'	S023°	12.5'
07	286°	22.6'	S023°	12.7'
08	301°	22.3'	S023°	12.8'
09	316°	22.0'	S023°	13.0'
10	331°	21.7'	S023°	13.1'
11	346°	21.4'	S023°	13.3'
12	001°	21.1'	S023°	13.4'
13	016°	20.8'	S023°	13.6'
14	031°	20.5'	S023°	13.7'
15	046°	20.2'	S023°	13.8'
16	061°	19.9'	S023°	14.0'
17	076°	19.6'	S023°	14.1'
18	091°	19.3'	S023°	14.3'
19	106°	19.0'	S023°	14.4'
20	121°	18.7'	S023°	14.5'
21	136°	18.4'	S023°	14.7'
22	151°	18.1'	S023°	14.8'
23	166°	17.8'	S023°	15.0'
December 15				
00	181°	17.5'	S023°	15.1'
01	196°	17.2'	S023°	15.2'
02	211°	16.9'	S023°	15.4'
03	226°	16.6'	S023°	15.5'
04	241°	16.3'	S023°	15.6'
05	256°	16.0'	S023°	15.8'
06	271°	15.7'	S023°	15.9'
07	286°	15.4'	S023°	16.0'
08	301°	15.1'	S023°	16.1'
09	316°	14.8'	S023°	16.3'
10	331°	14.5'	S023°	16.4'
11	346°	14.2'	S023°	16.5'

Hr	GHA		DEC	
12	001°	13.9'	S023°	16.6'
13	016°	13.6'	S023°	16.8'
14	031°	13.3'	S023°	16.9'
15	046°	13.0'	S023°	17.0'
16	061°	12.7'	S023°	17.1'
17	076°	12.4'	S023°	17.3'
18	091°	12.1'	S023°	17.4'
19	106°	11.8'	S023°	17.5'
20	121°	11.5'	S023°	17.6'
21	136°	11.2'	S023°	17.7'
22	151°	10.9'	S023°	17.9'
23	166°	10.6'	S023°	18.0'
December 16				
00	181°	10.3'	S023°	18.1'
01	196°	10.0'	S023°	18.2'
02	211°	09.7'	S023°	18.3'
03	226°	09.4'	S023°	18.4'
04	241°	09.0'	S023°	18.5'
05	256°	08.7'	S023°	18.7'
06	271°	08.4'	S023°	18.8'
07	286°	08.1'	S023°	18.9'
08	301°	07.8'	S023°	19.0'
09	316°	07.5'	S023°	19.1'
10	331°	07.2'	S023°	19.2'
11	346°	06.9'	S023°	19.3'
12	001°	06.6'	S023°	19.4'
13	016°	06.3'	S023°	19.5'
14	031°	06.0'	S023°	19.6'
15	046°	05.7'	S023°	19.7'
16	061°	05.4'	S023°	19.8'
17	076°	05.1'	S023°	19.9'
18	091°	04.8'	S023°	20.0'
19	106°	04.5'	S023°	20.1'
20	121°	04.2'	S023°	20.2'
21	136°	03.9'	S023°	20.3'
22	151°	03.6'	S023°	20.4'
23	166°	03.3'	S023°	20.5'
December 17				
00	181°	03.0'	S023°	20.6'
01	196°	02.7'	S023°	20.7'
02	211°	02.4'	S023°	20.8'
03	226°	02.1'	S023°	20.9'
04	241°	01.8'	S023°	21.0'
05	256°	01.5'	S023°	21.1'
06	271°	01.1'	S023°	21.2'
07	286°	00.8'	S023°	21.3'
08	301°	00.5'	S023°	21.4'
09	316°	00.2'	S023°	21.5'
10	330°	59.9'	S023°	21.5'
11	345°	59.6'	S023°	21.6'
12	000°	59.3'	S023°	21.7'
13	015°	59.0'	S023°	21.8'
14	030°	58.7'	S023°	21.9'
15	045°	58.4'	S023°	22.0'
16	060°	58.1'	S023°	22.1'
17	075°	57.8'	S023°	22.1'
18	090°	57.5'	S023°	22.2'

Hr	GHA		DEC	
19	105°	57.2'	S023°	22.3'
20	120°	56.9'	S023°	22.4'
21	135°	56.6'	S023°	22.5'
22	150°	56.3'	S023°	22.5'
23	165°	55.9'	S023°	22.6'
December 18				
00	180°	55.6'	S023°	22.7'
01	195°	55.3'	S023°	22.8'
02	210°	55.0'	S023°	22.8'
03	225°	54.7'	S023°	22.9'
04	240°	54.4'	S023°	23.0'
05	255°	54.1'	S023°	23.1'
06	270°	53.8'	S023°	23.1'
07	285°	53.5'	S023°	23.2'
08	300°	53.2'	S023°	23.3'
09	315°	52.9'	S023°	23.4'
10	330°	52.6'	S023°	23.4'
11	345°	52.3'	S023°	23.5'
12	000°	52.0'	S023°	23.6'
13	015°	51.7'	S023°	23.6'
14	030°	51.3'	S023°	23.7'
15	045°	51.0'	S023°	23.8'
16	060°	50.7'	S023°	23.8'
17	075°	50.4'	S023°	23.9'
18	090°	50.1'	S023°	23.9'
19	105°	49.8'	S023°	24.0'
20	120°	49.5'	S023°	24.1'
21	135°	49.2'	S023°	24.1'
22	150°	48.9'	S023°	24.2'
23	165°	48.6'	S023°	24.2'
December 19				
00	180°	48.3'	S023°	24.3'
01	195°	48.0'	S023°	24.4'
02	210°	47.6'	S023°	24.4'
03	225°	47.3'	S023°	24.5'
04	240°	47.0'	S023°	24.5'
05	255°	46.7'	S023°	24.6'
06	270°	46.4'	S023°	24.6'
07	285°	46.1'	S023°	24.7'
08	300°	45.8'	S023°	24.7'
09	315°	45.5'	S023°	24.8'
10	330°	45.2'	S023°	24.8'
11	345°	44.9'	S023°	24.9'
12	000°	44.6'	S023°	24.9'
13	015°	44.3'	S023°	25.0'
14	030°	43.9'	S023°	25.0'
15	045°	43.6'	S023°	25.1'
16	060°	43.3'	S023°	25.1'
17	075°	43.0'	S023°	25.1'
18	090°	42.7'	S023°	25.2'
19	105°	42.4'	S023°	25.2'
20	120°	42.1'	S023°	25.3'
21	135°	41.8'	S023°	25.3'
22	150°	41.5'	S023°	25.4'
23	165°	41.2'	S023°	25.4'
December 20				
00	180°	40.9'	S023°	25.4'

Hr	GHA		DEC	
01	195°	40.5'	S023°	25.5'
02	210°	40.2'	S023°	25.5'
03	225°	39.9'	S023°	25.5'
04	240°	39.6'	S023°	25.6'
05	255°	39.3'	S023°	25.6'
06	270°	39.0'	S023°	25.6'
07	285°	38.7'	S023°	25.7'
08	300°	38.4'	S023°	25.7'
09	315°	38.1'	S023°	25.7'
10	330°	37.8'	S023°	25.8'
11	345°	37.5'	S023°	25.8'
12	000°	37.1'	S023°	25.8'
13	015°	36.8'	S023°	25.8'
14	030°	36.5'	S023°	25.9'
15	045°	36.2'	S023°	25.9'
16	060°	35.9'	S023°	25.9'
17	075°	35.6'	S023°	25.9'
18	090°	35.3'	S023°	26.0'
19	105°	35.0'	S023°	26.0'
20	120°	34.7'	S023°	26.0'
21	135°	34.4'	S023°	26.0'
22	150°	34.0'	S023°	26.1'
23	165°	33.7'	S023°	26.1'
December 21				
00	180°	33.4'	S023°	26.1'
01	195°	33.1'	S023°	26.1'
02	210°	32.8'	S023°	26.1'
03	225°	32.5'	S023°	26.1'
04	240°	32.2'	S023°	26.2'
05	255°	31.9'	S023°	26.2'
06	270°	31.6'	S023°	26.2'
07	285°	31.2'	S023°	26.2'
08	300°	30.9'	S023°	26.2'
09	315°	30.6'	S023°	26.2'
10	330°	30.3'	S023°	26.2'
11	345°	30.0'	S023°	26.2'
12	000°	29.7'	S023°	26.2'
13	015°	29.4'	S023°	26.3'
14	030°	29.1'	S023°	26.3'
15	045°	28.8'	S023°	26.3'
16	060°	28.5'	S023°	26.3'
17	075°	28.1'	S023°	26.3'
18	090°	27.8'	S023°	26.3'
19	105°	27.5'	S023°	26.3'
20	120°	27.2'	S023°	26.3'
21	135°	26.9'	S023°	26.3'
22	150°	26.6'	S023°	26.3'
23	165°	26.3'	S023°	26.3'
December 22				
00	180°	26.0'	S023°	26.3'
01	195°	25.7'	S023°	26.3'
02	210°	25.3'	S023°	26.3'
03	225°	25.0'	S023°	26.3'
04	240°	24.7'	S023°	26.3'
05	255°	24.4'	S023°	26.3'
06	270°	24.1'	S023°	26.3'
07	285°	23.8'	S023°	26.3'

Hr	GHA		DEC	
08	300°	23.5'	S023°	26.2'
09	315°	23.2'	S023°	26.2'
10	330°	22.9'	S023°	26.2'
11	345°	22.5'	S023°	26.2'
12	000°	22.2'	S023°	26.2'
13	015°	21.9'	S023°	26.2'
14	030°	21.6'	S023°	26.2'
15	045°	21.3'	S023°	26.2'
16	060°	21.0'	S023°	26.2'
17	075°	20.7'	S023°	26.1'
18	090°	20.4'	S023°	26.1'
19	105°	20.1'	S023°	26.1'
20	120°	19.8'	S023°	26.1'
21	135°	19.4'	S023°	26.1'
22	150°	19.1'	S023°	26.0'
23	165°	18.8'	S023°	26.0'
December 23				
00	180°	18.5'	S023°	26.0'
01	195°	18.2'	S023°	26.0'
02	210°	17.9'	S023°	26.0'
03	225°	17.6'	S023°	25.9'
04	240°	17.3'	S023°	25.9'
05	255°	17.0'	S023°	25.9'
06	270°	16.6'	S023°	25.9'
07	285°	16.3'	S023°	25.8'
08	300°	16.0'	S023°	25.8'
09	315°	15.7'	S023°	25.8'
10	330°	15.4'	S023°	25.8'
11	345°	15.1'	S023°	25.7'
12	000°	14.8'	S023°	25.7'
13	015°	14.5'	S023°	25.7'
14	030°	14.2'	S023°	25.6'
15	045°	13.8'	S023°	25.6'
16	060°	13.5'	S023°	25.6'
17	075°	13.2'	S023°	25.5'
18	090°	12.9'	S023°	25.5'
19	105°	12.6'	S023°	25.5'
20	120°	12.3'	S023°	25.4'
21	135°	12.0'	S023°	25.4'
22	150°	11.7'	S023°	25.3'
23	165°	11.4'	S023°	25.3'
December 24				
00	180°	11.0'	S023°	25.3'
01	195°	10.7'	S023°	25.2'
02	210°	10.4'	S023°	25.2'
03	225°	10.1'	S023°	25.1'
04	240°	09.8'	S023°	25.1'
05	255°	09.5'	S023°	25.0'
06	270°	09.2'	S023°	25.0'
07	285°	08.9'	S023°	24.9'
08	300°	08.6'	S023°	24.9'
09	315°	08.3'	S023°	24.9'
10	330°	07.9'	S023°	24.8'
11	345°	07.6'	S023°	24.8'
12	000°	07.3'	S023°	24.7'
13	015°	07.0'	S023°	24.7'
14	030°	06.7'	S023°	24.6'

Hr	GHA		DEC	
15	045°	06.4'	S023°	24.5'
16	060°	06.1'	S023°	24.5'
17	075°	05.8'	S023°	24.4'
18	090°	05.5'	S023°	24.4'
19	105°	05.1'	S023°	24.3'
20	120°	04.8'	S023°	24.3'
21	135°	04.5'	S023°	24.2'
22	150°	04.2'	S023°	24.2'
23	165°	03.9'	S023°	24.1'
December 25				
00	180°	03.6'	S023°	24.0'
01	195°	03.3'	S023°	24.0'
02	210°	03.0'	S023°	23.9'
03	225°	02.7'	S023°	23.9'
04	240°	02.4'	S023°	23.8'
05	255°	02.0'	S023°	23.7'
06	270°	01.7'	S023°	23.7'
07	285°	01.4'	S023°	23.6'
08	300°	01.1'	S023°	23.5'
09	315°	00.8'	S023°	23.5'
10	330°	00.5'	S023°	23.4'
11	345°	00.2'	S023°	23.3'
12	359°	59.9'	S023°	23.2'
13	014°	59.6'	S023°	23.2'
14	029°	59.3'	S023°	23.1'
15	044°	58.9'	S023°	23.0'
16	059°	58.6'	S023°	23.0'
17	074°	58.3'	S023°	22.9'
18	089°	58.0'	S023°	22.8'
19	104°	57.7'	S023°	22.7'
20	119°	57.4'	S023°	22.7'
21	134°	57.1'	S023°	22.6'
22	149°	56.8'	S023°	22.5'
23	164°	56.5'	S023°	22.4'
December 26				
00	179°	56.2'	S023°	22.3'
01	194°	55.9'	S023°	22.3'
02	209°	55.5'	S023°	22.2'
03	224°	55.2'	S023°	22.1'
04	239°	54.9'	S023°	22.0'
05	254°	54.6'	S023°	21.9'
06	269°	54.3'	S023°	21.8'
07	284°	54.0'	S023°	21.8'
08	299°	53.7'	S023°	21.7'
09	314°	53.4'	S023°	21.6'
10	329°	53.1'	S023°	21.5'
11	344°	52.8'	S023°	21.4'
12	359°	52.5'	S023°	21.3'
13	014°	52.1'	S023°	21.2'
14	029°	51.8'	S023°	21.1'
15	044°	51.5'	S023°	21.1'
16	059°	51.2'	S023°	21.0'
17	074°	50.9'	S023°	20.9'
18	089°	50.6'	S023°	20.8'
19	104°	50.3'	S023°	20.7'
20	119°	50.0'	S023°	20.6'
21	134°	49.7'	S023°	20.5'

Hr	GHA		DEC	
22	149°	49.4'	S023°	20.4'
23	164°	49.1'	S023°	20.3'
December 27				
00	179°	48.8'	S023°	20.2'
01	194°	48.4'	S023°	20.1'
02	209°	48.1'	S023°	20.0'
03	224°	47.8'	S023°	19.9'
04	239°	47.5'	S023°	19.8'
05	254°	47.2'	S023°	19.7'
06	269°	46.9'	S023°	19.6'
07	284°	46.6'	S023°	19.5'
08	299°	46.3'	S023°	19.4'
09	314°	46.0'	S023°	19.3'
10	329°	45.7'	S023°	19.1'
11	344°	45.4'	S023°	19.0'
12	359°	45.1'	S023°	18.9'
13	014°	44.8'	S023°	18.8'
14	029°	44.4'	S023°	18.7'
15	044°	44.1'	S023°	18.6'
16	059°	43.8'	S023°	18.5'
17	074°	43.5'	S023°	18.4'
18	089°	43.2'	S023°	18.3'
19	104°	42.9'	S023°	18.1'
20	119°	42.6'	S023°	18.0'
21	134°	42.3'	S023°	17.9'
22	149°	42.0'	S023°	17.8'
23	164°	41.7'	S023°	17.7'
December 28				
00	179°	41.4'	S023°	17.6'
01	194°	41.1'	S023°	17.4'
02	209°	40.8'	S023°	17.3'
03	224°	40.5'	S023°	17.2'
04	239°	40.2'	S023°	17.1'
05	254°	39.9'	S023°	17.0'
06	269°	39.5'	S023°	16.8'
07	284°	39.2'	S023°	16.7'
08	299°	38.9'	S023°	16.6'
09	314°	38.6'	S023°	16.5'
10	329°	38.3'	S023°	16.3'
11	344°	38.0'	S023°	16.2'
12	359°	37.7'	S023°	16.1'
13	014°	37.4'	S023°	15.9'
14	029°	37.1'	S023°	15.8'
15	044°	36.8'	S023°	15.7'
16	059°	36.5'	S023°	15.5'
17	074°	36.2'	S023°	15.4'
18	089°	35.9'	S023°	15.3'
19	104°	35.6'	S023°	15.1'
20	119°	35.3'	S023°	15.0'
21	134°	35.0'	S023°	14.9'
22	149°	34.7'	S023°	14.7'
23	164°	34.4'	S023°	14.6'

Hr	GHA		DEC		Hr	GHA		DEC		Hr	GHA		DEC	
	December 29					December 30					December 31			
00	179°	34.1'	S023°	14.5'	00	179°	26.8'	S023°	10.9'	00	179°	19.6'	S023°	06.9'
01	194°	33.7'	S023°	14.3'	01	194°	26.5'	S023°	10.7'	01	194°	19.3'	S023°	06.7'
02	209°	33.4'	S023°	14.2'	02	209°	26.2'	S023°	10.6'	02	209°	19.0'	S023°	06.5'
03	224°	33.1'	S023°	14.0'	03	224°	25.9'	S023°	10.4'	03	224°	18.7'	S023°	06.3'
04	239°	32.8'	S023°	13.9'	04	239°	25.6'	S023°	10.3'	04	239°	18.4'	S023°	06.2'
05	254°	32.5'	S023°	13.8'	05	254°	25.3'	S023°	10.1'	05	254°	18.1'	S023°	06.0'
06	269°	32.2'	S023°	13.6'	06	269°	25.0'	S023°	09.9'	06	269°	17.8'	S023°	05.8'
07	284°	31.9'	S023°	13.5'	07	284°	24.7'	S023°	09.8'	07	284°	17.5'	S023°	05.6'
08	299°	31.6'	S023°	13.3'	08	299°	24.4'	S023°	09.6'	08	299°	17.2'	S023°	05.4'
09	314°	31.3'	S023°	13.2'	09	314°	24.1'	S023°	09.4'	09	314°	16.9'	S023°	05.2'
10	329°	31.0'	S023°	13.0'	10	329°	23.8'	S023°	09.3'	10	329°	16.6'	S023°	05.1'
11	344°	30.7'	S023°	12.9'	11	344°	23.5'	S023°	09.1'	11	344°	16.3'	S023°	04.9'
12	359°	30.4'	S023°	12.7'	12	359°	23.2'	S023°	08.9'	12	359°	16.0'	S023°	04.7'
13	014°	30.1'	S023°	12.6'	13	014°	22.9'	S023°	08.8'	13	014°	15.7'	S023°	04.5'
14	029°	29.8'	S023°	12.4'	14	029°	22.6'	S023°	08.6'	14	029°	15.4'	S023°	04.3'
15	044°	29.5'	S023°	12.3'	15	044°	22.3'	S023°	08.4'	15	044°	15.1'	S023°	04.1'
16	059°	29.2'	S023°	12.1'	16	059°	22.0'	S023°	08.3'	16	059°	14.8'	S023°	03.9'
17	074°	28.9'	S023°	12.0'	17	074°	21.7'	S023°	08.1'	17	074°	14.5'	S023°	03.7'
18	089°	28.6'	S023°	11.8'	18	089°	21.4'	S023°	07.9'	18	089°	14.2'	S023°	03.6'
19	104°	28.3'	S023°	11.7'	19	104°	21.1'	S023°	07.8'	19	104°	13.9'	S023°	03.4'
20	119°	28.0'	S023°	11.5'	20	119°	20.8'	S023°	07.6'	20	119°	13.6'	S023°	03.2'
21	134°	27.7'	S023°	11.4'	21	134°	20.5'	S023°	07.4'	21	134°	13.3'	S023°	03.0'
22	149°	27.4'	S023°	11.2'	22	149°	20.2'	S023°	07.2'	22	149°	13.0'	S023°	02.8'
23	164°	27.1'	S023°	11.1'	23	164°	19.9'	S023°	07.1'	23	164°	12.7'	S023°	02.6'

Declination Correction for Increased Accuracy

The Almanac data presented above will serve most backup navigation needs, meaning a noon latitude to well within ± 10 nmi, taking into account the limits of the Mark 3 sextant. For increased accuracy, you can get a better Declination using the table below. For example, if LAN occurred at 05h UTC on July 14, 2024, the uncorrected Sun Almanac gives N 21° 40.7'. From the table, we get a more accurate value by entering the almanac at 05+12 = 17h UTC, namely N 21° 36.1', which is the correct value for 05h on July 14, 2024. We would still use the GHA value listed in the Sun Almanac for 05h.

Declination Correction for Increased Accuracy*	
Year	Correction to UTC
2018, 2022, 2026	No Correction
2019, 2023, 2027	Subtract 6 hours
2020, 2024, 2028 (Jan. 01 - Feb. 29)	Subtract 12 hours
2020, 2024, 2028 (Mar. 01 - Dec. 31)	Add 12 hours
2021, 2025, 2029	Add 7 hours

*Correction Table courtesy of Greg Rudzinski.

Increments Table
0 - 7 Min

0 Min			1 Min			2 Min			3 Min		
Sec	°	′	Sec	°	′	Sec	°	′	Sec	°	′
0	0	0	0	0	15	0	0	30	0	0	45
4	0	1	4	0	16	4	0	31	4	0	46
8	0	2	8	0	17	8	0	32	8	0	47
12	0	3	12	0	18	12	0	33	12	0	48
16	0	4	16	0	19	16	0	34	16	0	49
20	0	5	20	0	20	20	0	35	20	0	50
24	0	6	24	0	21	24	0	36	24	0	51
28	0	7	28	0	22	28	0	37	28	0	52
32	0	8	32	0	23	32	0	38	32	0	53
36	0	9	36	0	24	36	0	39	36	0	54
40	0	10	40	0	25	40	0	40	40	0	55
44	0	11	44	0	26	44	0	41	44	0	56
48	0	12	48	0	27	48	0	42	48	0	57
52	0	13	52	0	28	52	0	43	52	0	58
56	0	14	56	0	29	56	0	44	56	0	59
60	0	15	60	0	30	60	0	45	60	1	0

4 Min			5 Min			6 Min			7 Min		
Sec	°	′	Sec	°	′	Sec	°	′	Sec	°	′
0	1	0	0	1	15	0	1	30	0	1	45
4	1	1	4	1	16	4	1	31	4	1	46
8	1	2	8	1	17	8	1	32	8	1	47
12	1	3	12	1	18	12	1	33	12	1	48
16	1	4	16	1	19	16	1	34	16	1	49
20	1	5	20	1	20	20	1	35	20	1	50
24	1	6	24	1	21	24	1	36	24	1	51
28	1	7	28	1	22	28	1	37	28	1	52
32	1	8	32	1	23	32	1	38	32	1	53
36	1	9	36	1	24	36	1	39	36	1	54
40	1	10	40	1	25	40	1	40	40	1	55
44	1	11	44	1	26	44	1	41	44	1	56
48	1	12	48	1	27	48	1	42	48	1	57
52	1	13	52	1	28	52	1	43	52	1	58
56	1	14	56	1	29	56	1	44	56	1	59
60	1	15	60	1	30	60	1	45	60	2	0

Increments Table

8 - 15 Min

8 Min Sec	°	′
0	2	0
4	2	1
8	2	2
12	2	3
16	2	4
20	2	5
24	2	6
28	2	7
32	2	8
36	2	9
40	2	10
44	2	11
48	2	12
52	2	13
56	2	14
60	2	15

9 Min Sec	°	′
0	2	15
4	2	16
8	2	17
12	2	18
16	2	19
20	2	20
24	2	21
28	2	22
32	2	23
36	2	24
40	2	25
44	2	26
48	2	27
52	2	28
56	2	29
60	2	30

10 Min Sec	°	′
0	2	30
4	2	31
8	2	32
12	2	33
16	2	34
20	2	35
24	2	36
28	2	37
32	2	38
36	2	39
40	2	40
44	2	41
48	2	42
52	2	43
56	2	44
60	2	45

11 Min Sec	°	′
0	2	45
4	2	46
8	2	47
12	2	48
16	2	49
20	2	50
24	2	51
28	2	52
32	2	53
36	2	54
40	2	55
44	2	56
48	2	57
52	2	58
56	2	59
60	3	0

12 Min Sec	°	′
0	3	0
4	3	1
8	3	2
12	3	3
16	3	4
20	3	5
24	3	6
28	3	7
32	3	8
36	3	9
40	3	10
44	3	11
48	3	12
52	3	13
56	3	14
60	3	15

13 Min Sec	°	′
0	3	15
4	3	16
8	3	17
12	3	18
16	3	19
20	3	20
24	3	21
28	3	22
32	3	23
36	3	24
40	3	25
44	3	26
48	3	27
52	3	28
56	3	29
60	3	30

14 Min Sec	°	′
0	3	30
4	3	31
8	3	32
12	3	33
16	3	34
20	3	35
24	3	36
28	3	37
32	3	38
36	3	39
40	3	40
44	3	41
48	3	42
52	3	43
56	3	44
60	3	45

15 Min Sec	°	′
0	3	45
4	3	46
8	3	47
12	3	48
16	3	49
20	3	50
24	3	51
28	3	52
32	3	53
36	3	54
40	3	55
44	3	56
48	3	57
52	3	58
56	3	59
60	4	0

Increments Table

16 - 23 Min

16 Min			17 Min			18 Min			19 Min		
Sec	°	′	Sec	°	′	Sec	°	′	Sec	°	′
0	4	0	0	4	15	0	4	30	0	4	45
4	4	1	4	4	16	4	4	31	4	4	46
8	4	2	8	4	17	8	4	32	8	4	47
12	4	3	12	4	18	12	4	33	12	4	48
16	4	4	16	4	19	16	4	34	16	4	49
20	4	5	20	4	20	20	4	35	20	4	50
24	4	6	24	4	21	24	4	36	24	4	51
28	4	7	28	4	22	28	4	37	28	4	52
32	4	8	32	4	23	32	4	38	32	4	53
36	4	9	36	4	24	36	4	39	36	4	54
40	4	10	40	4	25	40	4	40	40	4	55
44	4	11	44	4	26	44	4	41	44	4	56
48	4	12	48	4	27	48	4	42	48	4	57
52	4	13	52	4	28	52	4	43	52	4	58
56	4	14	56	4	29	56	4	44	56	4	59
60	4	15	60	4	30	60	4	45	60	5	0

20 Min			21 Min			22 Min			23 Min		
Sec	°	′	Sec	°	′	Sec	°	′	Sec	°	′
0	5	0	0	5	15	0	5	30	0	5	45
4	5	1	4	5	16	4	5	31	4	5	46
8	5	2	8	5	17	8	5	32	8	5	47
12	5	3	12	5	18	12	5	33	12	5	48
16	5	4	16	5	19	16	5	34	16	5	49
20	5	5	20	5	20	20	5	35	20	5	50
24	5	6	24	5	21	24	5	36	24	5	51
28	5	7	28	5	22	28	5	37	28	5	52
32	5	8	32	5	23	32	5	38	32	5	53
36	5	9	36	5	24	36	5	39	36	5	54
40	5	10	40	5	25	40	5	40	40	5	55
44	5	11	44	5	26	44	5	41	44	5	56
48	5	12	48	5	27	48	5	42	48	5	57
52	5	13	52	5	28	52	5	43	52	5	58
56	5	14	56	5	29	56	5	44	56	5	59
60	5	15	60	5	30	60	5	45	60	6	0

Increments Table

24 - 31 Min

24 Min			25 Min			26 Min			27 Min		
Sec	°	′	Sec	°	′	Sec	°	′	Sec	°	′
0	6	0	0	6	15	0	6	30	0	6	45
4	6	1	4	6	16	4	6	31	4	6	46
8	6	2	8	6	17	8	6	32	8	6	47
12	6	3	12	6	18	12	6	33	12	6	48
16	6	4	16	6	19	16	6	34	16	6	49
20	6	5	20	6	20	20	6	35	20	6	50
24	6	6	24	6	21	24	6	36	24	6	51
28	6	7	28	6	22	28	6	37	28	6	52
32	6	8	32	6	23	32	6	38	32	6	53
36	6	9	36	6	24	36	6	39	36	6	54
40	6	10	40	6	25	40	6	40	40	6	55
44	6	11	44	6	26	44	6	41	44	6	56
48	6	12	48	6	27	48	6	42	48	6	57
52	6	13	52	6	28	52	6	43	52	6	58
56	6	14	56	6	29	56	6	44	56	6	59
60	6	15	60	6	30	60	6	45	60	7	0

28 Min			29 Min			30 Min			31 Min		
Sec	°	′	Sec	°	′	Sec	°	′	Sec	°	′
0	7	0	0	7	15	0	7	30	0	7	45
4	7	1	4	7	16	4	7	31	4	7	46
8	7	2	8	7	17	8	7	32	8	7	47
12	7	3	12	7	18	12	7	33	12	7	48
16	7	4	16	7	19	16	7	34	16	7	49
20	7	5	20	7	20	20	7	35	20	7	50
24	7	6	24	7	21	24	7	36	24	7	51
28	7	7	28	7	22	28	7	37	28	7	52
32	7	8	32	7	23	32	7	38	32	7	53
36	7	9	36	7	24	36	7	39	36	7	54
40	7	10	40	7	25	40	7	40	40	7	55
44	7	11	44	7	26	44	7	41	44	7	56
48	7	12	48	7	27	48	7	42	48	7	57
52	7	13	52	7	28	52	7	43	52	7	58
56	7	14	56	7	29	56	7	44	56	7	59
60	7	15	60	7	30	60	7	45	60	8	0

Increments Table

32 - 39 Min

32 Min				33 Min				34 Min				35 Min		
Sec	o	'		Sec	o	'		Sec	o	'		Sec	o	'
0	8	0		0	8	15		0	8	30		0	8	45
4	8	1		4	8	16		4	8	31		4	8	46
8	8	2		8	8	17		8	8	32		8	8	47
12	8	3		12	8	18		12	8	33		12	8	48
16	8	4		16	8	19		16	8	34		16	8	49
20	8	5		20	8	20		20	8	35		20	8	50
24	8	6		24	8	21		24	8	36		24	8	51
28	8	7		28	8	22		28	8	37		28	8	52
32	8	8		32	8	23		32	8	38		32	8	53
36	8	9		36	8	24		36	8	39		36	8	54
40	8	10		40	8	25		40	8	40		40	8	55
44	8	11		44	8	26		44	8	41		44	8	56
48	8	12		48	8	27		48	8	42		48	8	57
52	8	13		52	8	28		52	8	43		52	8	58
56	8	14		56	8	29		56	8	44		56	8	59
60	8	15		60	8	30		60	8	45		60	9	0

36 Min				37 Min				38 Min				39 Min		
Sec	o	'		Sec	o	'		Sec	o	'		Sec	o	'
0	9	0		0	9	15		0	9	30		0	9	45
4	9	1		4	9	16		4	9	31		4	9	46
8	9	2		8	9	17		8	9	32		8	9	47
12	9	3		12	9	18		12	9	33		12	9	48
16	9	4		16	9	19		16	9	34		16	9	49
20	9	5		20	9	20		20	9	35		20	9	50
24	9	6		24	9	21		24	9	36		24	9	51
28	9	7		28	9	22		28	9	37		28	9	52
32	9	8		32	9	23		32	9	38		32	9	53
36	9	9		36	9	24		36	9	39		36	9	54
40	9	10		40	9	25		40	9	40		40	9	55
44	9	11		44	9	26		44	9	41		44	9	56
48	9	12		48	9	27		48	9	42		48	9	57
52	9	13		52	9	28		52	9	43		52	9	58
56	9	14		56	9	29		56	9	44		56	9	59
60	9	15		60	9	30		60	9	45		60	10	0

Increments Table

40 - 47 Min

Sec	40 Min °	'		Sec	41 Min °	'		Sec	42 Min °	'		Sec	43 Min °	'
0	10	0		0	10	15		0	10	30		0	10	45
4	10	1		4	10	16		4	10	31		4	10	46
8	10	2		8	10	17		8	10	32		8	10	47
12	10	3		12	10	18		12	10	33		12	10	48
16	10	4		16	10	19		16	10	34		16	10	49
20	10	5		20	10	20		20	10	35		20	10	50
24	10	6		24	10	21		24	10	36		24	10	51
28	10	7		28	10	22		28	10	37		28	10	52
32	10	8		32	10	23		32	10	38		32	10	53
36	10	9		36	10	24		36	10	39		36	10	54
40	10	10		40	10	25		40	10	40		40	10	55
44	10	11		44	10	26		44	10	41		44	10	56
48	10	12		48	10	27		48	10	42		48	10	57
52	10	13		52	10	28		52	10	43		52	10	58
56	10	14		56	10	29		56	10	44		56	10	59
60	10	15		60	10	30		60	10	45		60	11	0

Sec	44 Min °	'		Sec	45 Min °	'		Sec	46 Min °	'		Sec	47 Min °	'
0	11	0		0	11	15		0	11	30		0	11	45
4	11	1		4	11	16		4	11	31		4	11	46
8	11	2		8	11	17		8	11	32		8	11	47
12	11	3		12	11	18		12	11	33		12	11	48
16	11	4		16	11	19		16	11	34		16	11	49
20	11	5		20	11	20		20	11	35		20	11	50
24	11	6		24	11	21		24	11	36		24	11	51
28	11	7		28	11	22		28	11	37		28	11	52
32	11	8		32	11	23		32	11	38		32	11	53
36	11	9		36	11	24		36	11	39		36	11	54
40	11	10		40	11	25		40	11	40		40	11	55
44	11	11		44	11	26		44	11	41		44	11	56
48	11	12		48	11	27		48	11	42		48	11	57
52	11	13		52	11	28		52	11	43		52	11	58
56	11	14		56	11	29		56	11	44		56	11	59
60	11	15		60	11	30		60	11	45		60	12	0

Increments Table

48 - 55 Min

48 Min			49 Min			50 Min			51 Min		
Sec	°	′	Sec	°	′	Sec	°	′	Sec	°	′
0	12	0	0	12	15	0	12	30	0	12	45
4	12	1	4	12	16	4	12	31	4	12	46
8	12	2	8	12	17	8	12	32	8	12	47
12	12	3	12	12	18	12	12	33	12	12	48
16	12	4	16	12	19	16	12	34	16	12	49
20	12	5	20	12	20	20	12	35	20	12	50
24	12	6	24	12	21	24	12	36	24	12	51
28	12	7	28	12	22	28	12	37	28	12	52
32	12	8	32	12	23	32	12	38	32	12	53
36	12	9	36	12	24	36	12	39	36	12	54
40	12	10	40	12	25	40	12	40	40	12	55
44	12	11	44	12	26	44	12	41	44	12	56
48	12	12	48	12	27	48	12	42	48	12	57
52	12	13	52	12	28	52	12	43	52	12	58
56	12	14	56	12	29	56	12	44	56	12	59
60	12	15	60	12	30	60	12	45	60	13	0

52 Min			53 Min			54 Min			55 Min		
Sec	°	′	Sec	°	′	Sec	°	′	Sec	°	′
0	13	0	0	13	15	0	13	30	0	13	45
4	13	1	4	13	16	4	13	31	4	13	46
8	13	2	8	13	17	8	13	32	8	13	47
12	13	3	12	13	18	12	13	33	12	13	48
16	13	4	16	13	19	16	13	34	16	13	49
20	13	5	20	13	20	20	13	35	20	13	50
24	13	6	24	13	21	24	13	36	24	13	51
28	13	7	28	13	22	28	13	37	28	13	52
32	13	8	32	13	23	32	13	38	32	13	53
36	13	9	36	13	24	36	13	39	36	13	54
40	13	10	40	13	25	40	13	40	40	13	55
44	13	11	44	13	26	44	13	41	44	13	56
48	13	12	48	13	27	48	13	42	48	13	57
52	13	13	52	13	28	52	13	43	52	13	58
56	13	14	56	13	29	56	13	44	56	13	59
60	13	15	60	13	30	60	13	45	60	14	0

Increments Table

56 - 59 Min

	56 Min				57 Min				58 Min				59 Min	
Sec	o	'		Sec	o	'		Sec	o	'		Sec	o	'
0	14	0		0	14	15		0	14	30		0	14	45
4	14	1		4	14	16		4	14	31		4	14	46
8	14	2		8	14	17		8	14	32		8	14	47
12	14	3		12	14	18		12	14	33		12	14	48
16	14	4		16	14	19		16	14	34		16	14	49
20	14	5		20	14	20		20	14	35		20	14	50
24	14	6		24	14	21		24	14	36		24	14	51
28	14	7		28	14	22		28	14	37		28	14	52
32	14	8		32	14	23		32	14	38		32	14	53
36	14	9		36	14	24		36	14	39		36	14	54
40	14	10		40	14	25		40	14	40		40	14	55
44	14	11		44	14	26		44	14	41		44	14	56
48	14	12		48	14	27		48	14	42		48	14	57
52	14	13		52	14	28		52	14	43		52	14	58
56	14	14		56	14	29		56	14	44		56	14	59
60	14	15		60	14	30		60	14	45		60	15	0

Arc to Time Conversion

°	h	m	°	h	m	°	h	m	°	h	m
1	0	4	48	3	12	95	6	20	142	9	28
2	0	8	49	3	16	96	6	24	143	9	32
3	0	12	50	3	20	97	6	28	144	9	36
4	0	16	51	3	24	98	6	32	145	9	40
5	0	20	52	3	28	99	6	36	146	9	44
6	0	24	53	3	32	100	6	40	147	9	48
7	0	28	54	3	36	101	6	44	148	9	52
8	0	32	55	3	40	102	6	48	149	9	56
9	0	36	56	3	44	103	6	52	150	10	0
10	0	40	57	3	48	104	6	56	151	10	4
11	0	44	58	3	52	105	7	0	152	10	8
12	0	48	59	3	56	106	7	4	153	10	12
13	0	52	60	4	0	107	7	8	154	10	16
14	0	56	61	4	4	108	7	12	155	10	20
15	1	0	62	4	8	109	7	16	156	10	24
16	1	4	63	4	12	110	7	20	157	10	28
17	1	8	64	4	16	111	7	24	158	10	32
18	1	12	65	4	20	112	7	28	159	10	36
19	1	16	66	4	24	113	7	32	160	10	40
20	1	20	67	4	28	114	7	36	161	10	44
21	1	24	68	4	32	115	7	40	162	10	48
22	1	28	69	4	36	116	7	44	163	10	52
23	1	32	70	4	40	117	7	48	164	10	56
24	1	36	71	4	44	118	7	52	165	11	0
25	1	40	72	4	48	119	7	56	166	11	4
26	1	44	73	4	52	120	8	0	167	11	8
27	1	48	74	4	56	121	8	4	168	11	12
28	1	52	75	5	0	122	8	8	169	11	16
29	1	56	76	5	4	123	8	12	170	11	20
30	2	0	77	5	8	124	8	16	171	11	24
31	2	4	78	5	12	125	8	20	172	11	28
32	2	8	79	5	16	126	8	24	173	11	32
33	2	12	80	5	20	127	8	28	174	11	36
34	2	16	81	5	24	128	8	32	175	11	40
35	2	20	82	5	28	129	8	36	176	11	44
36	2	24	83	5	32	130	8	40	177	11	48
37	2	28	84	5	36	131	8	44	178	11	52
38	2	32	85	5	40	132	8	48	179	11	56
39	2	36	86	5	44	133	8	52	180	12	0
40	2	40	87	5	48	134	8	56			
41	2	44	88	5	52	135	9	0			
42	2	48	89	5	56	136	9	4			
43	2	52	90	6	0	137	9	8			
44	2	56	91	6	4	138	9	12			
45	3	0	92	6	8	139	9	16			
46	3	4	93	6	12	140	9	20			
47	3	8	94	6	16	141	9	24			

'	m	s	'	m	s
0	0	00	31	2	04
1	0	04	32	2	08
2	0	08	33	2	12
3	0	12	34	2	16
4	0	16	35	2	20
5	0	20	36	2	24
6	0	24	37	2	28
7	0	28	38	2	32
8	0	32	39	2	36
9	0	36	40	2	40
10	0	40	41	2	44
11	0	44	42	2	48
12	0	48	43	2	52
13	0	52	44	2	56
14	0	56	45	3	00
15	1	00	46	3	04
16	1	04	47	3	08
17	1	08	48	3	12
18	1	12	49	3	16
19	1	16	50	3	20
20	1	20	51	3	24
21	1	24	52	3	28
22	1	28	53	3	32
23	1	32	54	3	36
24	1	36	55	3	40
25	1	40	56	3	44
26	1	44	57	3	48
27	1	48	58	3	52
28	1	52	59	3	56
29	1	56	60	4	00
30	2	00			

Analemma

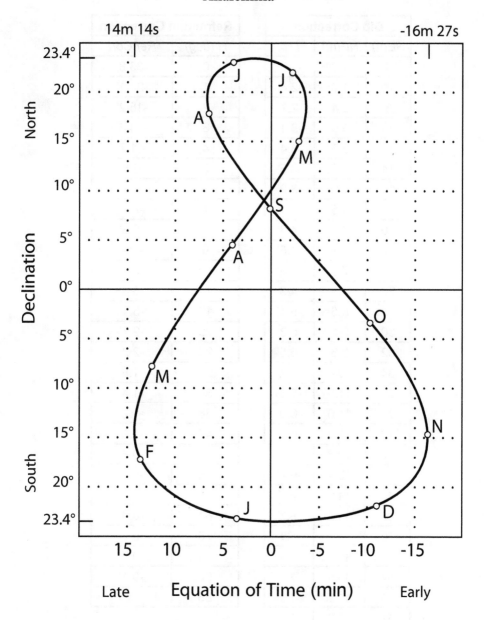

Dip Table and Refraction Table

Dip Correction		
HE(ft)	HE(m)	Dip
4	1.2	-1.9'
6	1.8	-2.4'
8	2.4	-2.7'
10	3.0	-3.1'
12	3.7	-3.4'
14	4.3	-3.6'
16	4.9	-3.9'
18	5.5	-4.1'
20	6.1	-4.3'
22	6.7	-4.5'
24	7.3	-4.8'
26	7.9	-4.9'
28	8.5	-5.1'
30	9.1	-5.3'
32	9.8	-5.5'
34	10.4	-5.7'
36	11.0	-5.8'
38	11.6	-6.0'
40	12.2	-6.1'
42	12.8	-6.3'
44	13.4	-6.4'
46	14.0	-6.6'
48	14.6	-6.7'
50	15.2	-6.9'
52	15.9	-7.0'
54	16.5	-7.1'
56	17.1	-7.3'
58	17.7	-7.4'
60	18.3	-7.5'

Refraction Correction	
H (deg)	Ref Corr
0	-33.8'
1	-24.1'
2	-18.2'
3	-14.3'
4	-11.7'
5	-9.8'
6	-8.5'
7	-7.4'
8	-6.6'
9	-5.9'
10	-5.3'
14	-3.8'
17	-3.1'
20	-2.7'
24	-2.2'
28	-1.8'
34	-1.4'
38	-1.2'
44	-1.0'
50	-0.8'
55	-0.7'
60	-0.5'
64	-0.4'
70	-0.3'
74	-0.2'
80	-0.1'
88	0.0'

Polaris Corrections

S	A	Q	S	A	Q	S	A	Q
180	000	+39	305	125	-31	070	250	-3
185	005	+38	310	130	-33	075	255	0
190	010	+36	315	135	-35	080	260	+3
195	015	+35	320	140	-36	085	265	+7
200	020	+33	325	145	-38	090	270	+10
205	025	+31	330	150	-39	095	275	+14
210	030	+28	335	155	-39	100	280	+17
215	035	+26	340	160	-40	105	285	+20
220	040	+23	345	165	-40	110	290	+23
225	045	+20	350	170	-40	115	295	+26
230	050	+17	355	175	-39	120	300	+28
235	055	+14	000	180	-39	125	305	+31
240	060	+10	005	185	-38	130	310	+33
245	065	+7	010	190	-36	135	315	+35
250	070	+3	015	195	-35	140	320	+36
255	075	0	020	200	-33	145	325	+38
260	080	-3	025	205	-31	150	330	+39
265	085	-7	030	210	-28	155	335	+39
270	090	-10	035	215	-26	160	340	+40
275	095	-14	040	220	-23	165	345	+40
280	100	-17	045	225	-20	170	350	+40
285	105	-20	050	230	-17	175	355	+39
290	110	-23	055	235	-14	180	000	+39
295	115	-26	060	240	-10			
300	120	-28	065	245	-7			

Printed in the USA
CPSIA information can be obtained
at www.ICGtesting.com
LVHW011631211023
761550LV00081B/1184